FAMILY COUNSELING
Strategies and Issues

Edited by

Jon Carlson and Judith Lewis
Governors State University, Illinois

LOVE PUBLISHING COMPANY®
Denver, Colorado 80222

Copyright © 1991 Love Publishing Company
Printed in the U.S.A.
ISBN 0-89108-219-0
Library of Congress Catalog Card Number 91-090265

Contents

Three Issues and Challenges 153

Preface

The nature of counseling has changed drastically in recent years. In the past, we tended to focus on providing the kinds of services that we knew best. Now, we know that we must tailor our interventions to the widely varying needs of a heterogeneous client population. The days of YAVIS (Young, Attractive, Verbal, Intelligent, Social) clients are gone. Because today's clients and their problems are non-traditional, today's counselors must be flexible, innovative, and ready to learn new skills.

Focusing on families, rather than solely on individuals, requires that counselors make some difficult adaptations. Assessment and intervention strategies are complex and require an understanding both of human beings and of the systems that affect them. Yet, despite its complexity, family counseling is rapidly becoming the treatment of choice for dealing with a variety of issues and problems. Counselors have learned that they must work with families if they hope to have a significant impact on their clients' lives.

Family Counseling: Strategies and Issues is designed to help counselors work more effectively with today's families. This book is divided into three parts. The introductory section provides an overview of the changing nature of contemporary families and describes the range of interventions involved in marital and family counseling and therapy. Section Two highlights specific strategies, including wellness-oriented family counseling, marital counseling, brief sexual counseling, mediation, and parental skill training. The chapters that make up Section Three, *Issues and Challenges*, address the question of how family counseling interventions can be used to help people cope with stressful and challenging situations. The authors represented in this section bring to light the diversity that characterizes today's changing families and present specific, concrete suggestions that counselors can follow.

This book has been tailored to the needs of practicing counselors. Each author has made use of his or her clinical experience to develop ideas for family counseling interventions that work. Our hope is that, ultimately, each counselor can play an important part, not just in helping families solve problems, but in helping them attain the highest possible levels of health.

Jon Carlson
Judith A. Lewis

One

Introduction to Today's Families

The time when one could define the "normal" or "typical" family is long past—if that time ever really existed. Today's families are most notable in terms of their variety. No single structure or set of interactional patterns can be identified as right or healthy for all families. If there is any one generalization that can be made about the healthy family, it is that such a family can accomplish its own goals and those of its members. Family counseling, then, must focus on helping each client system to be successful in its own terms.

The chapters that make up this section introduce the kind of broad, positively-stated framework that can make this kind of intervention possible. In the first chapter, "An Introduction to Family Counseling," Jon Carlson and Judith Lewis discuss the changing nature of contemporary families, emphasizing the fact that models developed for traditional families may no longer be appropriate. Now, counselors are faced with a difficult challenge. Just as we have become aware of the scope of possibilities for family organization, we have also learned that the impact of systems on individuals makes family counseling a treatment of choice. We need to use interventions that are based on careful assessment of the unique situation of each specific family. We

1

must also recognize that, as counselors, our forte is enhancing health, rather than merely diagnosing and addressing illness. Helping families move toward higher levels of functioning requires a broad repertoire of counseling skills that can be tailored to the needs of each system.

In Chapter Two, Robert Smith contributes an overview of marital and family therapy practice. Smith points out the dearth of empirically-supported research on healthy families, but provides a review of the literature that does help to shed light on some of the subtle differences between healthy and dys-functional systems. All approaches to family counseling and therapy share a concern with moving families toward health and a focus on the system, but there is variation among theories in how healthy systems are defined. Smith's summaries of structural, strategic, transgenerational, experiential, and behav-ioral family therapies help to make clear both the commonalities and the dif-ferences among these established theories. The nineteen specific interven-tions he describes in this chapter cut across all of the theories, making the need for a broad counselor repertoire of skills even more apparent.

This section concludes with Bonnie Robson's discussion of the impact of changing family patterns on children's development. Given the heterogene-ous nature of today's families, many children experience change from one type of family structure to another. Most commonly, children face the need to adapt to parental separation or divorce. The focus of this chapter moves from the system to the individual child, with the author recognizing that the impact of family changes on the child may be strongly affected by his or her develop-mental level. Robson reviews a number of interventions that can enhance children's adaptation to change. At the level of prevention, she suggests that educational programs for both parents and children can counteract some of the negative aspects of divorce, while legislation might prevent some of the dam-age brought about by custodial battles. In terms of direct intervention, she emphasizes early identification of vulnerable children; school-based support-ive group programs; and individual, family, or group counseling programs.

All of these chapters make one thing clear—change is a fact of life for today's families. As counselors, we need to accept this reality and develop the multi-faceted programs and flexible interventions that can make our clients' healthy adaptations possible.

1

An Introduction to Family Counseling

Jon Carlson and Judith A. Lewis

*Let the dead have the immortality of fame, but the living the
immortality of love.*

Tagore

The pervasive lifelong impact that families have upon individuals is finally being acknowledged, and treatment interventions are being conducted accordingly. The era of individual counseling is over. No longer will counselors remove, treat, and return individuals to their milieus without directly changing the system.

The who, what, when, where, and how of our lives are directly attributable to our families. We acknowledge how personalities, friendships, hobbies, careers have been shaped in at least some fashion by our family environment. Yet, what is this process and how does it take place?

"Family" is an ambiguous term that seems to be personally defined. It is different for each of us. But families once were more alike than they are today. Nontraditional families are becoming more commonplace, and the traditional nuclear family with a male provider and female homemaker is less and less a norm. Increases in divorce, more working mothers, declining birth rates, and longer life expectancy have become realities of contemporary families.

Today's counselors are being presented with new relationship combinations and problems. Traditional methods of assessment and intervention

3

based upon treatment for individual clients or models developed for traditional families are no longer appropriate. Counselors traditionally have been trained in dealing with problematic individuals; however, in today's world they must deal with couples, entire families, or a variety of combinations such as stepfamilies, single people living alone, childless families, mothers with out-of-wedlock children, and so on. Counselors are confronted by couples who are trying to decide if they should be together or remain together or separate. Counselors have to figure out if they are doing pre-marriage counseling, marriage counseling, divorce counseling, family counseling, or individual counseling.

Counselors are facing problems that were nonexistent or uncommon during their own upbringing. Issues of child custody between divorced parents, problems of stepfamily living with "yours, mine, and ours" children, and the impact of two-career couples are just a few of the possible challenges that today's counselors need to be prepared to face. These and the other issues discussed in this book require distinct counseling strategies. We no longer can refer to what was once a "typical" American family; we have to consider a variety of "typical" families. Perhaps the following facts and forecasts will help to highlight the rapid change.

- Two thirds of the marriages in 1990 will end in divorce or separation.
- One of five children is now born to an unwed parent.
- The number of teenage pregnancies is at an all-time high. Most teenage mothers are opting to keep their children, which increases the number of single-parent families.
- The number of unwed mature women who are economically self-sufficient having children is also at an all-time high.
- Married couples are divorcing earlier than ever before, which leaves younger children more and more likely to be impacted by the effects of divorce.
- More and more couples are getting divorced after 20 years of marriage, which calls for special strategies to deal with midlife divorce.
- Three fifths of all children born today will spend at least part of their childhood in a single-parent family.
- More than half of all black children live in one-parent households.
- More and more households are being formed by nonmarried couples.

The face of the American family has changed remarkably over the past few decades. These changes have made successful marriage, healthy child rearing, and the ability to maintain strong, lifelong bonds more difficult than ever.

FAMILY RULES AND SYSTEMS

As a result of our inability to bring about meaningful, lasting change, social scientists have begun to formulate problems differently. Two helpful frameworks are provided by family systems theory and structural family therapy.

Family Systems Theory

Family systems theorists conceptualize the family as an open system that functions in relation to its broader social/cultural context and evolves over the life cycle. Families operate according to rules and principles that apply to all systems (Bertalanffy, 1968; Miller, 1978; Walsh, 1982):

1. *Circular causality.* A family system can be defined as *a group of individuals interrelated so that a change in any one member affects other individuals and the group as a whole.* This in turn affects the first individual in a circular chain of influence. Every action in this sequence is also a reaction. Causality is thus seen as circular rather than linear.

2. *Nonsummativity.* The family as a whole is greater than the sum of its parts, and it cannot be described simply by summing up characteristics of individual members. The family organization and interactional patterns involve an interlocking of the behavior of its members.

3. *Equifinality.* According to the principle of equifinality, the same origin may lead to different outcomes and the same outcome may result from different origins. Watzlawick, Beavin, and Jackson (1967) refer to the error or genetic fallacy in confusing origin with significance in determining outcome. Rather, they assert, the influence of initial conditions or events will be outweighed by the impact of the family organization—its ongoing interactional patterns and responses to stress. Thus, one family may be disabled whereas another family may rally in response to the same crisis. Or two well functioning families may have evolved from quite different circumstances.

4. *Communication.* All behavior is regarded as communication transmitting interpersonal messages. Every communication has two functions: a *content* (report) aspect conveying factual information, opinions, or feelings; and a *relationship* (command) aspect which, in conveying how the information is to be taken, defines the nature of the relationship (Ruesch & Bateson, 1951). In an ongoing relationship this definition cannot be left unclear without pathological consequences. Families stabilize the process of defining relationships through mutual agreements or family rules.

5. *Family rules.* Relationship rules, both implicit and explicit, organize family interaction and function to maintain a stable system by prescribing and limiting members' behavior. They provide expectations about roles, actions, and consequences that guide family life. Through the operation of a *redundancy principle*, a family tends to interact in repetitious sequences so that family operations are governed by a relatively small set of patterned and predictable rules. Families develop different lifestyles based on their family rules.

6. *Homeostasis.* To maintain a steady, stable state in the ongoing interaction system, norms are delimited and enforced by homeostatic mechanisms. All family members contribute to the homeostatic balance through a mutually reinforcing feedback loop, such as in complementarity or reciprocal behavior. Too great a deviation from the family norm may be counteracted in the negative feedback process, to regulate tension and to restore the family equilibrium or homeostasis.

7. *Morphogenesis.* At the same time, flexibility is required for a family to adapt to internal and external change. Internally, the family must reorganize in response to new developmental challenges as its members and the family as a whole move through the life cycle. A shift of rules is required to move from one developmental stage to the next as new phase-appropriate needs and tasks demand new norms and options.

From a systems perspective, individual dysfunction is also seen as symptomatic of current family dysfunction. Although an individual's functioning and development are pathological, the symptoms may be functional and adaptive within the family context. The individual's problem may function as a homeostatic regulator restoring family stability by expressing and deflecting family tension. Psychopathology is thus defined as a relationship problem (Haley, 1970). The individual's symptomatic behavior is seen as embedded in a dysfunctional interaction pattern.

Regardless of the origin of symptoms, given the circular nature of causality, the family's response to the individual's distress will be an important factor in the readjustment or recovery of the individual symptom bearer. Dysfunctional family systems tend to maintain or reinforce the symptoms in ongoing interactional processes. If the dysfunctional relationship pattern is not altered, symptoms may shift from one member to another.

Structural Family Therapy

In addition to systems concepts, we have found the ideas of structural family therapy useful (Minuchin, 1974). This approach stresses the importance of family organization on the functioning of the family unit. Minuchin contends that all families have problems and that the difference between a healthy and an unhealthy family is the way they contend with these problems. Minuchin tries to help families function effectively and accomplish their goals. He believes that this is accomplished through clear subsystems and boundaries: A functional family has to be flexible enough to change, yet rigid enough to know who is in charge.

ASSUMPTIONS FOR TREATMENT

In the early days of counseling, identifying with a particular school of therapy was important. Now this is less important. Identifying what should be done and how to think to move a family toward healthier living is more important. Beavers (1990) developed the following global assumptions regarding families (pp. xii–xiii):

1. Family functioning in terms of systemic qualities of relationships, communication, and exchanges takes precedence over form or typology. Attempting to identify or label clinical typologies of symptomatic families (such as the "schizophrenogenic family") yields little useful information. Instead, functional and behavioral qualities of the unique system must be assessed.

2. Family competence ranging from healthy family functioning to severely dysfunctional is viewed along a progressive continuum rather than in categorical typologies. This helps us to assume a potential for growth and adaptation in all families.

3. Families at similar competence levels may show different functional styles of relating and interacting. Further, most competent families are able to balance and shift their functioning styles as developmental changes occur.

4. The successful therapist achieves an understanding of the presenting family and subtly alters factors such as therapeutic orientation, power differential, and operating style to join the family and catalyze its growth.

5. The successful therapist also appreciates the hierarchical structure of interacting systems within and surrounding the family, ranging from the biological/cellular through the individual to higher order systems, including extended family and larger social network. Although direct intervention with any one specific level or all levels may not be necessary in any given case, ignoring potentially important biochemical, neurological, or larger system influences may lead to failure.

6. Individual treatment for relationship difficulties including, but not limited to, marital or parent-child relationships is often an ineffective and complicating procedure.

By utilizing these guidelines, family counselors can provide effective treatment. Because no two families are alike, successful therapists need to have principles and guidelines such as these to underlie their ideographic interventions.

ASSESSMENT

Assessing family functioning as an ongoing system is a difficult and complicated process. Counselors often have to untangle the present and temporary situation, collect family histories extending over several generations, understand the purposes of the presenting problems, and basically just to sort out the labyrinth of potentially useful data (Reiss, 1980). Reiss suggests that several pathways for assessment are available to counselors. Among the available choices are:

- Whether to adopt a cross-sectional or a developmental view.
- Whether to conduct a family-based or an environmental-based inquiry.
- Whether to adopt a crisis or a character orientation.
- Whether to focus on family pathology or on family competence.
- Whether to emphasize underlying family themes or observable behavioral events.

How individual counselors make these choices is probably related to their theoretical orientation, counseling style, the family being appraised, and just what the counselor wants to learn. We have found that a systematic way to collect the multitude of information available is helpful. The counselor might use the genogram (McGoldrick & Gerson, 1985), the Circumplex Model (Olson, Russell, & Sprenkle, 1989), the Beavers System Model of Rating Family Competence (Beavers & Boeller, 1983), or the McMaster Model of Family Coping Skills (Westley & Epstein, 1969). In addition, counselors will need to utilize a clinical interview to find clues to the following (Goldenberg & Goldenberg, 1990, p. 66):

Why is the family seeking help now?
What are the sources of stress on this family?
Who has the symptom?
How severe is it?
Is it chronic or acute?
Why this person?

When did the problem or symptom first begin, and who is most affected by it?

What function does the symptom serve for family stability?

How often, when, and under what circumstances does the symptom occur?

Are interactive patterns discernible that may be related to the onset or termination of symptomatic behavior?

Is an enmeshed or disengaged family system operating?

What is the current level of family functioning?

Are noticeable alliances or coalitions operating?

How permeable are the boundaries between subsystems?

In what manner and with what degree of success has the family dealt with this or other problems in the past?

Has the family sought professional help before? If so, with what degrees of success?

How adaptable or rigid is the family?

How receptive is the family to help?

What apparent family interactive patterns are related to the perpetuation of this problem?

HEALTHY AND NORMAL FAMILIES

Counselors can be easily taken up with the various degrees of family function, but in order to set meaningful treatment goals, we also must understand what is normal and healthy. What is normal and healthy, however, means different things to different people, depending on their frame of reference. Normality has often been defined in four different ways (Walsh, 1982):

1. *Asymptomatic family functioning.* "Normal" can be defined as having no problems or symptoms. Many people believe if no symptoms are present, a person is healthy.

2. *Optimal family functioning.* In this approach, "normal" is defined as accomplishment of several positive ideal characteristics. Optimally functioning families are viewed at the top of a continuum, with average or asymptomatic families in the mid-range and severely dysfunctional families at the lower end.

3. *Average family functioning.* A family is viewed as normal from this perspective if it fits a pattern that is typical or average compared to most other families.

4. *Transactional family process.* In this concept, what is normal is defined in temporal and social context, and it varies with the different internal and external demands that require adaptation over the course of the family life cycle.

On May 10, 1990, leading experts convened in Washington, DC to identify successful families and to overview the various constructs and measurements of what an effective family is. From this meeting the researchers identified nine characteristics that constitute the basic dimensions of a strong, healthy family (Krysan, Moore, & Zill, 1990):

1. *Adaptability.* This dimension refers to the family's ability to accommodate to predictable life cycle changes as well as to stressful events. This capability is related to external resources, as well as to good communication and other internal family processes.
2. *Commitment to family.* This commitment involves both recognition of individual worth and acceptance of the value of the family as a unit.
3. *Communication.* A pattern of clear, open, and frequent communication is one of the characteristics of healthy families that is most often cited.
4. *Encouragement of individuals.* This dimension refers to the family's ability to encourage a sense of belonging while at the same time encouraging individual development.
5. *Expression of appreciation.* Extending appreciation means doing things consistently that are positive for the other person simply for their sake.
6. *Religious/spiritual orientation.* Many researchers list religiosity or spirituality among the characteristics of healthy families, although no consensus exists regarding the specific aspects of religion that are important to functioning.
7. *Social connectedness.* A connection with the larger society, extended family, friends, and neighbors, and participation in community activities typically makes available external resources to assist the family in adapting and coping.
8. *Clear roles.* In a clear and flexible role structure, family members know their roles and responsibilities and thus are able to function effectively in times of crisis as well as during normal times.
9. *Shared time.* Shared time means that family members devote both quality and quantity time, to the extent that this is enjoyable for family members.

Counselors, we hope, will understand the characteristics of effective successful families and will use these as goals to help families move forward to develop higher levels of functioning.

REFERENCES

Beavers, W. R. (1990) *Successful families.* New York: W. W. Norton.

Beavers, W. R., & Boeller, M. N. (1983). Family models: Comparing and contrasting the Olson Circumplex with the Beavers Model. *Family Process, 22,* 85–98.

Bertalanffy, von., L. (1968). *General systems theory: Foundation, development, applications.* New York: Braziller.

Goldenberg, H., & Goldenberg, I. (1990). *Counseling today's families.* Pacific Grove, CA: Brooks/Cole.

Haley, J. (1970). Approaches to family therapy. *International Journal of Psychiatry, 9,* 233–242.

Krysan, M., Moore, K. A., & Zill, N. (1990). *Identifying successful families: An overview of constructs and selected measures.* Washington, DC: Child Trends.

McGoldrick, M., & Gerson, R. (1985). *Genograms in family assessment.* New York: W. W. Norton.

Miller, J. G. (1978). *Living systems.* New York: McGraw-Hill.

Minuchin, S. (1974). *Families and family therapy.* Cambridge, MA: Harvard University Press.

Olson, D., Russell, C. S., & Sprenkle, D. H. (Eds.), (1989). *Circumplex model: Systematic assessment and treatment of families.* New York: Haworth.

Reiss, D. (1980). Pathways to assessing the family: Some choice points and a sample route. In C. K. Hofling & J. M. Lewis (Eds.), *The family: Evaluation and treatment.* New York: Brunner/Mazel.

Ruesch, J., & Bateson, G. (1951). *Communication: The social matrix of psychiatry.* New York: Norton.

Walsh, F. (1982). *Normal families.* New York: Guilford Press.

Watzlawick, P., Beavin, J., & Jackson, D. D. (1967). *Pragmatics of human communication.* New York: Norton.

Westley, W. A., & Epstein, N. B. (1969). *The silent majority.* San Francisco: Jossey-Bass.

2

Marital and Family Therapy: Direction, Theory, and Practice

Robert L. Smith

Life is not a matter of holding good cards, but of playing a poor hand well.

Robert Louis Sevenson

A comprehensive critique of the marital and family therapy (MFT) profession could fill volumes and still be considered incomplete. Sourcebooks, manuals, casebooks, and texts that are widely available cover many of the topics included here. Some of these have been authored by Becvar and Becvar (1988), Brown and Christensen (1986), Carter and McGoldrick (1989), Fenell and Weinhold (1989), Goldenberg and Goldenberg (1985), Gurman (1985), Nichols (1984), Piercy and Sprenkle (1986), and Sperry and Carlson (1991). Because marriage and family therapy is a dynamic field, harnessing all MFT vicissitudes in a single piece of writing is not possible. Therefore, I omit certain MFT topics, exclude some theories, and fail to address many of the issues. This overview, however, does address:

- The direction of marital and family therapy—a review of healthy family functioning.
- Major theories in marital and family therapy.
- Techniques most often applied during the practice of marital and family therapy.

If marital and family therapy is directed toward understanding, creating, and developing "healthy" or "healthier" marriages and families, clearer and more comprehensive roadmaps are needed. A limited body of research leads to speculation about healthy family functioning.

Currently, a number of well developed hypotheses have been proposed concerning family functioning. Many theories in marital and family therapy are not truly scientific if they are critiqued according to inductive or deductive methods of theory development. Yet, existing theories are acknowledged as quite useful, both in the training of therapists and for practitioners. Theoretical approaches discussed here are: structural, strategic, transgenerational, experiential, and behavioral.

An exaggeration of the presenting problem or family system often surfaces when attempting to describe how theoretical hypotheses relate to practice. This occurs when emphasizing the application of key theoretical constructs to day-to-day work with families. Several texts have used this approach (Becvar & Becvar, 1988; Brown & Christensen, 1986; Goldenberg & Goldenberg, 1985). Rather than following the case approach, I have chosen to identify those techniques often used during the practice of marital and family therapy. This allows the reader to adapt techniques according to presenting family cases.

DIRECTION: HEALTHY FAMILY FUNCTIONING

Carter (1986) states that it is essential for each of us to wrestle with several questions related to family therapy. At the top of her list is: "What is the purpose of family therapy?" Assume that the purpose of the marital and family therapy profession is to understand and strive toward healthy family functioning. This assumption, then, recognizes the existence of "dysfunctional" families. Societal problems support our second assumption. Dysfunctional behavior, divorce rates, murder, drug abuse, incest, and crime support the notion of dysfunction. The family literature discusses pathogenic family systems generationally trapped in a status quo. Enmeshment, scapegoating, disengagement, and violence exemplify dysfunctional family systems. Families are seen as maintaining themselves in an "unhealthy" manner, perpetuating problems from generation to generation.

For change in the family system to take place, the therapist and the family alike need direction, as well as examples and models from which to work. This sort of empirical evidence can help direct one as to what eventual change would be like, or what would be a "healthy functioning family." This information provides family therapists with notions, hypotheses, and direction.

I contend that the above fundamental question as to what is healthy family functioning has not been adequately addressed. Furthermore, identification of healthy family functioning possibly is so fugitive in nature that health can be described only from the point of view of cultural consensus without reference to the logic or cohesion of the family. Yet, Beavers (1982), Fisher, Giblin, and Hoopes (1982), Fisher and Sprenkle (1978), Kantor and Lehr (1975), Olson, Sprenkle, and Russell (1979), and Reiss (1981) have provided hunches as to characteristics of "healthy" family functioning.

Kantor and Lehr (1975) make reference to healthy versus dysfunctional family systems. They identified three family types. The first, "open" type, is viewed as healthy and is characterized by flexible rules and boundary arrangements. The family is democratic and makes honest exchanges with outside individuals and groups. The second type of family, a "closed" system, is "traditional," emphasizing family loyalty with minimum contact with outside systems. Rigidity exists in this family and creates dysfunctional systems. The third type, a "random" system, is a fragmented operational family. This system often becomes chaotic and dysfunctional because it has few rules and family policies. According to the Kantor and Lehr model, healthy family functioning exists in families that have clear rules, set boundaries, are flexible, and interact freely with outside systems.

Olson et al. (1979) and others see cohesion and adaptability as major factors governing healthy family functioning. *Cohesion* is viewed as the emotional bonding of family members with one another and the degree of individual autonomy they experience in the family system. *Adaptability* refers to the capability of a family system to change its power structure, rules, and role relationships in response to situational and developmental stressors. Healthy families, according to this model, exhibit a balance between these two dimensions. Healthy families are not enmeshed in each other's lives—not overly cohesive. Healthy families have the proper amount of adaptability—not overly adaptable and in flux or too rigid to prevent growth and change. More specifically, the healthy family has a *balance* as related to the following 10 specific aspects of cohesion (Olson et al., 1979):

1. Emotional attraction.
2. Differentiation.
3. Mature dependency.
4. Supportiveness.
5. Loyalty.
6. Psychological safety.
7. Reliability.
8. Family identification.
9. Physical caretaking.
10. Pleasurable interaction.

The healthy family is adaptable. It demonstrates a balanced flexibility, shared leadership, appropriate assertiveness, negotiation among members, appropriate rules, open feedback systems, and clear but interacting roles.

Healthy families (Reiss, 1981) are "environment-sensitive," because they believe the world is knowable and orderly. Healthy families expect each member to contribute to its understanding and mastery. Healthy family members are able to accept help and advice from others, are flexible, work together to overcome adversity, and examine alternative solutions.

Through extensive study, Beavers (1982) identified healthy families in relation to negotiation and transaction patterns. Research by Beavers identified healthy families as having a parental coalition that sets a level of functioning for the family. Healthy family members communicate their thoughts and feelings. In healthy families, members welcome contact with each other and expect transactions to be caring, open, and trusting. In healthy families, members respect personal autonomy. Families express humor, tenderness, warmth, and hopefulness. Beavers sees healthy families as having the capacity for and the seeking of intimacy.

Less healthy families seek control, concern themselves with power struggles, and tend to use intimidation. In fact, the following dimensions (Lewis, Beavers, Gossett, & Phillips, 1976) characterize healthy versus dysfunctional families: (1) a caring affiliative attitude versus an oppositional approach to human encounters, (2) high levels of initiative versus passivity, (3) high levels of reciprocity, cooperation, and negotiation, (4) high levels of personal autonomy, (5) openness in the expression of affect, a prevailing mood of warmth, affection, and caring, and (6) high degrees of spontaneity and humor (Fisher et al., 1982). In addition, communication is valued in healthy families. General skills of healthy family functioning as related to communication include: *spontaneity, feedback, metacommunication,* and *encouragement.*

When discussing healthy families, Becvar and Becvar (1988) define health as the family's success in functioning to achieve its own goals. They have observed the following dimensions as characteristic of healthy families:

1. A legitimate source of authority, established and supported over time.
2. A stable rule system established and consistently acted upon.
3. Stable and consistent nurturing behavior.
4. Effective and stable child-rearing and marriage-maintenance practices.
5. A set of goals toward which the family and each individual works.
6. Sufficient flexibility and adaptability to accommodate normal developmental challenges as well as unexpected crises.

The literature discussing healthy family functioning is interesting and even convincing. Yet, the statements and ideas about healthy family functioning are not supported by scientific rigor or empirical investigation. A concise summary of ideas regarding healthy versus unhealthy family functioning characteristics, as provided in the literature, is presented in Table 2.1.

Statements by family therapists and writers about healthy families are mostly hypothetical and abstract. I believe, in concurrence with Textor

TABLE 2.1
Healthy and Dysfunctional Family Characteristics:
A Review of the Literature

Healthy families are characterized as:	Dysfunctional families are characterized as:	Literature Source:
Flexible	Rigid	Kantor & Lehr, 1975
Possessing clear rules, family policies, clear boundaries	Chaotic and unruly	Kantor & Lehr, 1975
Having a balanced cohesion	Enmeshed	Olson, Sprenkle, & Russel, 1979
Possessing a balanced adaptability	In flux	Olson et al., 1979
Having individual autonomy	Overly bonded	Olson et al., 1979
Having appropriate assertiveness	Rigid or dogmatic	Olson et al., 1979
Using negotiation	Experiencing power struggles	Olson et al., 1979
Having appropriate rules	Chaotic or dogmatic	Olson et al., 1979
Working together	Disengaged	Reiss, 1981
Environment-sensitive	Rigid/closed	Reiss, 1981
Possessing a parental coalition	Dysfunctional at the top	Beavers, 1977
Communicating thoughts and feelings	Lacking in communication	Beavers, 1977
An expectancy of caring and trusting, with open contact by members and the family system	Distrusting, expecting the worst, oppositional	Beavers, 1977
Possessing humor, tenderness, warmth	Humorless, cold, lacking in feeling	Beavers, 1977
Having the capacity for intimacy	Lacking intimacy and seeking caring; controlling and power seeking	Beavers, 1977
Expressing spontaneity and encouragement	Lacking in spontaneity; using intimidation	Beavers, 1977; Fisher et al., 1982
Having a legitimate source of authority	Chaotic	Becvar & Becvar, 1988
Having a stable rule system	Random/chaotic	Becvar & Becvar, 1988
Nurturing	Cold	Becvar & Becvar, 1988
Using consistency in child rearing	Inconsistent	Becvar & Becvar, 1988
Having family and individual goals	Random/chaotic	Becvar & Becvar, 1988
Flexible and adaptable	Rigid/dogmatic	Becvar & Becvar, 1988

(1989), that empirical studies by psychologists, sociologists, social workers, and others about "healthy" families are sorely lacking. One explanation is that because family therapists rarely work with "healthy" families, the emphasis is less on a "health" concept and more on pathology. This phenomenon is somewhat akin to individual psychotherapy's utilization of the DSM-III-R and other schemes identifying mental health disorders. Yet, despite the lack of an empirically supported direction pertaining to family therapy when viewed from the "healthy family functioning perspective," a fairly comprehensive set of theories has been advocated in an effort to change family systems. The current major theoretical approaches are described next.

MAJOR THEORETICAL APPROACHES OF FAMILY THERAPY

Family therapists view the family in terms of interactions and relationships. Theories about family therapy have much in common, with the most fundamental being the *focus on the system*. Differences, in large part, are determined by what the therapist punctuates when working with the family. Most of today's theories of family therapy can be viewed as speculations or unsubstantiated hypotheses providing information about family functioning (Goldenberg & Goldenberg, 1985). Yet, these theoretical constructs often generate additional hypotheses leading to the implementation of intervention strategies.

Each theory has its own master or identified masters demonstrating their work. What works or does not work seldom if ever differentiates the theory from the therapist's personality, relationship-building skills, or professional status. Although much can be learned from the master demonstrations, I agree with Corsini (1984) in that the best theory and methodology have to be of one's own making.

The five major theories summarized here are believed to exemplify the "established" state of theory in family therapy. Additional theoretical principles, hypotheses, and hunches for working with families are evident in the literature, but to a lesser extent than structural, strategic, transgenerational, experiential, and behavioral approaches. The focus on "what is considered healthy" by each theory precedes key constructs and goals.

Structural Family Therapy*

HEALTHY FAMILY SYSTEMS

In structural family therapy the family's health is directly related to the configuration and operational structure of the family system (Becvar & Becvar, 1988). The healthy family builds on the spouse subsystem. Through this arrangement partners accommodate and support each other's uniqueness. A

---

*Salvador Minuchin

measure of autonomy is maintained while complementary roles are negotiated. The traditional family of two parents living together with children is not necessarily viewed as the ideal family or today's norm. In the healthy family the parental system provides the grounding, security, and support for the sibling subsystems. Healthy families have executive systems that are differentiated from their families of origin. Subsystems operate in the family system with adaptability, reciprocity, and accommodation.

In healthy families a mother-daughter or father-son subsystem does not interfere with, or disrupt, other family relationships and subsystems. Harmony with the family is stressed, producing a natural evolvement of a multitude of structural arrangements.

BASIC CONCEPTS

Several basic concepts underlie the structural approach to family therapy. One of the most important of these involves subsystems. The family system can contain several subsystems. The *marital subsystem* is the first to form, and it provides the basis of the family system (Becvar & Becvar, 1988; Brown & Christensen, 1986). Mutual satisfaction of the couple's needs, autonomy, and accommodation are important. Often referred to as the "spouse subsystem," this subsystem is formed at marriage. Autonomy is more readily established in this subsystem when enmeshment with respective

---

Structural Family Therapy

Systems
Subsystems
  Marital
  Parental
  Sibling
Boundaries
  Permeability
  Disengaged Families
  Enmeshment
Coalitions
Accommodations
Tracking
Mimesis

families of origin is absent and when roles and rules are negotiated. Complementarity is emphasized. Accommodation—allowing each partner to develop his or her talents and skills while keeping one's own individuality—is considered important.

The *parental subsystem*, often (but not necessarily) consists of the same two people that comprise the marital subsystem. The parental or executive subsystem, the second subsystem described in structural family therapy, could include a single parent and a friend, extended family members, or members of the community. The parental subsystem centers on child-rearing issues.

The parental subsystem's method of interacting with siblings is expected to change based upon the age and developmental stage of children. Although accommodation and negotiation are factors that play out during childrearing, the children in the family need to understand and see that parents are not peers. Parents are in charge. The family is not a democracy.

In structural family therapy the *sibling subsystem* provides children with their first experiences in relating with peers. Negotiation, accommodation, working out differences, and learning about mutual respect is looked for within the sibling subsystem. An important part of the sibling subsystem is its relationships with the parental subsystem. This negotiation process of working out problems becomes a focal point in structural family therapy. The relationships within and between subsystems define the structure of the family.

Boundaries—their presence, absence, use of, and changeability—are significant in structural family therapy. Boundaries are the interactional rules of who participates. They guide, tell, and determine what is said, when, by whom, and under what conditions. Each subsystem has its own rules and identity. The rules of the total family system, spoken or unspoken, combine to form the family system's boundary. Boundary difficulties can create barriers to healthy family functioning and can produce several dysfunctional patterns leading to the impediment of individual growth, allowing family members to take inappropriate roles in the family system, creating enmeshment, disengagement, or triangulation (triangulation is discussed under basic concepts of transgenerational family therapy).

The boundaries can be clear, rigid, or diffuse. *Clear boundaries* in a system are considered ideal. They are characterized as firm, flexible, nurturing, and supportive. Access across subsystems is present, including systems outside of the family that may, over time, change the roles and rules within the family system itself.

Rigid boundaries are impermeable, creating extremely autonomous individuals with little interaction. Minuchin (1974a) describes this as a "disengaged family" system. Families with rigid boundaries experience less communication across family subsystems, are less nurturing, and are least likely to change. With little access or permeability across family subsystems, adjustment and change are difficult. According to Minuchin, members of families with rigid boundaries rely on outside systems for support and nurturance.

Diffuse boundaries characterize *enmeshed* relationships. As contrasted with a family having rigid boundaries, members of this type of family are involved in everyone else's business. For example, an enmeshed family may allow children to consistently permeate and interfere with the spouse, or marital subsystem.

GOALS OF STRUCTURAL FAMILY THERAPY

The goals of structural family therapy relate to the status and characteristics of the family system. General goals include:

1. Movement toward and eventual presence of a parental subsystem with parental/executive authority. This is a coalition of support and accommodation.
2. A sibling subsystem characterized by a system of peers.
3. Independent activity fostering differentiation, if enmeshment is present.
4. Flexible and clear boundaries, if disengagement is present.
5. Establishment of the spouse subsystem as a distinct entity.

In structural family therapy the therapist works to change transactional patterns and realign the family structure. The process structural family therapists use to create change involves *joining* with the family (often called *accommodation*), *mimesis* (adopting the family's style and pace), and *tracking* the family's communication pattern.

In summary, the structural family therapist: (a) focuses on the family structure and subsystems, (b) identifies patterns, rules, and boundaries operating in the system, (c) hypothesizes structural changes desirable within the family system, (d) joins with the family by respecting the current family structure, (e) intervenes in the family in a direct manner, and (f) works with the family successes through praise and support (Becvar & Becvar, 1988).

Strategic Family Therapy*

HEALTHY FAMILY SYSTEMS

The concepts of *health, normal, abnormal,* and *dysfunction* are terms that strategic family therapists do not deal with lightly. They see families as operating logically or functionally rather than as "normal or abnormal." Yet, several of the cited masters of strategic family therapy indicate a direction toward health. For example, Haley (1976) sees the importance of a family hierarchical

---

*Jay Haley, Cloe Madanes, Gregory Bateson, Milton Erickson, Lynn Hoffman, Don Jackson, John Weakland

system and Selvini-Palazzoli, Boscolo, Cecehin, and Prata (1978) views healthy families as having fewer alliances. Other strategic family therapists see the importance of clear family rules and flexibility within the family.

BASIC CONCEPTS

Jay Haley (1973) defines strategic family therapy as being initiated by the clinician and designed according to the presenting problem. Goal setting takes place in accordance with the presenting problem. Assessment of the family system occurs by listening and looking for sequential patterns of behavior. Therapists ask themselves, for example, "What behaviors trigger a sequence of events?" The therapist often asks directly, "What is it that has to be worked on?" Emphasis is placed on measurable goals. The strategic therapist takes the final responsibility for selecting the goals.

The strategic approaches evolved from communication theory and general system theory. Strategic therapy also is known by other descriptions. Major constructs of focus for the strategic family therapist are symptoms, metaphors, hierarchy, and power.

Strategic therapists focus less on insight and more on *symptoms* that are seen as a way of maintaining a homeostatic balance in the family system. Symptoms provide a means by which family members communicate. The family uses symptoms when members are stuck. The symptom is seen as providing the family member with a way out or a means of functioning in the system. Strategic family therapists often view symptoms as *metaphors*

Strategic Family Therapy

Symptoms
Metaphors
Hierarchy
Power
Intervention
Paradoxical Directives
Positive Labeling
Mental Research Institute
Brief Family Center
Milan Center for Family Studies

(Haley, 1976; Madanes, 1981). The symptom might be used to avoid conflict, redirect attention from other issues, keep people away, manipulate, and so on.

In strategic family therapy the family system hierarchical structure is examined. Questions as to the existing hierarchy, maintenance of the system, and how symptoms, coalitions, communication patterns and generational interfaces can affect the hierarchy are reviewed.

Strategic therapists (e.g., Haley, 1976) see the importance of *power* in all relationships. In the family system the strategic therapist attempts to reestablish a hierarchy, with the parents being restored to a position superior to the children. Rules and consequences are stressed in the restoration of power.

GOALS OF STRATEGIC FAMILY THERAPY

Strategic family therapists emphasize clear goal statements. They consider observed behavior important. They often use intermediate goals. They apply strategies based upon goal statements. They give tasks or directives to the family to solve presenting issues and reach goal statements. The tasks can be straightforward or paradoxical. A number of adaptations of the strategic approach to family therapy have evolved, including work from the Mental Research Institute Brief Therapy Center (Palo Alto, California) and the Milan Center for Family Studies (Milan, Italy).

Transgenerational Family Therapy*

Transgenerational family has its roots in psychodynamic and systems theory. Transgenerational therapies, or extended family therapies, see the past as being active in the present.

HEALTHY FAMILY SYSTEMS

According to Bowen (1978), the partners in healthy marriages are capable of emotional intimacy without loss of autonomy. Family members experience differentiation as related to their families of origin. Healthy family and individual functioning is seen on a continuous scale. High levels of differentiation are generally tied to healthy functioning. Yet, based upon circumstances and stress conditions, symptoms of "abnormality" may exist from time to time. Bowen focuses on optimal functioning levels. Optimal-functioning individuals are inner-directed, establish personal goals, are rational and objective, and operate as their own persons.

Boszormenyi-Nagy and Ulrich (1981) describe healthy families as those that transmit a legacy of fairness and responsibility. In the healthy family, members are not deprived, nor are they overindulged. In healthy families,

---

*Boszormenyi-Nagy and Spark, Bowen, Kerr, Williamson, Fairbairn, Framo

open and honest communication serves as a method of what Boszormenyi-Nagy calls "balancing a ledger."

BASIC CONCEPTS

The major construct of transgenerational family therapy is that *the past is active in the present.* Understanding the past is therefore basic to transgenerational family therapy. Object relations theory provide some clues to the past. Fairbairn (1954) and Dicks (1967) both saw how object relations theory and past internalized functioning affects present behavior. Fairbairn saw individuals unconsciously attempting to influence or change intimate relationships according to internalized ideals. Dicks focused on marital complementarity and saw each partner seeking from the other what was missing in past relationships. Framo (1981) further saw people attempting to use current relationships to heal conflicts in one's own family of origin.

Family loyalty is another major construct of transgenerational family therapy. Family loyalty is examined in terms of unhealed wounds, generational legacies, and expectations. Transgenerational family therapists look at how family loyalties play a role in one's current functioning.

Bowen has made major contributions to transgenerational family therapy. His view of the nuclear family living within a family emotional system affected by extended family—living and dead—has provided tremendous insight into family functioning.

A key concept related to this theoretical foundational construct is that of *differentiation of self.* This includes differentiation of self from others in the family's emotional web, as well as the ability to differentiate one's feeling process from the intellectual process. According to Bowen, the differentiated person feels but is able to maintain objectivity.

Triangulation takes place, according to Bowen, when stress is introduced to the dyadic system. Under extreme stress, one of the marital partners, often

---

Transgenerational Family Therapy

Object Relations
Family Loyalty
Differentiation
Triangulation
Family Projection Process
Family of Origin
Genograms

the one most undifferentiated, seeks a third-party ally. This could be a friend, family member, work, and so forth. Bowen sees this effort to create a solution as being more likely a method of preventing a resolution.

Bowen further refers to the term *family projection process* when discussing how a child's level of differentiation approximates that of the parents. A key element in the family projection process is the extent to which parents project their own emotional conflicts onto children and thus create triangles within the family system.

GOALS OF TRANSGENERATIONAL FAMILY THERAPY

According to transgenerational family therapy, intergenerational issues create problems for the nuclear family. The major goal is to change intergenerational interference operating with the current family. Detriangulation is often a necessary intermediate goal.

Experiential Family Therapy*

HEALTHY FAMILY SYSTEMS

According to experiential family therapy, healthy family systems are open and flexible. Healthy family systems have the capacity for individual growth and change, as well as change in the system itself. Even under stress (Whitaker & Keith, 1981) healthy families tend to grow. Family members in these systems are free to play and experience different roles (Kempler, 1973; Satir, 1972). Healthy family systems, according to experiential family therapy, are "open systems," allowing individuals the freedom to move in and out of the family system.

BASIC CONCEPTS

The focus of experiential family therapy is on the here and now. Borrowing from a number of schools of thought including Perls (1969) (Gestalt) and Rogers (1961) (client-centered), experiential family therapists emphasize the construct of individuality, personal freedom, and self-fulfillment. Experiential family therapy does not rely on therapy but, rather, on the therapist's capacity to be involved with the family. Theory is seen as getting in the way of therapy.

Experiential family therapists promote self-expression and negotiation. They encourage family members to find self-fulfilling roles (Kempler, 1981). Because experiential family therapy is largely atheoretical, specific approaches tend to rely on the therapist's spontaneity (Whitaker, 1976).

------

*Whitaker, Satir, Kempler

Experiential Family Therapy

Atheoretical
Individuality
Freedom of Choice
Personal Growth
Co-Therapists
Paradoxical Intention
Family Sculpting

Whitaker views therapy as having three phases: *engagement, involvement,* and *disentanglement.* During this process the therapist becomes a part of and then separates from the family. Experiential family therapists challenge the family by redefining the symptom, using paradox, and suggesting fantasy. In addition, they frequently utilize psychodrama and sculpting.

GOALS OF EXPERIENTIAL FAMILY THERAPY

Growth is the goal of experiential family therapy. This does not necessarily mean the reduction of symptoms. Whitaker and Keith (1981) add *creativity* as a major goal of experiential family therapy. Under the general goal of growth, experiential family therapists strive for individuality, personal freedom, independence, and self-fulfillment.

Behavioral Family Therapy*

HEALTHY FAMILY FUNCTIONING

From a behavioral approach viewpoint, effective communication and problem-solving skills can be taught within the family structure (Patterson, 1971). A good, healthy relationship has a greater frequency of pleasant behavior than unpleasant behavior. Viewed from another perspective, good relationships involve a positive reward system. A healthy family system rewards positive, functional behavior and extinguishes or changes dysfunctional behavior.

BASIC CONCEPTS

The basic concepts of behavioral family therapy were founded upon the principles of behavior modification. *Reinforcement*, positive and negative, is

---

*Patterson, Levant, Jacobson, Wolpe

Behavioral Family Therapy

Reinforcement
Shaping
Successive Approximation
Baselines
Social Learning Theory

---

a key construct. Positive reinforcement within the family structure is examined, and often taught and encouraged. Negative reinforcement also is observed with the intention of identifying those reinforcers and modifying or eliminating them when necessary.

Shaping or the process of *successive approximation* is used to change behavior. Through this process, parts of a total behavior pattern are separated out to eventually reach a more complex set of behaviors (Bandura, 1974). Before making systematic interventions, *baselines* are recorded to determine the use of inappropriate behavior.

Social learning theory principles and constructs, such as modeling, time-out, and extinction are implemented. Behavioral family therapists often work with family subsystems. For example, they may work with the marital subsystem to make the marriage better or with the parental subsystem to increase effective parenting skills.

GOALS OF BEHAVIORAL FAMILY THERAPY

The goals of behavioral therapy are decided by the client. The therapist, in turn, decides on the appropriate interventions. General goals of behavioral family therapy are to eliminate undesirable behavior and substitute desirable behavior. Assisting family members in clarifying goals is an intermediate goal of behavioral therapy. Specific outcome behaviors are identified to determine when goals are met.

THE PRACTICE OF FAMILY THERAPY: TECHNIQUES

What takes place during the practice of marital and family therapy is often different from what one might expect as related to theory. Structural, strategic, and transgenerational family therapists at times may seem to be operating alike, using similar interventions with a family. Differences might become clear when the therapist explains a certain technique or intervention. Most of today's practicing family therapists go far beyond the limited number of techniques usually associated with a single theory. The following techniques are those that practicing clinicians most often use. The when, where, and how of each intervention always rests with the therapist's professional judgment and personal skills.

The Genogram

The genogram, a technique often used early in family therapy, provides a graphic picture of the family history. The genogram reveals the family's basic structure, demographics, functioning, and relationships (McGoldrick & Gerson, 1985). Through symbols, it offers a picture of three generations. Names, dates of marriage, divorce, death, and other relevant facts are included in the genogram. It provides an enormous amount of data and insight for the therapist and family members early in therapy. As an informational and diagnostic tool, the genogram is developed by the therapist in conjunction with the family.

The Family Floor Plan

The family floor plan technique has several variations. Parents might be asked to draw the family floor plan for their family of origin. Information across generations is therefore gathered in a nonthreatening manner. Points of discussion bring out meaningful issues related to one's past.

Another adaptation of this technique is to have members draw the floor plan for their nuclear family. The importance of space and territory is often inferred as a result of the family floor plan. Levels of comfort between family members, space accommodations, and rules are often revealed. Indications of differentiation, operating family triangles, and subsystems often become evident. Used early in therapy, this technique can serve as an excellent diagnostic tool (Coppersmith, 1980).

Reframing

Most family therapists use reframing as a method to both join with the family and offer a different perspective on presenting problems. Specifically, reframing involves taking something out of its logical class and placing it in another category (Sherman & Fredman, 1986). For example, a mother's repeated questioning of her daughter's behavior after a date can be seen as genuine caring and concern rather than that of a nontrusting parent. Through reframing, a negative often can be reframed into a positive.

Tracking

Most family therapists use tracking. Structural family therapists (Minuchin & Fishman, 1981) see tracking as an essential part of the therapist's joining process with the family. During the tracking process the therapist listens intently to family stories and carefully records events and their sequence. Through tracking, the family therapist is able to identify the sequence of events operating in a system to keep it the way it is. What happens between point A and point B or C to create D can be helpful when designing interventions.

Communication Skill-Building Techniques

Communication patterns and processes are often major factors in preventing healthy family functioning. Faulty communication methods and systems are readily observed within one or two family sessions. A variety of techniques can be implemented to focus directly on communication skill building between a couple or between family members. Listening techniques including restatement of content, reflection of feelings, taking turns expressing feelings, and nonjudgmental brainstorming are some of the methods utilized in communication skill building.

In some instances the therapist may attempt to teach a couple how to fight fair, to listen, or may instruct other family members how to express themselves with adults. The family therapist constantly looks for faulty communication patterns that can disrupt the system.

Family Sculpting

Developed by Duhl, Kantor, and Duhl (1973), family sculpting provides for re-creation of the family system, representing relationships to one another at a specific period of time. The family therapist can use sculpting at any time in therapy by asking family members to physically arrange the family. Adolescents often make good family sculptors as they are provided with a chance to nonverbally communicate thoughts and feelings about the family. Family sculpting is a sound diagnostic tool and provides the opportunity for future therapeutic interventions.

Family Photos

The family photos technique has the potential to provide a wealth of information about past and present functioning. One use of family photos is to go through the family album together. Verbal and nonverbal responses to pictures and events are often quite revealing. Adaptations of this method include asking members to bring in significant family photos and discuss reasons for bringing them, and locating pictures that represent past generations. Through discussion of photos, the therapist often more clearly sees family relationships, rituals, structure, roles, and communication patterns.

Individual and Team Feedback via Telephone

Strategic family therapists often are credited for their creative use of teams and the telephone as an intervention method. From behind a one-way mirror, an individual supervisor or supervision team can call the therapist regarding notions about therapy. The team can help the therapist join with the family in cases in which the therapist does not agree with a team member's assessment. Individual supervisors or team members also can use the telephone to call a specific family member during therapy.

Special Days, Mini-Vacations, Special Outings

Couples and families that are stuck frequently exhibit predictable behavior cycles. Boredom is present, and family members take little time with each other. In such cases, family members feel unappreciated and taken for granted. Caring days can be set aside when couples are asked to show caring for each other, or at least act in a caring manner. Specific times for caring can be arranged with certain actions in mind (Stuart, 1980). Adaptations of this technique include fantasizing a mini-vacation together or planning a special outing. Interesting insights can be obtained during the planning process.

Gift Giving

Similar to the previously described techniques, gift giving can serve as a method of recognizing a spouse or a family member. The gift might be a verbal statement to a family member or a tangible gift of some nature. True feelings of a helping nature are allowed to be expressed. How the gift is presented (e.g., verbal context, caring, supportive) as well as how it is received (e.g., positive, defensive) can provide valuable insights.

Contracting

Traditionally considered a technique of behavioral therapy, therapists from a variety of theoretical backgrounds now frequently use contracting. Contracting with a couple requires specificity in regard to time and place. Contracts can be verbal or written. The contract should be measurable, detailed, and of recognized importance to family members involved.

The Empty Chair

The empty chair technique, most often utilized by Gestalt therapists (see Perls, Hefferline, & Goodman, 1951), has been adapted to family therapy. In one scenario, a partner may express his or her feelings to a spouse (empty chair), then play the role of the spouse and carry on a dialogue. Expressions to absent family members, parents, and children can be arranged through utilizing this technique.

Family Choreography

In family choreography, arrangements go beyond initial sculpting; family members are asked to position themselves as to how they see the family and then to show how they would like the family situation to be. Family members may be asked to reenact a certain family scene and possibly resculpt it to a preferred scenario. This technique can help a stuck family and create a more lively situation.

Family Council Meetings

Family council meetings are organized to provide specific times for the family to meet and share with one another. The therapist might prescribe council meetings as homework, in which case a time is set and rules are outlined. The council should encompass the entire family, and any absent members would have to abide by decisions. The agenda may include any concerns of the family. Attacking others during this time is not acceptable. Family council meetings help provide structure for the family, encourage full family participation, and facilitate communication.

Strategic Alliances

This technique, often used by strategic family therapists, involves meeting with one member of the family as a supportive means of helping that person change. Individual change is expected to affect the entire family system. The individual often is asked to behave or respond in a different manner. This technique attempts to disrupt a circular system or behavior pattern.

Family Sociogram

The sociogram charts relationships among people. By devising a series of questions relevant to a given family, the therapist can gain information about special alliances and relationship power sources. This technique promotes identification of family roles and new insights by family members.

Family Rituals

The family therapist can prescribe rituals as a method of change. Often, rituals are directed to the family to add needed structure. Examples are dinner times, house clean-up time together, and a family homework time. Specific rules during these ritual times often are prescribed. These rules might include discussing positive items only, not criticizing others, and allowing everyone to talk.

Prescribing Indecision

The stress level of couples and families often is exacerbated by a faulty decision-making process. Decisions not made in these cases become problematic in themselves. When straightforward interventions fail, paradoxical interventions often can produce change or relieve symptoms of stress. Such is the case with prescribing indecision. The indecisive behavior is reframed as an example of caring or taking appropriate time on important matters affecting the family. A directive is given to not rush into anything or make hasty decisions. The couple is to follow this directive to the letter.

Putting the Client in Control of the Symptom

This technique, widely used by strategic family therapists, attempts to place control in the hands of the individual or system. The therapist may recommend, for example, the continuation of a symptom such as anxiety or worry. Specific directives are given as to when, where, with whom, and for what amount of time one should do these things. As the client follows this paradoxical directive, a sense of control over the symptom often develops, resulting in subsequent change.

The techniques suggested here are examples from those that family therapists practice. They are customized according to presenting problems and are basically atheoretical in nature. With the focus on healthy family functioning, therapists cannot allow themselves to be stuck according to a prescribed operational procedure, a rigid set of techniques or set of hypotheses. Therefore, creative judgment and personalization of application are encouraged.

Healthy family functioning, theoretical constructs concerning the family, and interventions to change the system are focal points of marital and family therapy. Although additional scientific inquiry is needed in each of these areas, we have seen progress.

REFERENCES

Bandura, A. (1974). *Social learning theory*. Englewood Cliffs, NJ: Prentice Hall.
Beavers, W. R. (1977). *Psychotherapy and growth: Family systems perspective*. New York: Brunner/Mazel.

Beavers, W. R. (1982). Healthy, midrange, and severely dysfunctional families. In F. Walsh (Ed.), *Normal family processes*. New York: Guilford Press.

Becvar, D., & Becvar, R. (1988). *Family therapy*. Boston: Allyn & Bacon.

Boszormenyi-Nagy, I., & Ulrich, D. (1981). Contextual family therapy. In A. S. Gurman & D. P. Knisbern (Eds.), *Handbook of family therapy* (pp. 159–186). New York: Brunner/Mazel.

Bowen, M. (1978). *Family therapy in clinical practice*. New York: Aronson.

Brown, J. H., & Christensen, D. N. (1986). *Family therapy: Theory and practice*. Monterey: Brooks/Cole.

Carter, B. (1986). Success in family therapy. *Family Therapy Networker, 10,* 16–22.

Carter, B., & McGoldrick, M. (1989). *The changing family life cycle*. Boston: Allyn & Bacon.

Coppersmith, E. (1980). The family floor plan: A tool of training, assessment, and intervention in family therapy. *Journal of Marital & Family Therapy, 6,* 141–145.

Corsini, R. (1984). *Current psychotherapies*. Itasca, IL: F. E. Peacock.

Dicks, H. (1967). *Marital tensions*. New York: Basic Books.

Duhl, F. S., Kantor, D., & Duhl, B. S. (1973). Learning space and action in family therapy: A primer of sculpting. In D. Bloch (Ed.), *Techniques of family psychotherapy: A primer*. New York: Grune & Stratton.

Fairbairn, W. (1954). *An object-relations theory of the personality*. New York: Basic Books.

Fenell, D. & Weinhold, B. (1989). *Counseling families*. Denver: Love Publishing.

Fisher, B. L., Giblin, P. R., & Hoopes, M. H. (1982). Healthy family functioning: What therapists say and what families want. *Journal of Marital & Family Therapy, 8,* 273–284.

Fisher, B. L., & Sprenkle, D. (1978). Therapists' perceptions of healthy family functioning. *International Journal of Family Counseling, 6,* 1–10.

Framo, J. (1981). The integration of marital therapy with sessions with family of origin. In A. Gurman & D. Kniskern (Eds.), *Handbook of family therapy*. New York: Brunner/Mazel.

Goldenberg, I., & Goldenberg, H. (1985). *Family therapy: An overview* (2d ed.). Monterey: Brooks/Cole.

Gurman, A. S. (Ed.) (1985). *Casebook of marital therapy*. New York: Guilford Press.

Haley, J. (1973). *Uncommon therapy: The psychiatric technique of Milton H. Erickson*. New York: Norton.

Haley, J. (1976). *Problem-solving therapy*. New York: Harper/Colophon Books.

Kantor, D., & Lehr, W. (1975). *Inside the family: Toward a theory of family process*. San Francisco: Jossey-Bass.

Kempler, W. (1973). *Principles of gestalt family therapy*. Costa Mesa: Kempler Institute.

Kempler, W. (1981). *Experiential psychotherapy with families*. New York: Brunner/Mazel.

Lewis, J., Beavers, W., Gossett, J., & Phillips, V. (1976). *No single thread: Psychological health in family systems*. New York: Brunner/Mazel.

Madanes, C. (1981). *Strategic family therapy*. San Francisco: Jossey-Bass.

McGoldrick, M., & Gerson, R. (1985). *Genograms in family assessment*. New York: Norton.

Minuchin, S. (1974a). *Families and family therapy*. Cambridge, MA: Harvard University Press.

Minuchin, S. (1974b). Structural family therapy. In G. Caplan (Ed.), *Child and adolescent psychiatry, sociocultural and community psychiatry* (2d ed., pp. 178–192). New York: Basic Books.

Minuchin, S., & Fishman, H. (1981). *Techniques of family therapy*. Cambridge, MA: Harvard University Press.

Nichols, M. P. (1984). *Family therapy—Concepts and methods*. New York: Gardner Press.

Olson, D., Sprenkle, D., & Russell, C. (1979). Circumplex model of marital and family systems: I. Cohesion and adaptability dimensions, family types, and clinical applications. *Family Process, 18*, 3–28.

Patterson, G. (1971). *Families*. Champaign, IL: Research Press.

Perls, F. S. (1969). *Gestalt therapy verbatim*. Lafayette, CA: Real People Press.

Perls, F. S., Hefferline, R. F., & Goodman, P. (1951). *Gestalt therapy*. New York: Julian Press.

Piercy, F. P., Sprenkle, D. H., & associates. (1986). *Family therapy sourcebook*. New York: Guilford Press.

Reiss, D. (1981). The family's construction of reality. Cambridge, MA: Harvard University Press.

Rogers, C. (1961). *On becoming a person*. Boston: Houghton Mifflin.

Satir, V. (1972). *Peoplemaking*. Palo Alto, CA: Science & Behavior Books.

Selvini-Palazzoli, M., Boscolo, L., Cecehin, G., & Prata, G. (1978). *Paradox and counterparadox*. New York: Jason Aronson.

Sherman, R., & Fredman, N. (1986). *Handbook of structural techniques in marriage and family therapy*. New York: Brunner/Mazel.

Sperry, L., & Carlson, J. (1991). *Marital therapy: Integrating theory and technique*. Denver: Love Publishing.

Stuart, R. (1980). *Helping couples change*. New York: Guilford Press.

Textor, M. R. (1989). The "healthy" family. *Journal of Family Therapy, 11*, 59–75.

Whitaker, C. A. (1976). The hindrance of theory in clinical work. In J. Guerin (Ed.), *Family therapy: Theory and practice* (pp. 154–164). New York: Gardner Press.

Whitaker, C. A., & Keith, D. V. (1981). Symbolic-experiential family therapy. In A. S. Gurman & D. P. Kniskern (Eds.), *Handbook of family therapy* (pp. 187–225). New York: Brunner/Mazel.

3

Changing Family Patterns: Developmental Impacts on Children

Bonnie E. Robson

The first half of our lives is ruined by our parents and the second half by our children.

Clarence Darrow

Today, children are likely to grow up experiencing more than one family pattern. The traditional structure of a family unit or household as a set of parents and children and possibly other blood relatives has been replaced by a multitude of possible family patterns. These include single parents, widowed, separated, divorced, adoptive, or selective families, and blended or remarried families, as well as the adoptive or biological two-parent families with intact first marriages.

Recently the interest of researchers, counselors, and the general public has focused on the effects of various patterns on individuals within the family. This chapter explores the impact of the change from one type of family structure to another on the development of children. It focuses on which developmental style or coping strategies and which environmental supports potentiate healthy adaptation to a change in family pattern. Using this knowledge, counselors can exert a positive influence on the process of normal development in ameliorating or preventing maladaptive responses.

THE PROBABILITY OF CHANGE IN FAMILY PATTERN

Most children who have lived in more than one family pattern have experienced parental separation or divorce (Bane, 1979; Norton & Glick, 1979). Since 1972, in the United States, more than one million children under age 18 have been affected each year by their parents' divorce (Carter & Glick, 1976) (although not all marital separations end in legal divorce proceedings). An estimated 40%-50% of children born in the 1980s will spend some time in a single-parent home (Hetherington, 1979; Statistics Canada, 1983).

Almost half of Canadian families and 45% of American families were predicted to be of the remarried form by the end of the 1980s (Visher & Visher, 1982). This is not surprising given that 80% of divorced men and 75% of divorced women remarry (widowed persons are much less likely to remarry) (Morrison & Thompson-Guppy, 1985). These statistics suggest that 25% of all children will be part of a remarried family; others will live with parents who are in a blended common-law union. Although the latter is not remarriage, the children will be required to form a relationship with an adult in the stepparent role. Even this readjustment is not the end of the divorce process for some children, as 47% of second marriages eventually dissolve (Morrison & Thompson-Guppy, 1985) and the children of these parents must adapt once more.

EFFECTS OF PARENTAL MARITAL STATUS

That children of divorce are over-represented in psychiatric populations has been known for two decades (Kalter, 1977; McDermott; 1970). These children show higher rates of delinquency and antisocial behavior, more neurotic symptoms, depression, conduct disorders, and habit formations such as sleep disturbances than do children in intact homes (McDermott, 1970; Morrison, 1974; Schoettle & Cantwell, 1980). In nonclinic populations the reported maladaptations are numerous. The children are more dependent, disobedient, aggressive, whining, demanding, and unaffectionate (McDermott, 1970). Hetherington, Cox, and Cox (1978) reported that children with divorced parents have generalized feelings of anxiety and helplessness and lower self-esteem. They perform less well on a variety of social and adjustment indices (Guidubaldi & Perry, 1985).

In interviewing 703 children from separated, divorced, and remarried families, Brady, Bray, and Zeeb (1986) found that they differed in both type and degree of problems. Although differences between children with separated parents and children with divorced parents were not significant, the children with separated parents showed more immature behavior, tensions, hyperactivity, and sleep disturbances. Children from remarried families "were found to demonstrate more behavior problems as characterized by conduct problems and hyperactive behavior" (p. 409).

DEMOGRAPHIC VARIABLES

In a 6-year follow-up of 60 children of divorcing parents who were compared with 64 children of nondivorcing parents, Hetherington, Cox, and Cox (1985) found that divorce had more adverse long-term effects on boys. Remarriage of the custodial parent was found to be associated with an increase in behavioral problems for girls and a decrease in problems for boys. Further, stability of the problem behaviors was found to be related to the gender of the children. "Early aggressive and antisocial behavior is more predictive of later behavior problems and lack of social competence than is early withdrawal and anxiety. Moreover, early externalizing behavior in girls, perhaps because it is less frequent and viewed as less sex appropriate, is the best predictor of later socially inept behavior" (p. 529). They suggested that these gender differences may be more prominent in younger children.

Brady, Bray, and Zeeb (1986) failed to find any significant interaction between parental marital status and the child's age and gender. Similarly, other studies have not found gender to be correlated significantly with divorce adjustment (Kalter, 1977; Kurdek, Blisk, & Siesky, 1981; Saucier & Ambert, 1986). In a psychiatric population McDermott (1970) found that the proportion of male to female patients was generally equivalent.

Firstborn children, who might feel more responsible for their parents and younger siblings, may experience more stress. The youngest child may have difficulty in later adolescence in identity formation and leaving home to pursue a career if leaving home means abandoning his or her single parent.

Studies of nonclinic populations have suggested that the child's age or specific developmental phase at the time of parental separation is related to the quality as well as the severity of the reaction (Kalter & Rembar, 1981; Wallerstein & Kelly, 1980). Further, the child's age appears to be related to adjustment to the divorce (Kurdek, Blisk, & Siesky, 1981; McDermott, 1970). Generally the younger the child is, the more vulnerable he or she appears to be, because younger children show the most behavioral disturbance (Brady, Bray, & Zeeb, 1986; Hetherington, Cox, & Cox, 1978; Kalter, 1977; Wallerstein & Kelly, 1980).

DEVELOPMENTAL REACTIONS

The child's developmental stage at the time of parental separation seems to be related to the reaction (Hetherington, Cox, & Cox, 1985; Wallerstein & Kelly, 1980; Robson, 1980, 1985). Thus, the following descriptions of the common reactions are divided into age-related (but not age-specific) groupings.

Infants and Preschool Children (0–5)

Following parental separation children under age 5 tend to regress in their development, showing feeding difficulties, toileting problems including soiling, smearing, and enuresis, and frequently disturbed sleeping patterns. Preschool and kindergarten children show, among other symptoms, intense separation anxiety manifested as fear that they will be left alone or abandoned by both parents.

The intensity of this reaction has two possible explanations. These children understand, albeit simplistically, that their parents no longer love each other; they are no longer living together. They reason that if this can happen to their parents, they, too, can be abandoned. An alternate explanation is that having lost one parent, they already have experienced abandonment. Fearing that they will be abandoned by the other parent, they regress to more childish behavior, recalling that when they were babies, they were loved and cared for and in close proximity to both of their parents.

Early responses of anger, fear, depression, and guilt are common in children of this age group. Preschoolers repeatedly state that they miss the nonresident parent. Although these statements may anger the custodial parent, he or she should be helped to realize that this expression of loss does not mean the child loves the resident parent any less; rather, the child wishes for both parents to be together again.

A child in this age group can develop an attachment to other parental figures and may come to view a resident stepparent as a psychological parent. This result can lead to ongoing discord between the biological parents, with subsequent negative effects on the child.

School-Age Children: Younger (6–8), Older (9–12)

Open denial of the separation or of any difficulties with the separation are frequent findings in early school-age children. Initially, parents may report that the child is adjusting well, but underlying feelings may not be readily apparent. As one illustration, Virginia, while drawing a picture of her father on the playroom blackboard, announced, "When he's not home, I pretend he's at work and it's okay. When I see him, then I'm sad." Thus, despite the denial, they view the separation as a profound loss. If these children are symptomatic, they appear depressed with anxious mood. They may be extremely hard to control and often have temper tantrums.

To differentiate the vulnerable from the invulnerable in this age group may be difficult for the counselor. The high-risk group seems to express more of a sense of guilt for having caused the separation. Nightmares are common. In addition, refusal to go to school, school failure, and unexplained illnesses are not uncommon.

School refusal may indicate that a child who, in the intermediate phase of the divorce process, 6 months to a year after the initial separation, is attempting to get the parents back together. Parents who are concerned about their child's sudden change in behavior sometimes meet to discuss what should be done. This, however, reinforces the behavior and confirms for the child that his or her actions can bring the parents back together. Despite the remarriage of one or both parents, children of 7 or 8 remain hopeful that their parents will reunite. For some children these fantasies persist as long as 10 years after the separation (Wallerstein, 1984).

Shock, surprise, denial, incredulity, and disbelief are characteristic of children within the older school-age group. This makes sense when we recall that these children adhere strongly to a sense of fair play. Rules are based on a strong identification with parental guidelines. When parents separate, the image of an all-knowing, all-good, ideal parent is destroyed, and children in this developmental phase can become intensely angry—usually at the nonresident parent. Once their initial anger subsides, they may assume that their parents are still angry with each other. Thus, they are vulnerable to a propaganda game in which they will accept, without question, bitter or false statements by one parent about the other.

Children in this developmental stage experience loyalty conflicts but fail to express them openly. They may attempt to resolve the conflict by becoming excessively dependent on one parent while completely rejecting the other. Susan, who is 9 years old, is unable to go out without her mother. She does not play with friends after school, preferring her mother's company. When the mother and daughter were interviewed, they sat huddled together on a couch. To pry them apart—even to get them to sit in separate chairs—was difficult at first.

These children frequently become enmeshed of their own volition in the custody struggle, and some hang on for years to the image of one parent as all good and the other parent as all bad. Some children engaged in the custody battle are permitted to read court transcripts and even testify on behalf of one parent. They are forced into a position of rejecting not only the other parent's behavior but also all those parts of that parent with which they had previously identified.

Shortly after his parents' separation, Kurt, who previously had shared an interest in soccer with his father, dropped the team despite his obvious enjoyment of the sport. This perceived need to reject all parts of one's life that were associated with the "other" parent can result in a lowered self-image and a concomitant decrease in level of functioning, both socially and academically.

Children in this age group may show anger at the time of a parent's remarriage. Anger that may have been directed at the noncustodial parent may be displaced onto the new marital partner. This can severely disrupt integration of the new family unit (Weiss, 1975).

Adolescents (13–18)

Parental divorce in adolescence can accelerate growth toward maturity, with many adolescents taking on more responsibility than their peers (Robson, 1980). This observation led many people to assert that the adolescent personality was minimally affected by divorce (Reinhard, 1977). If the spurt comes too early, however, it can intensify normal adolescent developmental conflicts and result in a premature attempt at mastery or a pseudo-adolescence (Wallerstein & Kelly, 1980).

Hetherington (1972) found that adolescent girls, fatherless through separation, tend to change in their interactions with males. They seek attention from men and demonstrate early heterosexual behavior, as compared with the daughters of widows, who tend to be more inhibited around men.

After surveying 1,519 high school students from three different districts, Saucier and Ambert (1986) found that adolescents from divorced families were most disadvantaged on a wide range of psychosocial variables. These included mental health, subjective reporting of their school performance, and perceptions of their life in the future, their parents, and their environment. Those authors also found that boys of widowed parents were more disadvantaged than girls with divorced parents.

Without conventional support systems and parental guidance, the independent capacity to make judgments and to establish interpersonal relationships is weakened. Lack of parental discipline, which is perceived as emotional withdrawal, is often a crucial factor constituting a further loss and an increased sense of abandonment.

College Students (18–22)

Only recently have young adults been considered when taking a developmental approach to the reactions of offspring to their parents' divorce or remarriage. Cooney, Smyer, Gunhild, Hagestad, and Klock (1986) studied 18 male and 21 female university students whose parents had been divorced 3 years or less. The authors found that in this age group the girls were more likely to experience the divorce as initially stressful.

The students appeared to lack networks, both formal and informal, and only 14% sought formal counseling. This low utilization rate may have been because of a lack of services or a lack of awareness of the availability of services. Entry into a university, with the loss of former peer support systems accompanied by the stress of an unfamiliar environment, is reported to delay adjustment to the parental separation. "The occurrence of multiple transitions was an important issue in the divorce experience in this age group" (Cooney et al., 1986, p. 473). The authors reported that this does not apply to all of the students because some found that living away from home provided protection from enmeshment in the family crisis.

Fifty percent of males and 62% of females reported a change in their relationship with their parents (Cooney et al., 1986). The women seemed more polarized in their post-separation parental relationships and experienced a deteriorating relationship with their fathers.

These are extremely important findings because the quality of relationships cannot be accounted for by custody decisions, as they might be with younger children. Although two thirds of the college students experienced anger directed at one or both parents, they were equally worried about their parents' future. More students reported being worried about their mothers' ability to cope with independent living situations.

A study of 400 18- and 19-year old college students revealed that those with divorced or separated parents were anxious about their own future marriages (Robson, 1985). They were less likely to want children. If they planned to marry, they thought they should delay it until they were older—perhaps in their late 20s. More of the students reported that they planned to live with their partners prior to marriage because of their anxiety that their own marriage might end in divorce. Wallerstein and Kelly (1980) found similar concerns in their interviews with younger adolescents.

ROLE OF THE COUNSELOR

From the preceding discussion of the severity and extent of typical reactions of children to their parents' separation, one can readily agree with Hetherington, Cox, and Cox (1978) that every family breakdown has its victim or victims. The results of Wallerstein's (1980) study are troubling. It revealed that one third of the children were still distressed and intensely unhappy 5 years after their parents' separation. Of course, two thirds of the children were coping well and described as emotionally healthy.

Thus, some children cope, and some do not. Viewing divorce as an inevitable disaster may be only one perspective; the divorce process might encourage healthy development for some children. This is not to suggest that these "invulnerable" children have escaped unscathed but, rather, that they may experience the divorce as a growth-enhancing process, albeit a painful and initially distressing event.

Primary Prevention

EDUCATION

Educational programs designed to enhance adjustment fit well with Caplan's (1964) definition of primary prevention as a "... community concept. It involves lowering the rate of new cases of mental disorder in a population over a certain period by counteracting harmful circumstances before they have had a chance to produce illness. It seeks to reduce the risk for a whole population" (p. 26). In this instance the population at risk consists of children who are exposed to parental separation and divorce. In discussing children's adjustment, Kurdek, Blisk, and Siesky (1981) stated that:

> Adjustment involves cultural beliefs, values and attitudes surrounding modern family life (the macro system), both the stability of the post divorce environment and the social supports available to the restructured single parent family (the exo system), the nature of the family interaction in the pre and post separation periods (the micro system), and the child's individual psychological competencies for dealing with stress (the ontogenic system). (p. 569)

The literature contains few reports of community intervention strategies designed to correct cultural misperceptions and attitudes (which might be stated as programming directed at the macro system). Educational programming may be in the forms of bibliotherapy, programs, public forums, information events, individual parent education groups, group education for children, formal school curriculum, and education for professionals. Gardner (1979) strongly advocated that educators be involved in all aspects of the divorce process.

Rubin and Price (1979) have recommended education within the school system as a preventive measure that can counteract the perpetuation of divorce in families. This type of intervention is especially important for married teenagers, because we know that this group is at high risk for marriage dissolution. By actively working with this population to further knowledge and problem-solving skills, a higher marital success rate may be ensured.

Warren and Amara (1984) found that parenting groups for custodial parents that begin after legal divorce proceedings are more effective than groups offered immediately after the separation. They further reported that participants in these 6-week groups who benefited most were the parents who had reported the greatest post-divorce stress.

Structured, educationally oriented groups exclusively for children of separated and divorced parents, either within the nursery or primary schools or within community centers and public libraries, have been recommended (Boren, 1983; Fine, 1982; Kurdek, Blisk, & Siesky, 1981; Nevins, 1981; Robson, 1982; Tableman, 1981). These community or nonclinic groups seem to be more effective when they are highly structured and when they adhere to a specific curriculum. Many organizations offer family-oriented parallel group programs similar to the program proposed by Isaacs and Levin (1984).

Freeman (1984) stated that children who participated in an 8-week semistructured educational group were significantly better adjusted than their wait-listed controls. They showed improved in-classroom behavior, and their parents reported that they were more achievement-oriented. They had developed more specific coping repertoires and responses to stress.

In one unique program Crossman and Adams (1980) used crisis theory and social facilitation programs with preschool children. This intervention was based on the assumption that children of divorce need adult-child interaction in addition to that provided by the mother, to mediate the negative consequences of having only one parent available. In a carefully designed double control study, preschool children with separated parents made marked gains in locus of control and intelligence testing.

LEGISLATION

Most recommendations for legislative changes advocate uniform state laws to avoid child snatching by a noncustodial parent. Others suggest changes to involve children in determining custody and visitation and to promote the concept of no-fault divorce (Atwell, Moore, Nielsen, & Levite, 1984; Payne & Dimock, 1983).

Conciliation counseling may assist families through the legal procedures surrounding a divorce and can help reduce adverse effects (Cleveland & Irvin, 1982; Lebowitz, 1983). Similarly, family mediation can simplify the procedures by proper preparation of the couple for the legalities. A full description of the place of family mediation in the divorce process is described by Haber, Mascari, and Sanders-Mascari (1983).

Much has been written about the best arrangements for custody and visitation of children. In recent years several states have followed the example of California in awarding joint custody as the preferred mode of custody. Joint custody acknowledges the continuation of parenting rights, responsibility, and duties of both parents but does not dictate place of residence or visiting and access practices. Wallerstein and Kelly (1980), Clingempeel and Reppucci (1982), and Steinman (1981) recommend joint custody, while Nehls and Morsenbesser (1980) and Goldstein, Freud, and Solnit (1973) caution against its overuse.

In examining 414 consecutive cases of divorce, Ilfeld, Ilfeld, and Alexander (1982) found a significant decrease in relitigation rates when joint custody was awarded. This is not surprising when one considers that a requirement for successful joint custody is the ability to negotiate. In 18 cases the joint custody award was made over the opposition of both parents, and their relitigation rate was the same as when sole custody was awarded.

Is joint custody the best alternative? Certainly some children find a joint custody arrangement that requires frequent changes of residence unsettling and anxiety-provoking (Steinman, 1981). In conclusion, joint custody can work, but it is not effective in all cases.

Direct Intervention

EARLY IDENTIFICATION

To be most effective, programs should be provided first for children and adolescents who are at high risk for maladaptive responses to their parents' separation. The previously described research indicated that the children more at risk are boys (Hetherington, Cox, & Cox, 1985), children with poor academic achievement (Rutter, 1979), firstborn children (Despert, 1962), and children whose parents are only recently separated (Wallerstein, 1980).

Several researchers (Chess, Thomas, Korn, Mittleman, & Cohen, 1983; Ellison, 1983; Rutter, 1971) have implicated ongoing parental discord as a high risk factor for maladaptive patterns. Alternatively, children and adolescents who had a supportive peer group and were able to rely on their custodial parent and siblings were less vulnerable (Kalter, 1977; Robson, Homatidis, Johnson, & Orlando, 1986).

The quality and availability of support services, both before and after the separation, seem to differentiate the vulnerable and the invulnerable. Because vulnerable children make less use of their families for support and rely more heavily on fewer friends who also are more likely to have separated parents, peer support groups for these children would seem to be an efficacious preventive program.

SCHOOL-BASED SUPPORTIVE GROUP PROGRAMS

The education of teachers, administrative personnel, and parents can provide a firm basis for the success of school-based programs. Supportive groups that are moderately structured and time-limited seem to constitute ideal programming for adolescence and late latency (ages ± 10–12) children for the reasons indicated earlier (Rubin & Price, 1979). During these group sessions, children often project and portray their parents as mean, selfish, abusive, and violent. Ultimately, the parents do emerge as having strengths as well as weaknesses.

Children's divorce groups led by elementary school counselors have been found to be extremely successful (Wilkinson & Bleck, 1976). This type of group, which is based on a developmental model of counseling and includes play activities and crafts, is synopsized by developmental phase in Table 3.1 From personal experience, common themes of these groups are loneliness, fears of separation or abandonment, and feelings of guilt.

While acknowledging that preventive programs based on a crisis intervention model can be effective initially, Kalter, Pickar, and Lesowitz (1984) believe that children go through a reworking of "nodal developmental points." They caution that divorce should be viewed not as a single life event but, rather, as a process. Thus, they recommend that groups within the school setting should assist children "to negotiate points." They caution that divorce should be viewed not as a single life event but, rather, as a process. Thus, they recommend that groups within the school setting should assist children "to negotiate more effectively the developmental tasks associated with both divorce and post-divorce experiences" (p. 614). Although they worked with students in grades five and

TABLE 3.1
School-Based Groups for Children of Separation or Divorce

Developmental Phase	Early School Age (6–8)	Latency (8–12, 9–11)	Early Adolescence (13–15)	Middle and Late Adolescence (15–18)(18–22)
Symptoms	Pervasive sadness, suffering, experience loss Fearful nightmares Guilt Reconciliation desired	Shock and surprise Intense anger Blaming and rejecting one parent Dependency conflicts	Shock, not surprise Pain, "loss of family" Anger at loss Pseudo-maturity Acting-out, delinquency, promiscuity	
Group Size	5–6	5–7	5–6	6–8
Gender	Both genders	Same gender	Same gender	Both genders
Length of Time	1 hour	1–1½ hours	1 hour	1-½ hours
Setting	One room; table, chairs around it Carpeted floor space	Two rooms — group room and activity space; sturdy chairs	Group room; video playback and taping Sturdy chairs	Group room; avoid swivel chairs; lamps, pictures Regular seating, coffee tables
Equipment, Supplies and Materials	Pillows, craft supplies, paper, scissors, glue, crayons, etc. Simple games — Bingo, Twister, ET, Simon Says, Star Wars, Candyland Plasticine, Polaroid camera, display area Juice, milk, cookies	Indoor/outdoor sports — floor hockey, soccer, softballs Film Dress-up materials, hats, belts, make-up Polaroid camera, craft supplies, string, paper, cooking supplies Juice, milk, cookies	Suggestion box Paper, pens Films Simple dress-up props, collage materials Soda	Soda, coffee, tea (15–18) No refreshments (18–22)
Activities	Individual — crafts or games (2 per session) plus refreshment time (starts with snack)	One per session — alternate large motor with quieter End with refreshment	Films, guest speakers, videodrama, discussion Refreshments available at outset	Discussion Refreshments available at outset (15–18)
Counselor Activity	Group preparation Interpretation of positive transference. Avoid splitting Modeling Individual in group Structure, rules, boundaries Coaching Rules — listen when someone is talking, stay in room, keep hands off others and others' work	Coaching approach Interpret group process during planning Define boundaries Provide security Stimulate ideas, topics Promote group cohesion, psychodrama	Focus on group process Define boundaries Assist in maintaining structure and focus Role play Participate Relate group to reality	Group as whole Use reasoning Use events to develop group insights Use modeling Allow for verbal confrontation with adult Relate group to reality
Parent Involvement	Regular contact (once a week/ once a month)	Group meetings irregular, discussed with group Parents available to transport and wait for children if necessary Parent groups	Initially 6–8 weeks	As indicated; not necessary

TABLE 3.1 (continued)

Developmental Phase	Early School Age (6–8)	Latency (8–12, 9–11)	Early Adolescence (13–15)	Middle and Late Adolescence (15–18)(18–22)
Goals	Have peer support Reduce anxiety Reduce unrealistic or catastrophic expectations of adults Link feelings with language Help child focus on individual needs Improve concentration and school motivation through improved self-image	Have peer support Reduce guilt See both sides of parents Gain insight Improve behavior Control, reduce impulsiveness Improve self-image Improve interpersonal skills	See both sides of parents Tolerate ambivalence Not use alcohol and drugs for loneliness Improve self-image Gain insight	Share and care Try for cohesion and confrontation in supportive environment Develop capacity to resolve conflicts in school and family Develop hope for future Improve self-esteem
Themes	Anger Blame Rights and fair play Intolerance of mistakes Sadness linked with anger	Anger Blame Rights and fair play Intolerance of mistakes Sadness linked with anger	Hostility Violence Rejection Too much responsibility too soon Hunger and pain	Loneliness Fear of future Existential anxiety Loss of adolescence Sexuality

six, they also recommend groups for students at other nodal developmental points and possibly at the point of entry or leaving junior or senior high school and as preparation for college or university entrance.

Themes that emerge for students of about 10–12 years are anxiety over parental fighting, loyalty conflicts, worry about custody decisions, loss of family and loss or partial loss of the father, worry and anger about parents' dating, and concern about stepparents' discipline (Kalter et al., 1984). In adolescent school-based groups, anxiety-charged issues include marital infidelity and family violence. Teens express fear about parents' dating—and about parents who are not socially active. Adolescents feel an increased sense of responsibility and guilt if the parent is not socially active, but when the parent expresses a wish to remarry, the adolescent is concerned about having to revert from the adult position that he or she currently occupies back into a child role.

In addition, anxieties about homosexuality are increased during adolescence. Although this is a normal developmental fear during adolescence, it appears to be increased among students with divorced parents. They express fears about disturbed gender identity formation as a result of living with only one parent—particularly if that parent has preferred an opposite-sex child. Not being of the preferred gender is an issue for both males and females.

Discussion of loyalties is prominent in group sessions when holidays and vacations are imminent—especially summer and Christmas. Girls' groups tend to confirm research demonstrating lower self-concept among girls whose parents are separated (Parish & Taylor, 1979). A persistent theme in girls' groups was that they felt deprived of a normal teenage life and that they felt abnormal and unlike their peers.

An advantage of students participating in school-based groups is the opportunity to observe participants more closely in peer interactions. Close observation can enable the counselor to select students who might benefit from a more individualized approach or who might warrant referral to a clinical setting for treatment.

School-based groups, compared with community-based groups, are less likely to require parallel parent groups. Adolescent groups prefer not to have parents regularly involved, and groups may be more productive when they are free from direct parental interference. To participate actively and openly, adolescents need to be reassured about confidentiality.

FAMILY OR INDIVIDUAL COUNSELING

Reviewing the literature that deals with disruption of the family unit, few reports advocate a family approach. Hayes and Hayes (1986) addressed the issues in counseling for remarriage families. Beal (1979) recommended family counseling as a preventive measure. Multiple family group therapy, as employed by Messinger, Walters, and Freeman (1978), promotes change and realignment with the family.

Parental *support*, not education, is recommended to assist very young children in adapting to separation and divorce of their parents. As Rutter (1971) pointed out, a good relationship with one parent can be highly preventive of later difficulties. Parents who participate in parent support groups report improved self-esteem as they acquire better parental coping skills (Kessler, 1978; Thiessen, Avery, & Joanning, 1980). And if they feel more positive about their own skills, they are likely to have improved relationships with their children.

Parents of preschoolers need support in maintaining appropriate limits in the face of their child's often extreme regression. Parents who already are stressed may become intensely angry and displace onto their preschooler their anger at the failure of the marriage. If the child is encopretic and smearing or crying and stating repeatedly that he or she wants the absent parent, the resident parent is likely to get even angrier. Preschoolers need to cope cognitively with the separation, but 80% of them are given no explanation for the loss or partial loss of one parent (Wallerstein, 1980).

When parent counseling alone is insufficient to promote security and reassurance, filial therapy, in which the parent is trained to interact in a therapeutic-like play session with the child, is recommended. Filial therapy is especially helpful when a child seems to have an ambivalent attachment to the resident parent and an anxious-avoidant attachment to the nonresident parent (Robson, 1982).

Individual secondary prevention or treatment programs should be oriented to the child's developmental phase. Individually oriented programs usually are reserved for secondary prevention or treatment of symptomatic children. One exception is the specific high-risk population of children "kidnapped" by their noncustodial parent. Individual counseling is recommended with these children to avoid post-traumatic stress syndrome, which is specific to this group (Terr, 1983).

Early school-age children seem to respond extremely well to individual play therapy sessions in which issues of the "neurosis of abandonment," as defined by Anthony (1974), can be represented symbolically. Play therapy assists the child in achieving mastery of the stressful situation by repetition of the feared event in the play situation. Short-term play therapy, supported by frequent visiting with the nonresident father, has been extremely effective in reducing boys' anxiety symptoms such as nightmares or fears of robbers, murderers, or monsters.

CLINICAL GROUP COUNSELING PROGRAMS

More symptomatic older children and adolescents in clinic settings similar to those in school-based programs seem to respond well to group therapy. Older school-age children have a tendency to take sides and become embroiled in parental conflict and intractable custody disputes (Robson, 1982). In this situation, family counseling with the unfavored parent and the child or children is imperative. Separate individual counseling for the favored (usually the custodial) parent is recommended in conjunction with family counseling. The custodial parent must be helped to overcome his or her own anger and resentment at the situation and to support the children in a more reality-oriented approach to visitation.

Adolescents who show more severe reactions, such as acting-out through delinquent behavior or promiscuity or marked withdrawal, can benefit from an intensive psychotherapeutic group experience, which may protect them from developing a personality disorder. The creative drama and videotape playback employed in these groups increases the individual's awareness, facilitates expression of fantasy and feelings, and promotes problem solving (Stirtzinger & Robson, 1985).

The video playback technique is unique in that it allows the adolescent to both invest in the process and maintain a safe distance. In light of these adolescents' loss of alliance with parents and their difficulty in forming a treatment alliance, video playback allows each group member to maintain a sense of control. It allows the adolescent to be an active participant, either as part of the audience or as the director of a drama. Thus, the individual is permitted to identify with the group in a role function rather than as a dependent patient.

Creative drama can be viewed as a complex form of play. The adolescent is developmentally intermediate between needing the discharge of play and the ability to bind and delay inherent in talking therapy. Creative drama is intermediate between concrete, symbolic play with toys and personal revelation. It permits displacement on the characters.

In my experience with early adolescent clinic groups, family violence seems to be portrayed with increasing frequency. In client dramatizations fathers set themselves on fire and threaten the family with guns, whereas mothers take overdoses or suddenly abandon the family. There is much sexual stereotyping, often linked with violence and anger (Robson, 1986).

Confusion over the cause of separation and the need to blame is captured in plays about family conflicts. In these plays parents frequently are portrayed as fighting over their adolescent's behavior—such as failing to clean up his or her room or not finishing homework or getting into trouble at school. Portrayal of the parents' continued fighting may represent an ambivalent wish to have the parents reunite. Fathers usually are blamed for the break-up; mothers are viewed as stupid and inadequate. Stepmothers typically are seen in the classic Cinderella sense. Parents who remarry often bear another child, so expression of the theme of being "replaced" by an infant also is common in these groups.

The older adolescent clinic groups, in my experience, tend to be more metaphorical. Through discussion these adolescents rework their understanding of their parents' separation, issues of dating, or the loss of a boyfriend or girlfriend. These themes may reflect a greater sense of parents as individuals with needs of their own. Dramatized solutions to the dilemmas, however, are at times magical and childish, with the main character suddenly becoming a famous rock star, lawyer, or journalist—an individual who goes into the world successfully, needing help from no one.

Families sometimes are portrayed as arguing endlessly with no resolution, but later themes frequently involve asking for and receiving help. A loss of discipline may represent the loss of the family as a unit. The adolescent's strivings for independence and identity can be intensified in an attempt to seek the appropriate discipline. A struggle that extends beyond the family unit into the community suggests that the parent (or both parents) needs support and guidance in providing consistency and structure. Individual counseling for the single custodial parent or separate counseling with the same counselor for both the resident and the nonresident parent may be indicated.

CONCLUSION

The percentage of students in elementary, secondary, and even postsecondary schools who recently have experienced a change in their family pattern is increasing. This demands the development of more innovative, preventive programming for the students affected, This programming is vital if counselors are to ward off maladaptive responses in later years and help both adults and children cope with changing family patterns.

REFERENCES

Anthony, E. J. (1974). Children at risk from divorce: A review. In E. J. Anthony & C. Koupernik, *The child in his family* (pp. 461–477). New York: Wiley.

Atwell, A. E., Moore, U. S., Nielsen, E., & Levite, Z. (1984). Effects of joint custody on children *Bulletin of American Academy of Psychiatric Law, 12*, 149–157.

Bane, M. J. (1979). Marital disruption and the lives of children. In G. Levinger & O. C. Moles (Eds.), *Divorce and separation* (pp. 276–286). New York: Basic Books.

Beal, E. W. (1979). Children of divorce: A family systems perspective. *Journal of Social Issues, 35*, 140–154.

Boren, R. (1983). The therapeutic effects of a school-based intervention program for children of the divorced. *Dissertation Abstracts International, 43* (12-A), 3811–3812.

Brady, C. P., Bray, J. H., & Zeeb, L. (1986). Behavior problems of clinic children: Relation to parental marital status, age and sex of child. *American Journal of Orthopsychiatry, 56*, 399–412.

Caplan, G. (1964). *Principles of preventive psychiatry*. New York: Basic Books.

Carter, H., & Glick, P. E. (1976). *Marriage and divorce: A social and economic study*. Cambridge, MA: Harvard University Press.

Chess, S., Thomas, A. Korn, S., Mittleman, M., & Cohen, J. (1983). Early parental attitudes, divorce and separation and adult outcomes: Findings of a longitudinal study. *Journal of American Academy of Child Psychiatry, 22*(1), 47–51.

Cleveland, M., & Irvin, K. (1982). Custody resolution counseling: An alternative intervention. *Journal of Marital & Family Therapy, 8*, 105–111.

Clingempeel, G. W., & Reppucci, N. D. (1982). Joint custody after divorce: Major issues and goals for research. *Psychology Bulletin, 92*, 102–127.

Cooney, T. M., Smyer, M. A., Hagestad, G. O., & Klock, R. (1986). Parental divorce in young adulthood. Some preliminary findings. *American Journal of Orthopsychiatry, 56*, 470–477.

Crossman, S. M., & Adams, G. R. (1980). Divorce, single parenting and child development, *Journal of Psychology, 106*, 205–217.

Despert, J. (1962). *Children of divorce*. New York: Doubleday.

Ellison, E. S. (1983). Issues concerning parental harmony and children's psychosocial adjustment. *American Journal of Orthopsychiatry, 53*(1), 73–80.

Fine, S. (1982). Children in divorce, custody and access situations: The contribution of the mental health professional. *Journal of Child Psychology & Psychiatry, 21*, 353–361.

Freeman, R. (1984). *Children in families experiencing separation and divorce: An investigation of the effects of brief interventions*. Toronto: Family Service Association of Metropolitan Toronto Press.

Gardner, R. A. (1979). Social, legal and therapeutic changes that should lessen the traumatic effects of divorce on children. *Journal of the American Academy of Psychoanalysis, 6*, 231–247.

Goldstein, J., Freud, A., & Solnit, A. J. (1973). *Beyond the best interest of the child*. New York: Free Press.

Guidubaldi, J., & Perry, J. D. (1985). Divorce and mental health sequelae for children: A two year follow-up of a nationwide sample. *Journal of American Academy of Child Psychiatry, 24*, 531–537.

Haber, C. H., Mascari, J. B., & Sanders-Mascari, A. (1983). Family mediation: An idea whose time has come. *Counseling & Human Development, 18*, 1–8.

Hayes, R. L., & Hayes, B. A. (1986). Remarriage families: Counseling parents, stepparents, and their children. *Counseling & Human Development, 18*, 1–8.

Hetherington, E. M. (1972). Effects of father absence on the personality development in adolescent daughters. *Developmental Psychology, 7*, 313–326.

Hetherington, E. M. (1979). Divorce: A child's perspective. *American Journal of Psychiatry, 34*, 851–858.

Hetherington, E. M., Cox, M., & Cox, R. (1978). The aftermath of divorce. In J. Stevens & M. Mathews (Eds.), *Mother-child relations*. Washington, DC: National Association for the Education of Young Children.

Hetherington, E. M., Cox, M., & Cox, R. (1985). Long term effects of divorce and remarriage on the adjustment of children. *Journal of American Academy of Child Psychiatry, 24*, 518–530.

Ilfeld, F. W., Jr., Ilfeld, H. Z., & Alexander, J. R. (1982). Does joint custody work? A first look at outcome data of relitigation. *American Journal of Psychiatry, 139*, 62–66.

Isaacs, M. B., & Levin, I. R. (1984). Who's in my family? A longitudinal study of drawings of children of divorce. *Journal of Divorce, 7*, 1–20.

Kalter, N. (1977). Children of divorce in an out-patient psychiatric population, *American Journal of Orthopsychiatry, 47*, 40–51.

Kalter, N., Pickar, J., & Lesowitz, M. (1984). School-based developmental facilitation groups for children of divorce: A preventive intervention. *American Journal of Orthopsychiatry, 54*, 613–623.

Kalter, N., & Rembar, J. (1981). The significance of child's age at the time of parental divorce. *American Journal of Orthopsychiatry, 51*, 85–100.

Kessler, S. (1978). Building skills in divorce adjustment groups. *Journal of Divorce, 2*, 209–216.

Kurdek, L. A., Blisk, D., & Siesky, A. (1981). Correlates of children's long-term adjustment to their parents' divorce. *Developmental Psychology, 17*, 565–579.

Lebowitz, M. L. (1983). The organization and utilization of child-focused facility for divorcing, single-parent and remarried families. *Conciliation Courses Review, 21*, 99–104.

McDermott, J. R. (1970). Divorce and its psychiatric sequelae in children. *Archive of General Psychiatry, 23*, 421–427.

Messinger, L., Walters, K. N., & Freeman, S. J. J. (1978). Preparation for remarriage following divorce: The use of group technique. *American Journal of Orthopsychiatry, 48*, 263–272.

Morrison, J. (1974). Parental divorce as a factor in childhood psychiatric illness. *Comprehensive Psychiatry, 15*, 95–102.

Morrison, K., & Thompson-Guppy, A. (1985). *Stepmothers: Exploring the myth.* Ottawa: Canadian Council on Social Development.

Nehls, N., & Morsenbesser, M. (1980). Joint custody: An exploration of the issues. *Family Process, 19*, 117–125.

Nevins, V. J. (1981). Evaluation of effectiveness of a group treatment intervention with children of divorce. *Dissertation Abstracts International, 42* (2-B), 781.

Norton, A. M., & Glick, P. S. (1979). Marital instability in America. In G. Levinger & O. C. Moles (Eds.), *Divorce and separation* (pp. 6–19). New York: Basic Books.

Parish, T. S., & Taylor, J. C. (1979). The impact of divorce and subsequent father absence on children's and adolescents' self concepts. *Journal of Youth & Adolescence, 8*, 427–432.

Payne, J. D., & Dimock, J. L. (1983). Legal and psychiatric approaches to marriage breakdown or divorce. *Psychiatric Journal University of Ottawa, 8*, 189–197.

Reinhard, D. (1977). The reaction of adolescent boys and girls to the divorce of their parents. *Journal of Clinical Child Psychology, 6*, 21–23.

Robson, B. (1980). *My parents are divorced, too.* New York: Everest House.

Robson, B. E. (1982). A developmental approach to the treatment of children of divorcing families. In L. Messinger (Ed.), *Therapy with remarriage families* (pp. 59–78). Rockville, MD: Aspen Systems Corp.

Robson, B. (1985). Marriage concepts of older adolescents. *Canadian Journal of Psychiatry, 30*, 169–172.

Robson, B. (1986). School-based groups for children and adolescents of divorce. *Canadian Home Economics Journal, 36*, 13–22.

Robson, B., Homatides, G., Johnson, L., & Orlando, F. (1986). *Toronto family study.* Toronto: Toronto Board of Education Publication.

Rubin, L. D., & Price, J. H. (1979). Divorce and its effects on children. *Journal of School Health, 49*, 552–559.

Rutter, M. (1971). Parent-child separation: Psychological effects on the children. *Journal of Child Psychology & Psychology, 12*, 223–260.

Rutter, M. (1979). Invulnerability or why some children are not damaged by stress. In S. J. Shamsie (Ed.) *New Directions in children's mental health* (pp. 53–75). New York: Spectrum.

Saucier, J., & Ambert, A. (1986). Adolescents' perception of self and of immediate environment by parental marital status: A controlled study. *Canadian Journal of psychiatry, 31*, 505–512.

Schoettle, J. C., & Cantwell, D. P. (1980). Children of divorce: Demographic variables, symptoms and diagnoses. *Journal of American Academy of Child Psychiatry, 9*, 453–476.

Statistics Canada. (1983). The experience of children in joint custody arrangement: A reprint of a study. *American Journal of Orthopsychiatry, 51*, 403–414.

Steinman, S. (1981). The experience of children in joint custody arrangement: A reprint of a study. *American Journal of Orthopsychiatry, 51*, 403–414.

Stirtzinger, R., & Robson, B. (1985). Videodrama and the observing ego. *Journal of Small Group Behaviour, 16*(4), 539–548.

Tableman, B. (1981). Overview of programs to prevent mental health problems of children. *Public Health Reports, 96*, 38–44.

Terr, L. C. (1983). Childsnatching: A new epidemic of an ancient malady. *Journal of Pediatrics, 103*, 151–156.

Thiessen, J. D., Avery, A. W., & Joanning, H. (1980). Facilitating post divorce adjustment among women: A communication skills training approach. *Journal of Divorce, 4*, 4–22.

Visher, E. B., & Visher, J. S. (1982). Step families in the 1980's. In L. Messinger (Ed.), *Therapy with remarriage families* (pp. 105–119). Rockville, MD: Aspen Systems Corp.

Wallerstein, J. S. (1980). The impact of divorce on children. *Psychiatric Clinics of North America, 3*, 455–468.

Wallerstein, J. S. (1984). Children of divorce: Preliminary report of a ten year follow-up of young children. *American Journal of Orthopsychiatry, 54*, 444–458.

Wallerstein, J. S., & Kelly, J. B. (1980). *Surviving the breakup: How children and parents cope with divorce*. New York: Basic Books.

Warren, N. J., & Amara, I. A. (1984). Educational groups for single parents: The parenting after divorce programs. *Journal of Divorce, 8*(2), 79–96.

Weiss, R. S. (1975). *Marital separation*. New York: Basic Books.

Wilkinson, G. S., & Bleck, R. T. (1976). Children's divorce groups. *Elementary School Guidance & Counseling, 11*, 205–213.

TWO

Strategies

The term *family counseling* means different things to different people. If we consider family counseling along a continuum, we find at one end the family systems purists who "focus entirely on the family as the unit of both change and pathology" (Kolevzon & Green, 1985, pp. 26–27) and who direct all interventions on the family unit as a whole. At the other end of the continuum we find counselors who use family interventions for the purpose of shedding light on the problems of specific family members and whose focus stays primarily on the individual.

This book is based on a broader and more flexible orientation. A variety of interventions can be used to affect family functioning and enhance individual development. An awareness that the family is a system makes it apparent that changes in any one area will, directly or indirectly, affect other facets of family dynamics. Counselors need to have in their repertoires a number of tools that can be adapted to meet the needs of specific families. Counselors also need to know that, although family counseling interventions can be used to remedy existing problems, they also can serve a preventive role, helping people navigate the normal transitions of family life.

In this section we highlight a range of interventions showing that the counselor can choose his or her focus from among a number of helping alternatives. Jon Carlson and Dan Fullmer suggest a health or wellness model of family counseling. Their chapter reviews some of the characteristics of a healthy family and suggests a strength-oriented model that can be used to work toward the goal of family wellness.

Charles Huber, in "Marital Counseling: An Adlerian Approach," focuses on the married couple. Like Carlson and Fullmer, he uses a positive, health-oriented approach, based on the process of encouragement.

In "Sexual Counseling," Ron Pion, Jack Annon, and Jon Carlson outline methods that can be used to resolve sexual conflict. Their focus in this chapter is not on serious problems that may require intensive, highly specialized therapy but, rather, on sexual problems that can be resolved effectively through brief counseling procedures that belong in the family counselor's repertoire.

Family counselors also should be aware of the important contribution to family life that mediation has made. Charles Huber, J. Barry Mascari, and Aviva Sanders-Mascari discuss mediation as a useful tool for bringing about equitable solutions to pressing problems. Although mediation has been widely recognized as a method that can help people avoid being victimized by adversarial divorce processes, it also has proven effective for dealing with conflicts within intact families.

Finally, Jon Carlson and Brenda Faiber describe the necessary skills for effective parenting. Parent education has become an important tool for today's family counselor. The belief that most families need training, rather than treatment, guides this chapter and, in fact, provides an underpinning for all of the chapters in this section. Family counselors who have a variety of tools in their repertoire can empower families so that democratic family life and enhanced human development become the norm.

REFERENCE

Kolevzon, M. S., & Green, R. G. (1985). *Family therapy models: Convergence and divergence*. New York: Springer.

4

Family Counseling: Principles for Growth

Jon Carlson and Dan Fullmer

Sticks in a bundle are unbreakable.
Kenyan proverb

The national barometer of mental health seems to be dropping at an ever accelerating rate as more and more people become symptom-ridden victims of stress. Psychoses, neuroses, high blood pressure, ulcers, backaches, headaches, nervous tics, and bodily discomforts are all common place. In today's world of emphasis on technology and change, the situation seems to be changing—for the worse. Preventive interventions are not occurring, and remedial efforts are still producing a 50% chance of recovery—the same percentage as no treatment at all. This is a time when people must decide to live a healthy life or to have a new car, to have a body or to be a body, to continue to just exist or to begin to live and grow.

Typical mental health treatment (counseling, therapy, analysis) involves reducing, or *shrinking*, the symptoms of the injured, sick, or identified patient. Research, however, indicates that this procedure is, for the most part, inefficient (in terms of use of money, resources, and time) and largely ineffective (especially in terms of permanent rather than short-term changes). This situation need not be. Approaches to mental health that are anchored in *expanding* our educational and growth-centered perspectives produce effec-

57

tive, efficient, and permanent mental health. These approaches practice equality and collaboration, center upon complete systems rather than elemental analysis, and flow or work with the natural flow of living.

Research indicates that the family is the prime source for establishment of healthy and "growthful living" as well as the breeding ground for our pathology. "Growthful living," or wellness, is more than just being alive. Human development is a lifelong process, and growth can be facilitated or arrested at any stage. The family plays a major role in personality formation and development, and we are just now realizing its lifelong importance. Our nuclear families are the first and most important educational delivery system for children, and, yet, for many understandable reasons we as a nation continue to fail to equip families to do the necessary job (White, 1976).

The counseling profession has not been effective in helping people. Research does not seem to support our traditional or current paradigms. The purpose here is to acquaint the reader with the rationale, essential principles, and constructs of family counseling, provide a description of the healthy family, present a set of directions on how to use a strength-oriented educational approach with families, and discuss how counselors can use these ideas in a school setting.

RATIONALE FOR FAMILY WORK

Although family counseling has existed for some time, it has come into prominence in both professional and public eyes over the last 25 years. The AACD (American Association of Counseling and Development) and APA (American Psychological Association) have both added divisions for the study of family. This recognition and acceptance have resulted from a growing awareness that the individual cannot be responsible for all the problems that he or she encounters, many of which come from outside pressures and influences including the family and social environment. Often, the problems of children are the result of family interaction, and family counseling has become the treatment of choice.

No one model or pattern can be used for conducting family counseling. The approach depends upon the problems, the conditions surrounding them, and the counselor's theoretical orientation (Sperry & Carlson, 1991). Nevertheless, several basic, universal principles are important for all family work.

General systems theory (Bertalanffy, 1968) applies the principle of *synergy*. Synergy is defined as: "The whole is more than the sum of its parts." Extending the principle to family practice, it is claimed that if one family member changes behavior, all other family members need to change enough to cope with the new conditions, especially the emotional climate in the family network. Fullmer's (1971) relationships theory of behavior focuses on the relationship definition between family members (i.e., mother-father, father-daughter, sibling peer group, symbiotic parent-child, friendship). The basic principle is that behavior is the expression of each individual's personal experience of meaning acted out of the relationship definition perceived by each significant other in the dyad. Adlerian or individual psychology has a well developed system for family work (Sherman & Dinkmeyer, 1987). The primary focus for application has been on child-rearing practices. The central principle treats the individual's behavior as goal-directed. The child's goal is to achieve a place of importance in his or her environment. The motivation principle is a will to belong or find a meaningful place in society.

The variety of approaches continues to grow, as does the number of counselors using family systems approaches. The "Related Readings" at the end of this chapter are sources for exploring the various approaches and can serve as a starting place for readers who desire further background in family counseling.

PRINCIPLES USED IN FAMILY WORK

The foundation on which behavior is based can be expressed in principles that represent the key components in the family counseling model described here. The principles incorporate motivation, needs, communication, identity, and power. Through an understanding of the following principles, counselors can learn to understand, communicate, and facilitate effectively within a family context.

Principle 1: Context is fundamental to meaning.

The concept of "context" is simply the setting one is in. Given your behavior in an elevator, look quickly at your behavior in your bedroom. How are the two alike? How are they different? Notice your emotional response when you imagine yourself making love in the elevator. What you feel is what we refer to as "meaning." This principle can be seen within a family setting where a child is encouraged to fight at home but not at school; where the wife is sensuous when the lights are out and frigid when the lights are one; using loose and colorful language when eating at home and being sent to the car when using these words in a public restaurant. The behaviors are the same, but the meanings or feelings are different.

Meaning has feelings because it is tied to the emotional system, the basis of the relationship system. What you feel is the way communication takes place within your family context. Processing one's own feelings is what leads to meaning. Feelings of anger, joy, sadness, elation, sorrow, and so on determine the meaning of the event. Feelings are the connection between the emotional system (myself) and the relationship system (others) (Papero, 1990). *Your perception determines what you are going to do.*

Principle 2: Relationships are substance and behavior is form.

The concept of relationship is illustrated by the complex feelings one gets when faced with an enemy as contrasted with a friend. The enemy relationship feels like flight or fright, but the friendship feels warm and free. Our behavior in each instance serves to express the meaning we are experiencing. The form may vary for each instance, but undoubtedly we will each display a consistent pattern of behavior with latitude for unique variation. *How you feel is how you act.* The "why" of your feeling is relationship definition.

When someone does things for someone else, the message may be "I love you and care for you" or "I'll dominate and trap you," depending upon the relationship. Relationship is substance and behavior is form. A mate may agree to participate in family counseling (behavior) one week to placate or "butter you up" to *control*, and may not agree to participate the next week to show you who is boss and to *control*. Although the relationship remains unchanged, the behavior is different.

Principle 3: Patterns of behavior repeat themselves in cycles.

Patterns of behavior are derived from the redundance in communication as people repeat themselves again and again and receive acceptable results. The redundant behavior can be either verbal or nonverbal, both verbal and nonverbal, and contextual-verbal/nonverbal.

Take a quick imaginary trip through your past 48 hours. What do you find? A counselor typically does the same thing at a given moment of time each day. Nobel Prize winners Konrad Lorenz (1965) and Nikko Tinbergen (1951) have observed that much of the motor behavior of any species can be described by specifying only a few dozen fixed action patterns. Your schedule is a concrete example of redundant patterns of behavior. *What is stable is predictable. What is unstable is unpredictable. Redundance in pattern is the predictable way of life.*

One specific example of our consistent patterns can be found in the "buzz phrases" (Sperry and Hess, 1974) we frequently and automatically use in conversation. Buzz phrases are simply words, explanations, exclamations, or questions that a person uses consistently. In fact, some people actually can be identified with one or more of their buzz phrases. Researchers have found that from one half to two thirds of a person's verbalizations may be reduced to 15 to 30 buzz phrases. The buzz phrases, of course, relate to the person's dominant goal. Some possible buzz phrases associated with certain goals are (Sperry, 1975, p. 24):

Buzz	**Goal**
"How do you like my . . . ?"	Attention or
"Have you ever gone to . . . ?"	Elevation
"I'll bet you didn't know . . ."	
"If this job's too hard for you . . ."	Power or
"I want it done *this* (my) way. . . ."	Control
"Who does he think he is?"	
"Just you wait and see!"	Revenge
"It's impossible to get anything through his thick skull."	
"Well, I didn't volunteer for this job anyway."	Inadequacy
"I'll try, but I know I can't do it."	
"Remember how things used to be . . ."	Time-wasting
"Say, what did you do over the weekend?"	
"Don't get so excited. It's nothing."	Peacemaking
"There must be *something* we can do about it."	
"Wow, that's really something!"	Excitement
"I might as well try it. I've done everything else."	

When we take this concept into a family and quickly map the individual patterns, it frequently is immediately apparent where the conflicts are likely to happen. The myriad of familial problems recurs in a predictable fashion as the same action chains or patterns are triggered. Each family is like and individual in that it has a characteristic way or pattern of generating conflict. Your action chain is another way to see how your relationships are defined.

Principle 4: Action chains express definition and relationships.

The concept of an action chain (Hall, 1976) comes from observing what you do following a given cue or stimulus. All behaviors actually consist of sequences, or chains of behaviors. The links in the chains are each composed of simpler behavioral components.

For example, the behavior "going to bed" can be broken down into a set of component behaviors: proceeding to the bedroom; taking off clothes; putting on sleeping attire; using bathroom and toilet facilities; saying good-night to spouse; turning out light; getting into bed. Each of these component behaviors could be broken down into even smaller components. Taking off clothes, for instance, may be composed of: untying right shoe; reaching down and removing shoe with hands; untying left shoe; reaching down and removing left shoe; removing right sock; removing left sock; removing pants; removing sweater; removing shirt; removing underwear; removing jewelry. *You are chained to your routine of actions.*

Chains are learned by taking simple behaviors already in the individual's repertoire and combining them into more complex behaviors. Each behavior in a chain has a dual function—serving as a reinforcer for the previous response and as a stimulus for the next one. The action chain utilized depends on what a situation means to the individual.

For example, if someone compliments you, you probably will activate an action chain and pass it on to someone else at the first opportunity. If someone gives you a put-down, you probably will activate an action chain and pass it on to someone else. The action chain expresses the meaning each experience has for you, completing the communication of your definition of relationship with the sender.

Principle 5: Families from a given culture will display similar behavior in a given context.

Context is the manifestation of culture parameters or rules for the way it is supposed to be. *What I do is natural because it is culturally correct. What you do is unnatural because it is culturally incorrect.* A family teaches children the culture of which it is a part. The family is an entire culture on a small scale (microcosm). Rarely does a given family master a culture's entire rule system; therefore, each family represents a unique pattern in a given culture.

Because each family emphasizes unique patterns and symbols, the range of microcosm equals the number of families in the culture. Yet, each family resembles each other family within a given culture in the global dimensions such as language, values, attitudes, and basic patterns of behavior. This phenomenon provides the basic rationale for working with multiple families in groups. The healthy family is able to accommodate the wide range of differences encountered in other families without losing its own uniqueness.

Context as a concept defines meaning to an individual in any given situation. The culture's rules for "the way it is supposed to be" form the person's emotional system, complete with physiological and biochemical consequences. The way you feel in a given situation is the manifestation of the principle. The human potential movement claimed that feelings could be the basis of behavior. The fallacy is in omission of the fact that individuals can create a new context and, therefore, new feelings by their own initiative.

Principle 6: People learn social behaviors all at once, in gestalts, not in pieces.

The context in social behavior may be more important than the specifics of what is learned. The conditions under which you come into your learning (knowledge and behavior) may be more important than the context of the learning (Loukes, 1964). *It is not what you do; it is the way you do it.*

For example, think of what is learned about sex if you are raped as your initial experience. Or think of the child who learns toilet behavior from a mother who always rewards successful execution with candy. The context may teach many values in addition to the central content in the learning experience. The counselor's attitude toward the family sets the tone for what will occur. The first few minutes of contact between people, according to Zunin and Zunin (1972), usually determine whether a successful relationship will develop. The counselor's prejudgments in regard to prejudices, values, and attitudes influence the depth of subsequent interactions.

Principle 7: The healthy family solves problems through support and trust from within the group.

The power of the family bond endures because no matter when you go to your family, it will take you in. No other human group has approached that characteristic functioning in the families of the world. After more than 50 years in the kibbutz, for example, the grandparents relate to the children in much the same way as in most extended families—with a strong emotional bond.

The strong emotional bond is the base for a healthy family. The family bond helps to solve problems because it is the source of support and the essence of trust. With this emotional base a healthy family can use the most effective means of problem solution and conflict resolution. The most effective means for solving problems is to redefine the family's relationship to the source of the problem. This can be done by stepping outside the context containing the problem. Communications experts call it *meta-communicating.* Essentially, the process requires each participant in any encounter to step outside the frame or context and look at the larger stage or picture. *The view from out here is different from the view from within.* The counseling process centers on helping families learn this method in order to become self-healing.

Principle 8: Encouragement is fundamental to creative behavior.

Individuals must gain the courage to violate their own rules for behaving if they are to achieve new behavior (Bateson, 1972). Learning is fun if the risk is manageable. If the risk is too great, the result is traumatic. Pathology in behavior frequently is generated by the anxiety or fear of failure. Failure is the deterrent to foolishness. To risk, to go beyond what you know and can predict the consequences of, requires you to violate your rule of safety. Whenever you violate your rules and survive the pathology generated, you stand to learn in significant terms or degrees. Bateson calls this "trans-contextual learning." You begin in context A and wind up in context B.

Transpersonal experience is similar in social learning terms. You are as usual in context A; then a transformation happens (you learn something new) and find yourself changed and living in context B. I left home at age 20. Five years later I returned home to visit. Home was different, though the same people were there. My experience of home was from the perceptions in context B. I cannot go home again in terms of the old context A perceptions. Experience is altered by the new perception achieved in context B.

This process has to be anchored in a stable and secure setting. Individuals and their families gain security through understanding and accepting their assets and where they are in life. *Tell me what is right with me—not what is wrong.* Security does not result from a diagnosis of liabilities or a concentration on one's problems or weaknesses. This results in insecurity, discouragement, depression, and failure.

Counselors should model encouraging behavior, identify existing strengths in the family, and facilitate activities that increase the possibilities of future encouraging behaviors (Dinkmeyer & Losoncy, 1980). Counselors should make frequent use of confrontation—not confronting individuals with their mistakes but, rather, with their strengths. Research has not shown much support for negative confrontation (Berenson & Mitchell, 1974) but strongly supports positive changes resulting from positive confrontation (Jacobs & Spradlin, 1974: Lieberman, Yalom, & Miles, 1972).

Principle 9: Overemphasis on individual achievement leads to erosion of basic support within families.

A social system that has produced Howard Hughes, Albert Einstein, Henry Ford, B. F. Skinner, William Douglas, Tom Dooley, and Muhammed Ali has had a powerful emphasis upon individual achievement. *The price society pays for outstanding individual achievement is ultimate destruction of the basic social support system, the family group.* In *Earthwalk*, Slater (1974) hypothesizes that this will lead to ultimate destruction of the world. You can decide for yourself if the price is right.

Counselors have to be constantly aware of keeping a balance between individual and family achievement. This same balance is necessary for our survival in larger or world affairs (Slater, 1974).

Principle 10: People do not change: They become more and more like themselves.

In a healthy environment this principle is true. In a traditional environment the principle is modified to read: People change; they become more and more like themselves. The shrinking, correcting, evaluation paradigm leads to reductionism, almost to zero or nothingness. The person, for example, may feel a void or nothingness and powerlessness. Contrast this unhealthy condition to the growth paradigm that encourages people to become more and more like themselves. *Happiness is finding more and more where there used to be less and less.*

NECESSARY COMPETENCIES FOR HEALTHY AND GROWTHFUL FAMILY LIFE

Family competencies are defined as those vital elements responsible for maintaining the growth and health of the family unit. To help teach people to become healthy and growthful, we need to know what we want to teach. Imagine math teachers teaching a unit on algebra if they aren't too sure what equations are, or mechanics instructing on carburetion when they are unfamiliar with fuel systems. This is, however, the situation in mental health. We previously have had little agreement on standards of growthful living for an individual, let alone a family.

The following are among the essential competencies for healthy and growthful family life. These are not isolated variables but, rather, form clusters, constellations, and chains that are dynamic, fluid, interrelated, and variable at different stages in a family's life cycle (Otto, 1975, p. 11):

- *Uniqueness* of each member is allowed to develop.
- The constructive use of *power* is facilitated, and each member learns to achieve intellectually, socially, and emotionally.
- *Flexibility*, and creative coping with the ever-changing environment, is a must. The ability to adapt to each other's needs creates a collaborative environment.
- Accurate *communication* among all members of the family is fostered.
- An atmosphere of *belonging* is essential. The family should represent a stronghold where changing needs can be met, a system in which individual problems can be resolved conjointly.
- A supportive climate that provides enough *security* for family members to attempt various endeavors is healthy for the family and its members.
- *Democratic principles* of family management are needed.
- Frequent use of *feedback* and *feedforward* helps members assess themselves and grow.

- *Problem solving* and *decision making* are needed for healthy living.
- The use of *consequences* and *consistency* in everyday family interactions is also regarded as a competency.

Otto (1975) sets forth "primary strength clusters" that should be nourished, developed, and expanded throughout the lifespan of a family. He believes that these clusters have a great deal to do with a family's adaptability, resiliency, and optimum functioning. A partial list includes:

- The capacity to give love, affection, and support to each other.
- Open communication and listening.
- The ability to give encouragement.
- Each family member helping the other to develop his or her unique potential.
- The capacity for understanding.
- Sensitivity to each other.
- Empathy.
- Fostering curiosity, creativity, and the spirit of adventure.

The family counselor can learn to encourage primary strength clusters or positive action chains and facilitate their continued development through teaching family members this process. By encouraging appropriate segments of these chains, the entire chain is affected and "strength syndromes" are created. Table 4.1 demonstrates how to encourage specific behaviors and how these behaviors are linked to bigger action chains or clusters.

TABLE 4.1
Encouragement of Action Chains

Positive Behavior	Positive Mental Health Principle or Larger *Action Chain*	Facilitative Response
Doing a job that is yours	Having social interest or concern for others	"I like the way you see a job that needs to be done and do it!"
Waking up with a smile and making a nice remark (e.g., "good morning")	Encouraging others and demonstrating ability and willingness to live cooperatively	"You sure seem to know how to make me smile."
Asking for other family members' opinions	Democratic decision making	"It feels good to be a part of the family and to know that what I have to say matters to you."

THE STRENGTHS-ORIENTED EDUCATION MODEL

Using a strengths-oriented model in education and in family living has many ramifications. The single element most significant to behavior change for any individual is a *new life situation*. The introduction of family and group counseling has created situational changes that have led to more opportunity for new expectations and, consequently, new behavior.

The second element significant to a strengths-oriented education model is *encouragement*. New life situations create anxiety. Anxiety must be counterbalanced by hope. Hope comes from the encouragement to risk oneself in a new situation.

In contrast to the prevailing weaknesses model, the strengths model does not require retooling. You are OK as you are—just give it a try. The task is to get the other person to try to act in a new situation. If he or she does, the reinforcement helps maintain the new relationship definition and the new self definition acquired. Going back to the previous behavior even becomes difficult. As long as a situation in life does not change, the tendency will be to maintain the familiar behavior. The same is true for changed behavior, but the new situation must become stable.

Weaknesses make us losers. Strengths make us winners. In the strengths-oriented model, relationships are made (tamed) and maintained over time. The rules we live by create the situation or define the relationships in which we behave. Strengths make us OK. Weaknesses make us not OK. If I am OK, I can try to imitate new behavior demonstrated in an old situation. I am free to create new behavior in a new situation. If I am not OK, none of the above is likely to happen.

To be a winner, a person has to have rules by which to live that permit exercise or expansion and, consequently, growth. To be a loser, a person has to have rules by which to live that require "exorcise" or shrinkage by casting out or reducing the not OK part of yourself. Win or lose, the myth of unchangeability in people persists. Evidence is legion that the situation in which people find themselves influences behavior more than do inner traits of personality (Weisstein, 1970; Bakker, 1975). Cohen (1953), Milgram (1965), and Zimbardo (1971) have each concluded that the situation influences behavior beyond the individual's personal expectations. Thus, the unpredictability of human behavior has persisted.

Counseling and education have given lip service to the idea that we should begin with individuals wherever they are when we find them. To start where the person is constitutes the cardinal rule for a strengths-oriented education model. This does not allow a chance to bring individuals up to grade level or put them back into their mythical group. They must be treated as unique, and new situations must be created for them to learn and grow. When this was done in our Peer Counselor-Consultant Training Program (Fullmer,

1976b), the new behavior the students were able to create made the significant difference in the way they saw themselves. Low self-esteem became aspiration to post-high school training in the spirit of a winner, whereas, prior to training, the despair of losing prevailed. Peer counseling training is one way to actualize a strengths-oriented education model in a school.

Two systems are suggested for counselors working with families. The first is aimed at *skill development for parents* (Carlson & Faiber, 1976; Dinkmeyer & McKay, 1989). Parent education has been gaining acceptance as a necessary role of the counselor. It is important for helping people help themselves. A second system or model, however, has gained prominence. Counselors can use *family counseling as a form of group counseling.* Two family counseling cases illustrate how the 10 stated principles were applied from the perspective of counseling in a school context. To change behavior, the life situation has to be changed, encouraged, and stabilized. The aim is to change the life situation or family system. Thus, individuals will behave in new ways.

Case 1

The school counselor was experienced in family counseling. The case involved the family of a seventh grade girl in a suburban setting. The presenting complaint was disruptive behavior and deterioration in the girl's behavior generally, especially in school achievement. Because her teachers found no obvious reasons, the counselor invited the parents to come in for an information session.

During the initial session with the family, several items of information were disclosed. The most significant change in the family's life situation was that the father, 41, had just lost his job, which had provided the family with a very comfortable living. A check of dates between his daughter's change in behavior at school and the father's job situation confirmed the guess that her behavior change came a short time after father lost his job.

Several of the 10 principles are apparent in this case. The relationship between father and daughter was robust (Principle 2). Principle 4 claims that action chains express definitions of behavior. The heavy emphasis on individual achievement in the family (Principle 9) seemed to have intensified the daughter's reaction.

The case was handled successfully by encouraging (Principle 8) them each to assess their individual and family strengths and to develop ways of communicating to each other what pleases them. The family came for three additional sessions. During the family counseling, the daughter learned of resources in her family (both financial and psychological) of which she had been unaware. A new pattern of behavior was proposed to meet and stabilize the new situation. The girl's schoolwork improved, and her behavior modified in a new and more acceptable fashion.

Case 2

The counselor decided to try family counseling with a case of a first grade boy referred by a teacher. The counselor had used parent conferences before, but this was the first time she tried to convene the entire family to help.

The referral stated that the boy was unable to handle social interaction without becoming panicky. Sometimes he would withdraw, and other times he would become hyperactive. In either mood it was difficult to reach him and to help him restore the balance of normal affect. During each event he was unable to participate with the group in the room or on the playground. He had been removed from a private school a week earlier for similar behavior. The public school he attends is not in his neighborhood because of the existing busing policy in his district. Consequently, the boy, in his second month of school, has to attempt to make it under adverse conditions. The child has the additional drawbacks of being from a disadvantaged community and being ethnically different from the majority of children in his class. His new school is in a affluent neighborhood.

The counselor began by using the family counseling method of asking for help from outside resource persons. She started with the mother of the boy. The boy is from a single-parent family; he has three older siblings and one younger brother. None of the other school-age children were experiencing any reported difficulties in school. The counselor visited the mother at home because the mother does not have private transportation. The counselor was welcomed into the home and experienced the impact of being out of her familiar context because of the cultural "differentness" (Principle 5). She had to learn from the mother what behavior is appropriate, and the mother displayed strengths and a depth of understanding that initially proved disarming to the counselor until she realized that her first impression of the case came out of her own culture and was inappropriate.

The happy ending did not come easily. Time was required to bridge the cultural gap. The new learning for each participant, including counselor, teacher, and student peers, came with application of Principle 1, that new context(s) supplied new meaning(s). Principle 2 was applied when the counselor came to the mother for help to gain understanding of the new situation. The action chain forged by the counselor defined the relationship with the mother as one of mutual trust, and the reciprocity of the helping relationship flourished. For the counselor, Principle 6 fits the learning she needed for new social behavior.

APPLICATION TO SCHOOL COUNSELING

Few school counselors have skills to work with families, because few school counselors have permission to enter this domain. Role statements separate home and school. Professional counselors have debated the legitimacy of whether school counselors have the right to go into the home. The real issue, however, is whether we have an obligation to help in the most effective manner available. Most school counselors deal on the periphery of family work, however, through parent conferencing and involvement with students who have home problems. These marginal approaches bring about marginal results, as the real issues are being overlooked.

By switching the focus to direct family work, permanent change can take place. Individuals learn to become more creative and more understanding, to communicate better with the world in general, and to live and work with other people. School counselors traditionally have been noneffective because they have searched for inner traits when they should have been looking for the social context.

> Man's behavior is not primarily determined by unchangeable personality traits or other essential characteristics; on the contrary, his behavior is extremely changeable as a function of the situation in which he finds himself. Change the situation and the person's behavior will change. If one wants to predict his behavior, it is more important to know the situation than the person. (Weisstein, 1970)

In dealing with the entire family, permanent direct change can occur. The community and school feel secondary gains as their social context is changed when the "new" family ripples out.

Through family counseling, some individuals are helped that could not be reached with other methods. Individuals experience dissonance as previous behaviors no longer work when contexts are modified. Many ineffectual responses are reinforced and, even though somewhat troublesome, accepted.

METHODS

The counselor may choose from any or all of the following suggested interventions:

Family Education

A family education program is a formal learning experience that teaches families in a didactic setting how to live in a healthy fashion. Topics might include communication, family planning and decision making, conflict resolution, family activities and recreation, vacations, stages of family development, encouragement, sexual issues, and birth order.

Family Demonstration Model

Each week a different family volunteers to receive counseling on normal problems in front of an audience. The counselor uses this format to teach or educate all present. From any given group an estimated 80% to 90% of the parents can make direct use of the information that the family in focus receives (Christensen, 1972; Christensen & Schramski, 1983).

Family Involvement Communication System (FICS)

The FICS model provides a human relations "umbrella" approach for parent and teacher input and participation in a school's guidance program. This system offers a variety of strategies to enhance the educational growth of children by providing information and assistance to families who are experiencing normal and problematic growth (Shelton & Dobson, 1973).

Multiple Family Group Counseling (MFGC)

MFGC is a short-term treatment in which several families are brought together in weekly group sessions. MFGC combines the advantage of group therapy and family counseling and increases the counselors' effectiveness and the size of the population they reach (Sauber, 1971).

Family Counseling

Assisting families with normal or abnormal problems is an important counselor function. Treatment involving the family unit directly affects the situation in which an individual lives rather than dealing with the "identified patient." Treating the living unit rather than the "symptom bearer" has proven effective for problems of different types and magnitudes.

CHECKLIST OF HEALTHY FAMILY CHAINS OR STRENGTHS

	Never				Repeatedly
1. Regular periods of relaxation, recreation and rest are scheduled.	1	2	3	4	5
2. Positive feedback and encouragement are noted frequently.	1	2	3	4	5
3. In daily conversation, assets are mentioned more than liabilities.	1	2	3	4	5
4. Family activities are scheduled frequently and family has a lot of fun together (many common interests).	1	2	3	4	5
5. Decision making is done in a democratic fashion.	1	2	3	4	5
6. Communication among family members is accurate (including facts and feelings).	1	2	3	4	5

Checklist of Healthy Family Chains or Strengths (continued)

	Never				Repeatedly
7. Family problems are dealt with as they come up—never staying at odds long (willing to forgive) or burying problems.	1	2	3	4	5
8. Family work responsibilities are divided fairly and equitably.	1	2	3	4	5
9. Sharing daily experience is done on a regular basis and with respect.	1	2	3	4	5
10. Rules are made cooperatively.	1	2	3	4	5
11. Personal goals and family goals are interfaced in an agreeable fashion (a sense of mission).	1	2	3	4	5
12. The family's physical needs are provided for.	1	2	3	4	5
13. The family's spiritual needs are provided for.	1	2	3	4	5
14. The family's emotional needs are provided for.	1	2	3	4	5
15. Support of family members and security are ever present—liking/loving, caring for each other, freedom of expression.	1	2	3	4	5
16 Growth-producing relationships and experiences are initiated and maintained both within and outside of the family.	1	2	3	4	5
17. Constructive and responsible community involvement is created and maintained.	1	2	3	4	5
18. Growth is evidenced through and with children.	1	2	3	4	5
19. The family has the ability for self-help, as well as to accept outside help when appropriate.	1	2	3	4	5
20. The family uses "injuries" and "crises" as experiences from which to grow.	1	2	3	4	5
21. Time is spent together and alone.	1	2	3	4	5
22. A good circle of friends is available.	1	2	3	4	5
23. Good humor is valued.	1	2	3	4	5
24. Family finances are understood and agreed upon.	1	2	3	4	5
25. Good food and nutrition are present.	1	2	3	4	5
26. Family traditions and celebrations are practices.	1	2	3	4	5
27. Family members share respect for self and each other and are sensitive to each other's needs.	1	2	3	4	5
28. Family has ability to plan ahead rather than to react.	1	2	3	4	5

Other strategies available to counselors include:

- Referral to other sources: psychologists, mental health centers, clergy.
- A community-wide family clinic where several professionals volunteer their services on a minimal or no-fee basis. Lay people, paraprofessionals, graduate students, and so on may intern under a professional's supervision.
- Family life education courses for junior and senior high school students (Dinkmeyer, McKay, Dinkmeyer, Dinkmeyer, & Carlson, 1985).
- Newsletters and other printed materials that provide information and activities to help families with normal issues such as caring, sharing, thinking positively, communicating, recreation, finances.
- Parent education to develop strong relationship and management skills (Dinkmeyer & McKay, 1989)
- Marriage enrichment (Dinkmeyer & Carlson, 1984; Dinkmeyer & Carlson, 1989).

Family counseling is an efficient and effective process that counselors need to utilize. A wide variety of theoretical approaches and techniques is available. Procedures focusing on strengths and encouragement are the most successful.

REFERENCES

Bakker, C. B. (1975). Why people don't change. *Psychotherapy, 12*(2), 164–172.

Bateson, G. (1972). *Steps to an ecology of mind.* New York: Ballantine.

Berenson, B. G., & Mitchell, K. M. (1974). *Confrontation for better or worse.* Amherst, MA: HRD Press.

Bertalanffy, von, L. (1968). *General system theory: Foundations, development, application.* New York: Braziller.

Carlson, J., & Faiber, B. R. (1976). Necessary skills for parenting. *Focus on Guidance, 8*(7), 1–12.

Christensen, O. C. (1972). Family education: A model for consultation. *Elementary School Guidance & Counseling, 7*(2), 121–129.

Christensen, O. C., & Schramski, T. (1983). *Adlerian family counseling.* Minneapolis: Educational Media.

Cohen, E. A. (1953). *Human behavior in the concentration camp.* New York: Grosset & Dunlap.

Dinkmeyer, D., & Carlson, J. (1984). *Training in marriage enrichment.* Circle Pines, MN: American Guidance Service.

Dinkmeyer, D., & Carlson, J. (1989). *Taking time for love: How to stay happily married.* New York: Prentice Hall.

Dinkmeyer, D., & Losoncy, L. E. (1980). *The encouragement book.* New York: Prentice Hall.

Dinkmeyer, D., & McKay, G. (1989). *Systematic training for effective parenting.* Circle Pines, MN: American Guidance Service.

Dinkmeyer, D., McKay, G., Dinkmeyer, D., Dinkmeyer, J., & Carlson, J. (1985). *PREP for effective family living.* Circle Pines, MN: American Guidance Service.

Fullmer, D. W. (1971). *Counseling: Group theory and system.* Scranton, PA: Intext.

Fullmer, D. W. (1976). *Peer counselor-consultant training manual.* Honolulu: Hawaii Department of Education.

Hall, E. T. (1976). *Beyond culture.* Garden City, NY: Anchor Press/Doubleday.

Jacobs, A., & Spradlin, W. (1974). *The group as agent of change.* New York: Behavioral Publications.

Lieberman, M. A., Yalom, I. D., & Miles, M. B. (1972). *Encounter groups: First facts.* New York: Basic Books.

Lorenz, K. (1965). *Evaluation and modification of behavior.* Chicago: University of Chicago Press.

Loukes, H. (1964). Passport to maturity. *Phi Delta Kappan, 46,* 54–57.

Milgram, S. (1965). Liberating effects of group pressure. *Journal of Personality & Social Psychology, 1,* 127–134.

Otto, H. A. (1975). *The use of family strengths concepts and methods in family life education.* Beverly Hills, CA: Holistic Press.

Papero, D. V. (1990) *Bowen family systems theory.* Boston: Allyn & Bacon.

Sauber, S. R. (1971). Multiple family group counseling. *Personnel & Guidance Journal, 49*(6), 459–465.

Shelton, J. E., & Dobson, R. L. (1973). FICS: An expanded view of counselor-consultation. *Elementary School Guidance & Counseling, 7*(3), 210–215.

Slater, P. (1974). *Earthwalk.* New York: Bantam.

Sperry, L. (1975). *Developing skills in contact counseling: A workbook.* Reading, MA: Addison-Wesley.

Sperry, L., & Carlson, J. (1991). *Marrital therapy.* Denver: Love Publishing Co.

Sperry, L., & Hess, L. R. (1974). *Contact counseling: A workbook.* Reading, MA: Addison-Wesley.

Tinbergen, N. (1951). *The study of instinct.* Fairlawn, NJ: Oxford University Press.

Weisstein, N. (1970). Kinder, Kuche, Kirche as scientific law: Psychology constructs in the female. In R. Morgan (Ed.), *Sisterhood is powerful.* New York: Vintage Books.

White, B. (1976). Exploring the origins of human competence. *APA Monitor, 7*(4), 4–5.

Zimbardo, P. G. (1971). *The psychological power and pathology of imprisonment.* Statement prepared for the U.S. House of Representatives Committee on the Judiciary (Subcommittee No. 3, R. Kastenmeier, Chm: Hearings on Prison Reform), October 25.

Zunin, L., & Zunin, N. (1972). *Contact: The first four minutes.* Los Angeles: Nash.

RELATED READINGS

Ackerman, N. W. (1958). *The psychodynamics of family life: Diagnosis and treatment of family relationships.* New York: Basic Books.

Ackerman, N. W. (1966). *Treating the troubled family.* New York: Basic Books.

Ackerman, N. W. (1984). *A theory for family systems.* New York: Gardner Press.

Allred, G. H. (1974). *On the level: With self, family and society.* Provo, UT: Brigham Young University Press.

Andreozzi, L. L. (1985). *Integrating research and clinical practice.* Rockville, MD: Aspen Systems Corp.

Andrews, E. E. (1974). *The emotionally disturbed family.* New York: Jason Aronson.

Ault-Riché, M. (1986). *Women and family therapy.* Rockville, MD: Aspen Systems Corp.

Bagarozzi, D., Jurich, A., and Jackson, R. W. (1983). *Marital and family therapy: New perspectives in theory, research and practice.* New York: Human Sciences Press.

Baruth, L. G., and Huber, C. H. (1984). *An introduction to marital theory and therapy.* Monterey: Brooks/Cole Publishing Co.

Bentovin, A., Barnes, G. G., and Cooklin, A. (1982). *Family therapy: Complementary frameworks of theory and practice (Vol. 1 & 2).* New York: Grune & Stratton.

Bjorksten, O. J. W. (1985). *New clinical concepts in marital therapy.* Washington, DC: American Psychiatric Association Press.

Block, D. A. (1973). *Techniques of family therapy: A primer.* New York: Grune & Stratton.

Bowen, M. (1971). The use of family theory in clinical practice. In J. Haley (Ed.), *Changing families.* New York: Grune & Stratton.

Breunlin, D. C. (1985). *Stages: Patterns of change over time.* Rockville, MD: Aspen Systems Corp.

Campbell, D., & Draper, R. (1985). *Application of systemic family therapy: The Milan approach.* Orlando, FL: Grune & Stratton.

Coleman, S. B. (1985). *Failures in family therapy.* New York: Guilford Press.

Curran, D. (1985). *Stress and the healthy family.* Minneapolis: Winston Press.

Dreikurs, R., Gould, S., & Corsini, R. J. (1974). *Family council.* Chicago: Henry Regenery.

Einstein, E. (1985). *The step-family: Living, loving and learning.* Boulder, CO: Shambhala Publications.

Feldman, H., & Feldman, M. (1985). *Current controversy in marriage and family.* Beverly Hills, CA: Sage Publications.

Fishman, H. C., & Rosman, B. L. (1985). *Evolving models for family change.* New York: Guilford Press.

Foley, V. D. (1986). *An introduction to family therapy* (2d ed.). Orlando, FL: Grune & Stratton.

Framo, J. L. (Ed.) (1972). *Family interaction: A dialogue between family researchers and family therapists.* New York: Springer.

Friesen, J. D. (1985). *Structural-strategic marital and family therapy.* New York: Gardner Press.

Fullmer, D. W., & Bernard, H. E. (1968). *Family consultation.* Boston: Houghton Mifflin.

Galvin, K. M., & Brommel, B. J. (1986). *Family communication: Cohesion and change* (2d ed.). Glenview, IL: Scott Foresman & Co.

Geismar, L. L., & Wood, K. (1986). *Family and delinquency: Resocializing the young offender.* New York: Human Sciences Press.

Gelles, R. J., & Cornell, C. P. (1985). *Intimate violence in families.* Beverly Hills, CA: Sage Publications.

Glick, I. D., & Kessler, D. R. (1974). *Marital and family therapy.* New York: Grune & Stratton.

Goldenberg, I., & Goldenberg, H. (1985). *Family therapy: An overview* (2d ed.). Monterey, CA: Brooks/Cole Publishing Co.

Grebe, S. C. (1985). *Divorce and family mediation.* Rockville, MD: Aspen Systems Corp.

Grunwald, B. B., & McAbee, H. V. (1985). *Guiding the family: Practical counseling techniques.* Muncie, IN: Accelerated Development.

Gullotta, T. P., Adams, G. R., & Alexander, S. J. (1986). *Today's marriages and families: A wellness approach.* Monterey, CA: Brooks/Cole Publishing Co.

Gurman, A. S. (1985). *Casebook of marital therapy.* New York: Guilford Press.

Haley, J. (1969). *The power tactics of Jesus Christ and other essays.* New York: Avon.

Haley, J. (1971). *Changing families.* New York: Grune & Stratton.

Haley, J. (1973). *Uncommon therapy.* New York: Ballantine.

Haley, J., & Hoffman, L. (Eds.) (1967). *Techniques of family therapy.* New York: Basic Books.

Handel, G. (1985). *The psychosocial interior of the family* (3d ed.). Hawthorne, NY: Aldine Publishing Co.

Horne, A. M., & Ohlsen, M. M. (1982). *Family counseling and therapy.* Itasca, IL: F. E. Peacock Publishers.

Howells, J. G., & Guirguis, W. R. (1985). *The family and schizophrenia.* Madison, CT: International Universities Press.

Howells, J. G., & Lickorish, J. R. (1984). *Family relations indicator.* Madison, CT: International Universities Press.

Jackson, D. D. (Ed.). (1968). *Communication, family and marriage.* Palo Alto, CA: Science and Behavior Books.

Kantor, D., & Lehr, W. (1975). *Inside the family.* San Francisco: Jossey-Bass.

Kaufman, E. (1985). *Substance abuse and family therapy.* Orlando, FL: Grune & Stratton.

Koledzon, M. S., & Green, R. G. (1985). *Family therapy models convergence and divergence.* New York: Springer Publishing Co.

L'Abate, L. (1985). *The handbook of family psychology and therapy* (Vol. 1 & 2). Homewood, IL: Dorsey Press.

L'Abate, L., Ganahl, G., & Hansen, J. C. (1986). *Methods of family therapy.* Englewood Cliffs, NJ: Prentice Hall.

L'Abate, L., & McHenery, S. (1983). *Handbook of marital interventions.* New York: Grune & Stratton.

Laing, R. D. (1969). *The politics of the family and other essays.* New York: Pantheon.

Laing, R., & Esterson, A. (1964). *Sanity, madness and the family.* Baltimore: Penguin.

Lansky, M. R. (1981). *Family therapy and major psychopathology.* New York: Grune & Stratton.

Lansky, M. R. (1985). *Family approaches to major psychiatric disorders.* Washington, DC: American Psychiatric Press.

Levant, R. F. (1936). *Psychoeducational approaches to family therapy and counseling.* New York: Springer Publishing Co.

Luthman, S. G., & Kirschenbaum, M. (1974). *The dynamic family.* Palo Alto, CA:

Science & Behavior Books.

McGoldrick, M., Pearce, J. K., & Giordano, J. (1982). *Ethnicity and family therapy*. New York: Guilford Press.

Miller, S., Nunnally, E. W., & Wackman, D. B. (1975). *Alive and aware: Improving communications in relationships*. Minneapolis: Interpersonal Communication Programs.

Minuchin, S. (1974). *Families and family therapy*. Cambridge, MA: Harvard University Press.

Moynihan, D. P. (1986). *Family and nation: The Godkin lectures, Harvard University*. Orlando, FL: Harcourt Brace Jovanovich.

Nerin, W. F. (1986). *Family reconstruction: A long day's journey into light*. New York: W. W. Norton & Co.

Newberger, E. H., & Bourne, R. (1985). *Unhappy families*. Littleton, MA: PSG Publishing Co.

Otto, H. A. (1975). *The use of family strengths concepts and methods in family life education*. Beverly Hills, CA: Holistic Press.

Papp, P. (1983). *The process of change*. New York: Guilford Press.

Patterson, G. R. (1975). *Families: Applications of social learning to family life*. Champaign, IL: Research Press.

Patterson, G. R., Reid, J. B., Jones, R. R., & Conger, R. E. (1975). *A social learning approach to family intervention*. Eugene, OR: Castalia.

Peseschkian, N. (1986). *Positive family therapy: The family as therapy*. New York: Springer-Verlag New York, Inc.

Richman, J. (1985). *Family therapy with suicidal people*. New York: Springer Publishing Co.

Roy, R. (1985). *The family and chronic pain*. New York: Human Sciences Press.

Sager, C. J., & Kaplan, H. S. (Eds.), (1972). *Progress in group and family therapy*. New York: Brunner/Mazel.

Satir, V. (1967). *Conjoint family therapy* (rev. ed.). Palo Alto, CA: Science & Behavior Books.

Satir, V. (1972). *Peoplemaking*. Palo Alto, CA: Science & Behavior Books.

Sauber, S. R., L'Abate, L., & Weeks, G. R. (1985). *Family therapy: Basic concepts and terms*. Rockville, MD: Aspen Systems Corp.

Sherman, R., & Dinkmeyer, D. (1987). *Systems of family therapy: An Adlerian integration*. New York: Brunner/Mazel.

Sherman, R., & Fredman, N. (1986). *Handbook of structured techniques in family therapy*. New York: Brunner/Mazel.

Speck, R., & Atteneave, C. (1973). *Family networks*. New York: Pantheon.

Springer, J. R., & Woody, R. H. (1985). *Healthy promotion in family therapy*. Rockville, MD: Aspen Systems Corp.

Turk, D. C., & Kerns, R. D. (1985). *Health, illness and family: A life-span perspective*. New York: Wiley-Interscience.

Umbarber, C. C. (1983). *Structural family therapy*. New York: Grune & Stratton.

Wahllroos, S. (1974). *Family communication*. New York: Macmillan.

Will, D., & Wrate, R. M. (1986). *Integrated family therapy*. New York: Methuen.

Ziffer, R. L. (1985). *Adjunctive techniques in family therapy*. Orlando, FL: Grune & Stratton.

Zuk, G. H. (1971). *Family therapy: A triadic-based approach.* New York: Behavioral Publications.

Zuk, G. H. (1974). *Process and practice in family therapy.* Haverford, PA: Psychiatry & Behavioral Science Books.

5

Marital Counseling

Charles H. Huber

*Chains do not hold a marriage together. It is threads, hundreds of
tiny threads which sew people together through the years.*
Simone Signoret

As an interpersonal relationship, marriage holds a pivotal place in human
development. The evidence supporting this position is fourfold (Wamboldt &
Reiss, 1989).

1. Marriage is a relational state to which people overwhelmingly gravitate.
   More than 90% of men and women marry at least once during their life-
   times. Furthermore, at least 80% of divorced persons eventually remarry
   (Cherlin, 1981).
2. Clear rewards are associated with success in marriage. For example, happiness in marital and family life is found consistently to be a central
   determinant of the extent to which individuals experience life as meaningful and gratifying (Campbell, Converse, & Rogers, 1976; Freedman,
   1978).
3. Many marriages are troubled. The divorce rate for new marriages has lev-
   eled off at around four of every 10 (National Center for Health Statistics,
   1985). Moreover, marital problems constitute the most common chief

complaint presented to mental health professionals (Veroff, Kulka, & Douvan, 1981)..

4. Marital failure is costly. Whether indexed as participant dissatisfaction/ distress, relationship instability/dissolution, or interactional dysfunction, marital difficulties unequivocally increase the risk of physical and emotional disorders in married partners and their children (Emery, 1982; Hetherington, Cox, & Cox, 1982).

Accordingly, it is no surprise that many of the major schools of marital and family therapy focus on the marital dyad as a key subgroup within the family system. These schools, however, contain a diverse assortment of theoretical constructs and therapeutic procedures. Although some overlap and consensus exist, significant disagreement also exists, with many important questions remaining to be researched (Wamboldt, Wamboldt, & Gurman, 1985). With the vested interest that the mental health professions have in the marital process given the importance of marital outcome in human development, I assert that the task of maintaining a clear, therapeutically useful understanding of the mechanisms whereby some marriages succeed and others fail commands a high priority. Toward this end, this chapter offers one perspective for facilitating positive counseling outcomes founded on a concise, consistently supported theoretical model explaining the etiology of marital success and failure.

MARRIAGE FROM AN ADLERIAN PERSPECTIVE

From an Adlerian point of view, successful marriage requires two partners, each individually willing to work toward mutual enhancement and cooperation. Herein lies the problem, the area in which marital concerns and conflicts most frequently arise. The Adlerian perspective has the premise that marital distress results from partners' attempts to experience a cooperative, mutually enhancing relationship by expecting their mates to contribute the bulk of effort, rather than they themselves (as well as their mates) contributing actively to the common good.

It is fair to assume that most couples who present themselves for counseling genuinely prefer progress to a stalemate or increased distress. Yet a significant number of these couples remain frozen in noncooperative positions, each insisting that the other make the first move. Ensnared in an endless series of noncooperative demands they both feel helpless to initiate change. Fineberg and Walter (1989) illustrated this "couples dilemma" as a four-celled figure, shown in Figure 5.1.

Both partners have the choice to initiate cooperative efforts or wait for the other to do so. In addition to the overtly stated goal of mutual cooperation (Cell A) and the stalemated status quo (Cell D), two other possibilities are present. In each of these, one partner waits for the other partner to initiate cooperative effort between them (Cells B and C). Because most couples in conflict harbor the idea that everything would be best if only the other would initiate cooperative effort, and worst if they were to give in to their partners' demands for them to take the bulk of effort upon themselves, Cells B and C tend not to be acted upon. Couples entering counseling therein find themselves maintaining the status quo, less desirable mutual stalemate of Cell D.

TABLE 5.1
The Couple's Dilemma

	Partner 2	
	Initiate cooperative interaction	Wait for other to initiate cooperative interaction
Initiate cooperative interaction	Cell A: Mutual cooperation	Cell B: Partner 2 waits, and Partner 1 initiates cooperative interaction
Partner 1		
Wait for other to initiate cooperative interaction	Cell C: Partner 1 waits, and Partner 2 initiates cooperative interaction	Cell D: Mutual stalemate

Note: Adapted from D.E. Fineberg & S. Watter, "Transforming Helplessness: An Approach to the Therapy of 'Stuck' Couples," *Family Process, 28,* 291–299.

These couples need assistance in altering their position of "stuckness" maintaining the stalemate—in a stalemate that exists despite the real preference of both for mutual cooperation instead of deadlock. To facilitate this change, the counselor's priority must be to help alter the position of one or both members of a couple, from helplessly demanding that the other change, to a perception of empowering, and the advantages of initiating change themselves, each through their own individual actions. When one or both partners shift the stance from stuck ("My partner needs to change first") to empowerment ("I can contribute to transforming this situation by my own actions"), counseling efforts can move forward (Fineberg & Walter, 1989).

Long ago Adler (1931) pointed out the importance of this position as the standard for a successful marriage:

> Each partner must be more interested in the other than himself. This is the only basis on which love and marriage can be successful...it should be the effort of each to ease and enrich the life of the other. In this way, each will be safe; each will feel that he is worthwhile and that he is needed. The fundamental guarantee of marriage, the meaning of marital happiness, is that feeling that you are worthwhile, that you cannot be replaced, that your partner needs you, that you are acting well, and that you are a fellow man and true friend. (p. 266)

The Adlerian perspective posits marital relationships as systems. A system consists of several individual parts that are essential and related to one another in achieving certain outcomes. Actions, reactions, and interactions occur as the parts move and change positions. Take, for example, a heating system regulating room temperature. As soon as the heat drops below, say 68 degrees, the thermostat sends an electrical impulse to the furnace, which heats up and brings the room temperature back to 68 degrees. Marital partners likewise act upon their mates and the marriage in a similar fashion. Their positive actions trigger and facilitate positive reactions and interactions. Their negative actions, however, similarly trigger and facilitate negative reactions and interactions.

Thus, instead of proposing, "If only my mate would change, I'd gladly act differently," partners empowered to impact in the most advantageous and adaptive manner would take the stance, "If I change my behavior, my mate can't continue his (or hers)." The most minor changes in the position and consequent actions of one partner often are reflected immediately in the other's behaviors. The counselor can assist marital partners to recognize the advantages of this and thereby become empowered to successfully change their behavior and contribute to their partner's simultaneously doing so, all the while facilitating a more cooperative, mutually enhancing marital relationship, by focusing on four main areas of intervention:

1. Perceiving marriage as a goal-oriented endeavor.
2. Enhancing communications.
3. Managing conflict.
4. Being able to impact by using consequences and encouragement.

MARRIAGE AS A GOAL-ORIENTED ENDEAVOR

The Adlerian perspective on marriage holds that marital partners seek a sense of belonging and feelings of significance and status in their marriage. Partners behave (constructively or destructively) in ways that they perceive can lead toward achieving these goals. In addition, because these goals are attained through interactions with each other, problems that do arise are directly influenced by the consequences and reactions of each other. Thus, when partners feel worthwhile as partners, their "marital interest" will be high, and they will function as cooperative, mutually enhancing mates. In contrast, low self-esteem as a partner and low marital interest typically result in unproductive and destructive methods of gaining a sense of belonging and feelings of significance and status in the marriage.

Extracting from the works of noted Adlerian Rudolf Dreikurs' work, Huber (1981) posited that marital partner's destructive behaviors are generally directed toward one of four goals:

1. Excuse for shortcomings.
2. Attracting attention.
3. Gaining power.
4. Vengeance.

Destructive behavior in marriage can be defined as the actions of one or both partners that lead them to engage in negative interpersonal conflict. These partners are discouraged, feeling stuck in being unable to achieve belongingness and significance in their relationship through more constructive means. Some actively promote distressful situations by being openly hostile and contradictory. Others involve their mates with them through passively destructive actions such as laziness, stubbornness, intentional "forgetfulness," and general lack of cooperation. The basic belief motivating these destructive behaviors is, "I must have importance!"

Initial counselor intervention involves empowering each partner by explaining how their behaviors, both positive and negative, are goal-directed, and then showing them how to identify which of the aforementioned four goals provide(s) the basis for any destructive behavior being exhibited in their relationship interactions. This is done in two ways:

1. Teaching partners to be aware of how they feel when their mate acts in a destructive manner.
2. Teaching partners to monitor what they do in reaction to their partner's displaying the destructive behavior.

Table 5.2 summarizes these two points to be addressed for each of the four goals.

John is a television sports fan who enjoys nothing better than spending all his weekend hours watching football, basketball, hockey, and anything else related to sports. He has been becoming quite annoyed recently because Jane disturbs his TV viewing with requests for him to do things around the house. John usually accedes to her requests immediately or offers to do the tasks between programs, which he does. But he's finding that after he completes each task, Jane returns a short time later with a further request.

TABLE 5.2
Identifying Destructive Goals in Marriage

Goal	How did I feel when the behavior occurred?	What did my partner do when I tried to correct the behavior?
1. Excuse for shortcomings	Confused Frustrated Discouraged Like giving up	Resisted taking any responsibility Increased attempts to project blame on partner
2. Attracting attention	Annoyed Aggravated	Initially stopped when given attention Soon repeated behavior when further attention was desired
3. Gaining power	Challenged Angry Argumentive "He/she can't say/do that to me!"	Continued or intensified destructive actions Sought to "win" at all costs
4. Vengeance	Hurt Confused by what appears to be senseless, destructive behavior	Showed hurt feelings Attempted to get even

The goal of Jane's behavior can be identified by referring to Table 5.2. How did John feel? What was Jane's response to John's reaction to her behavior? John felt annoyed, and Jane temporarily stopped her attention-seeking behavior when he reacted to it, but she repeated the behavior when she felt the need for further attention. Her goal: attracting attention.

Once partners can identify the goal of their mate's destructive behavior, the counselor's next step is to teach what can be done that will tend to correct it. Corrective actions are those that will lessen or prevent, rather than initiate or intensify, conflict in response to the destructive behavior exhibited. These actions will differ, depending upon a partner's specific goal. Means of reacting in a corrective manner to each of the four goals are suggested next.

Excuse for Shortcomings

Partners who avoid personal responsibility for their inadequacies and mistakes and correspondingly blame and project responsibility for them onto their mates are discouraged. This may be all-encompassing or may be only in specific areas in which they feel especially lacking.

If a partner is exhibiting destructive behaviors that indicate a goal of excusing shortcomings, the most essential step for a mate to take is to not criticize his or her partner's behavior. This would probably only create a conflict, upsetting the mate even more, and the partner will likely intensify attempts to find fault. Usually this does nothing to facilitate correction and merely reinforces feelings of not belonging and insignificance in the relationship. A mate's main task is to encourage his or her partner to try things, and then to recognize any positive attempt, no matter how small. The focus should be on strengths and assets.

This reinforcement should not be delayed until a task or endeavor is completed. Encouragement should be offered at the first possible opportunity. Smiles, hugs, kisses, and compliments are excellent sources of acknowledgement. Change may take time, so mates themselves should be cautioned to be patient and, above all, to not allow themselves to become discouraged.

Attracting Attention

Partners who engage in destructive behaviors for the sake of attracting attention believe they belong and have significance in the relationship only when their mates are involved with them. The counselor should point out to couples that everyone needs to be recognized and noticed, but when this occurs at inappropriate times (e.g., one partner is on the way out the door to meet a friend) and leads to negative feelings and conflict, it is considered destructive behavior.

One way of adaptively responding to this form of destructive behavior is to ignore it as much as possible, in which case it frequently will lessen or stop. But the partner must remember that every effort should be made later to acknowledge the attention-seeking partner when he or she is acting constructively and caringly. If attention is awarded for appropriate behavior, the partner wanting attention will have less desire to seek attention in destructive ways. Also, because partners seeking to attract attention do want to belong and feel they are significant in the relationship, acknowledgment from their mates will contribute to a continuance, if not increase, of constructive and caring behaviors.

Another means to suggest to couples for handling this type of situation is for the mate of a partner who is destructively desiring to attract attention to offer his or her partner the choice of two options. One option would be related to the destructive behavior and the other a logical consequence of continuing that behavior. For example, if a mate were interrupting his or her partner during a phone conversation, the interrupted mate could ask the partner if he or she would wait until the end of the conversation before speaking. The other option would be to move to a phone in another room and continue the conversation there.

Besides being an effective way of lessening attention-seeking behavior, the use of options also tends to prevent the mate's response to his or her partner from escalating the situation into a possible power struggle. The partner attempting to attract attention is given a choice, not a demand.

A final point for the counselor to stress is that initiating and maintaining conflict are means of attracting and gaining a mate's full attention. Many partners would rather annoy and argue than be ignored if they perceive the former to be their only means of belonging and feeling significant within the marriage.

Gaining Power

Partners whose goal is to gain power usually can perceive themselves as belonging and significant in their marriage only when they are in control or when they are proving that their mates cannot boss them. Responding to power-seeking behaviors with "I won't let him (or her) get away with this" can only lead to continuing conflict. Even if a mate were to win an argument with the power-seeking partner, chances are that the relationship would be damaged further as a consequence.

The counselor must emphasize to a mate that upon realizing that he or she is becoming involved in a power struggle with the partner, he or she must make a firm attempt to refrain from getting angry and must immediately withdraw from the conflict physically, if not psychologically. Many people have difficulty doing this because they feel that to withdraw is to lose. But by withdrawing, a mate is really saying, "I know we'll never be able to work this out while we're both angry and hostile to each other." The two should discuss the conflict and the destructive behaviors that are a part of it at a neutral time, not during the heat of a struggle.

Another way of responding to a partner who is attempting to gain power is for the mate to admit that the partner has power and work to enlist cooperation by assisting him or her to use that power constructively. The counselor might encourage couples to examine who has what responsibilities in the marriage and, if an uneven distribution is found, arrange that these responsibilities be shared in more equitably.

Phrasing requests in a way that minimizes opportunities for a power struggle to erupt also can be helpful in responding to a power-seeking partner. Instead of the mate saying, "I want you to . . ." or "Would you do . . . ," more likely corrective responses would include, "Let's . . ." and, "We need to. . . ."

Vengeance

Partners who pursue vengeance as their goal are convinced that they are not lovable. They feel a sense of significance and perceive that they belong only when they are able to hurt their partners as they feel hurt. They find their belongingness and significance by being cruel and unlikable. Most mates' typical reaction is to retaliate and attempt to get even. Unfortunately, vengeance-seeking partners intensify their destructive actions as they see the effectiveness of these actions through their mates' hurt and hostile responses.

In attempting to deal with a vengeful partner, the mate must be encouraged to try to avoid being hurt and, especially, to refrain from retaliating in kind. A vengeance-oriented partner's response to retaliation is not likely to be, "Thanks, I needed that" but, rather, to feel more hurt, unloved, and discouraged. Instead, showing good will, even when confronted with destructive behaviors, will let the vengeance-seeking partner know that his or her feelings are being understood. Mates must make all attempts to build a more trusting relationship and convince their partners that they can be loved and belong, that they are significant in the marriage for their positive qualities.

The counselor should help couples consider the idea that they can be committed to each other without having to approve of each other's behavior at all times. Also, the counselor should emphasize that vengeance-seeking partners often test their mate's commitment. This frequently occurs by their doing something hurtful just at a time when progress in the marriage seems real. At these times, mates must attempt to remain positive and not affirm their partners' destructive notion that they can belong and be significant only through hurtful actions.

ENHANCING COMMUNICATIONS

Enhanced communications between partners is vitally important if marital distress is to be dealt with, as well as prevented from arising as frequently in the future. To have and maintain a cooperative, mutually satisfying relationship, marital partners must talk *and* listen to each other. The counselor often has to convey to couples the idea, "Both my mate and I are important!" This initially involves urging partners to accept each other's right to speak and be heard. Although they may not agree on everything, couples can demonstrate an acceptance of each other's right to say what they wish.

Empathy

Communication enhancement requires *wanting* to listen. "Listening is loving" is a phrase that aptly sums up this crucial understanding. Listening with empathy means listening to what is being said, and also communicating back to the speaker in a way that says, "I understand what you're telling me." For example:

Partner: "I've had it with night school! I'm quitting."
Mate: "You're disgusted with school and feel it's not worth all the effort."

Listening with empathy involves recognizing what a partner is communicating—the feelings (e.g., disgust) and the content related to the feelings (e.g., school), and then stating these feelings and content so the partner can feel understood and accepted. Partners who listen with empathy act as sounding boards for their mates to see themselves more clearly and realize that they are being heard and understood and, therefore, what they have to say is important.

Listening with empathy requires practice and concentrated effort. The counselor should point out that listening with empathy will frequently feel awkward if this is not something a couple is accustomed to. The following step-by-step procedure can be effective in lessening these feelings of awkwardness and simultaneously increasing feelings of empowerment by offering a structured way to impact positively on the marital interaction:

1. Give full attention to what your partner is saying. Listen to what is being said (words) and the manner in which it is said (tone of voice, facial expressions, etc.).
2. When your partner has stopped talking, recall the feelings being expressed. (Many partners have difficulty identifying "feelings words," so the counselor may have to take time to explain the various emotions, identifying them through examples, role play, etc.).
3. Recall the content, and relate it to the feelings. Consider why the partner is feeling this way.
4. Formulate a response that includes the feeling and the content related to that feeling. Then say it.

For example:

Partner: "The work is too much! I'll never get it done."

1. Listen carefully.
2. Recall the feeling—"overwhelmed."
3. Recall the content—"work—never get it done."
4. Formulate a response and say it—"You're overwhelmed at work and think you'll never get it all done."

Assertive Expression

Though listening is crucial, effective and continuing communication also involves speaking, especially when it concerns the need to confront destructive behaviors. Empowerment must entail expressing oneself assertively to increase the probability of being listened to.

One means by which the counselor can facilitate the use of assertive expression is through "I-messages." An I-message is a statement in which a partner communicates to his or her mate how that mate's destructive behavior makes the speaker feel and what he or she thinks about it. The message focuses on the speaker, not on the person it is directed to. It simply reports what the person is feeling and thinking, with no attempt to find fault or blame.

One way the counselor can help couples understand the value of I-messages is to contrast them with "You-messages," which are usually critical and communicate blame, disapproval, and objection.

For example:

> "*You*'re acting like a child."
> "Why did *you* do that?"
> "[You] Do it the way I say to."

In contrast, when partners simply state to their mates how some destructive behavior makes them feel and what they think regarding it, the message sent generally turns out to be an I-message:

> "I get very worried when I don't know what's happening."
> "I feel awfully discouraged about not getting the job done right."

I-messages are much less apt to provoke hostility and conflict in a relationship. To communicate to one's partner the effect his or her behavior is having on oneself is much less provoking than to suggest that the other person is to be blamed or at fault. Using I-messages tends to influence their use by the other partner. Conversely, the use of You-messages can similarly encourage You-messages by the partner. This is one reason that, in struggle-ridden marriages, disagreements frequently degenerate into mutual name-calling and reciprocally blaming conflicts.

Counselors should stress to couples that I-messages are best communicated in a way that is as calm and nonjudgmental as possible. An I-message stated in an angry, accusing tone becomes merely a disguised You-message. Further, one partner's destructive behavior by itself is typically not what contributes most to a mate's upset but, rather, how that behavior interferes with the mate's needs, wants, or expectations. Therefore, the focus in communicating an I-message is on the consequences a behavior is creating for the mate, not on the behavior itself. Dinkmeyer and McKay (1976) outlined a three-step procedure for constructing effective I-messages, a modification of which is:

1. Describe the destructive *behavior* causing the interference in terms of "I" (just describe; don't blame): "When I . . . "
2. State the *feeling* about the consequence the behavior produces: " . . . I feel . . . "

3. Conclude with stating the *consequence*, stressing the word *because*, to put the focus on the consequence, not the behavior itself: " . . . because . . . ."

For example:

Situation: Partner comes home very late. Mate had no reason to expect the later arrival.

1. Communicate the behavior: "When I don't know you're going to be late . . . "
2. Communicate the feeling: " . . . I feel worried that something may have happened . . . "
3. Communicate the consequences: " . . . because I didn't know where you were."

In summary, the completed message would be: "When I don't know you're going to be late, I feel worried that something may have happened, because I didn't know where you were." After the partners become comfortable using I-messages via the formula, the counselor should urge them to practice responding more in their own words. In response to the situation above, an individual might say, for example, "If I don't know you'll be late, sometimes I get upset and even frantic later on, not knowing what might have happened to you."

Reframing

The value of empathic listening and assertive expression as presented here can contribute significantly to partners' empowerment to break through the stuckness they are experiencing. Often, however, simply communicating a more positive perception of a situation can have equally empowering effects. Individuals who are at different vantage points can perceive the very same words differently. As the ancient philosopher Epictetus stated more than 2,000 years ago, "Men [and women] are disturbed not by things but by the views they take of them." This thought provides the basis for reframing: Changing a marital partner's conceptual or emotional perception of a situation and placing it in another frame.

Reframing doesn't necessarily change the situation; in fact, the situation may be unchangeable. The change made through reframing is in the meaning given to the situation. Consider the following illustration:

Partner: "I don't see how we will ever be happy together."
Mate: "I guess we'll have to work a lot harder if we're going to get more out of the marriage than we do now."

The mate's response reframed the unhappy partner's perception of the situation, increasing the probability that it might be viewed more optimistically and hopefully. Once a problem is successfully reframed, ways to improve the situation are more likely to be brainstormed, considered, and carried out.

CONFLICT MANAGEMENT

The presence of conflict is not what leads to marital distress but, the inability of couples to manage it constructively. By empowering marital partners to cope more effectively with, and thus better manage, conflict situations, increasing closeness and greater satisfaction in the relationship tend to be forthcoming. Couples need not avoid conflict, just manage it better. And management does not necessarily mean compromise (which is frequently used as a recommended solution in conflict situations). Management occurs when both partners can feel that each has gained something. Compromise, by contrast, is a process in which both partners give up or lose something. One effective means by which the counselor can empower couples to better manage their conflicts is through the ideas and process incorporated in Adlerian Rudolf Dreikurs' four principles of conflict management:

1. Create mutual respect.
2. Pinpoint the issue.
3. Seek areas of agreement.
4. Mutually participate in decision making.

Every poorly managed marital conflict involves a violation of one or more of these principles.

Create Mutual Respect

Creating mutual respect means neither fighting nor giving in. Fighting violates respect for one's partner; giving in violates respect for oneself. Mutual respect involves acknowledging that the initial step in managing conflict lies in understanding and accepting each other's point of view, and the value of mutual, not individual, "winning."

To begin to manage a conflict, partners must ask themselves whether their mates are less worthy of their respect because of their different point of view. The topic of contention typically isn't what maintains a conflict; rather, it is the position that partners hold toward it and each other. To keep a conflict going, both partners have to actively cooperate. To stop it, one partner only has to decide to withdraw. This does not mean to give in but, instead, to stop arguing and to start looking for possible reasons, or goals, for one's own and the mate's destructive behaviors.

If partners can understand how to identify and respond adaptively to the four goals of destructive behavior discussed earlier in this chapter, they should be reminded that the conflict may have been instigated by one mate's action but is perpetuated by the other's reactions. Tentatively identifying the destructive goal, responding more adaptively, and then communicating by listening with empathy and reframing the situation or being assertively expressive can begin to create a climate in which conflict management can optimally take place. A climate of mutual respect thus can be readily fostered.

Pinpoint the Issue

The "real" issue is usually not what partners are actually arguing about. The real issue is their troubled marital relationship. A partner who resists a request that his or her mate may perceive to be completely reasonable is not resisting the request but, instead, what he or she sees as an attempt at domination or control. Partners may argue over money, friends, in-laws, children, and so on. Underlying each disputed issue is the problem of personal involvement on the part of each partner—concerns such as who is right, who is being treated unfairly, the desire to win, threats to personal status, prestige, or security.

Dreikurs, Gould, and Corsini (1974) suggested that the "real" issue in most interpersonal conflicts is one of the following:

1. A threat to personal status: "Why should I give in?"
2. A question of prestige: "What will he/she/they think?"
3. A matter of superiority: "If I'm not on top, I'll be on bottom."
4. The right to decide: "Why should I let him/her decide for me?"
5. The right to control: "If I don't boss him/her, he/she won't do it right."
6. The right of judgment: "Whose way is the best way?"
7. The idea of retaliation: "He/she won the last time."
8. The wish for revenge: "I'll get even this time."

By not recognizing the important role of personal involvement in marital conflict, partners often escalate minor disagreements into major battles. Pinpointing and then dealing directly with the real issue can significantly empower partners in moving toward meaningful conflict management.

Seek Areas of Agreement

Fighting represents an agreement to fight. Thus, to better manage conflict, couples must make new agreements. Instead of agreeing to argue, attempting to dominate or control, partners can agree to work toward a more common, mutual means of interacting. Marital partners, particularly when embroiled in conflict, rarely consider that any type of mutual interaction, be it conflict or close intimacy, is based on agreement, full cooperation, and accord.

By recognizing that they cannot experience conflict without communicating their intention to fight and then gaining each other's cooperation and support to do so, partners can become empowered to lessen existing hostility. It takes only one of them to refuse to continue his or her role in the agreed-to conflict. The agreement is changed when only one partner (or both) simply decides what he or she alone can do, instead of pointing out what the mate should do to end the discord. Reaching a new agreement ultimately comes down to one (or both) partner being willing to change his or her own behavior, perhaps declaring, "This is what I'm willing to do—no strings attached." This should be the initial area of agreement sought in any martial conflict. Other agreements tend to readily follow.

Mutually Participate in Decision Making

Decision making can be viewed as an unequal, superior-inferior interaction wherein one partner (the superior) decides, while his or her mate (the inferior) is given no role in the process, only the outcome; or, alternatively, as a joint venture in which both partners contribute to the process and take responsibility for participating in any outcome decided upon. Reframing both partners as mutual decision makers and assertively acting on that reframing can have a dramatic impact on the way in which decisions are made and adhered to.

Johnson (1972) has offered a six-step decision-making strategy for the cooperative management of conflict situations. I have found an adaptation of that strategy to be an empowering outline for couples to apply. This adapted strategy is described in Table 5.3.

CONSEQUENCES AND ENCOURAGEMENT

As has been emphasized in the preceding portions of this chapter, marital partners who see themselves as stuck are almost certain to be ineffective in impacting more favorably on each other. One or both partners must move from a belief that "my partner must change first" to a conviction that "I can influence the nature of this relationship through creative action on my part." All the interventions discussed so far have had the same focus: to help empower marital partners to reformulate their preferences with regard to initiating change rather than to wait for their mate to do so. Two particularly productive concepts for further doing this are natural and logical consequences and encouragement.

Natural and Logical Consequences

Natural consequences are those in which a partner experiences the consequences of his or her own behavior. They represent the reality of the social order, the natural course of events without outside interference (usually some intervention, verbal or otherwise, from one's mate). For instance, if a husband decides to keep postponing mowing the grass, he will find that the higher the grass grows, the more difficult it is to mow. The natural consequences of his not mowing the grass is more work when he does decide to mow it. Natural consequences are imposed by the reality of the situation itself. His wife need not precipitate any argument with him about getting the task done. She merely can maintain the role of a friendly bystander. He eventually will realize the advantages of mowing the lawn more frequently himself.

TABLE 5.3
Outline for The Cooperative Resolution of Marital Conflict

Considering the situation and attendant attitudes:

1. How do you define the problem between yourself and your partner? Remember to consider the possible "real issue" involved.
   Husband:
   Wife:

2. What behavior(s) of yours contributes to or represents the problem?
   Husband:
   Wife:

3. How appropriate are the above behaviors to the situation in which the problem occurs?
   Husband:
   Wife:

4. What is the smallest definition of the problem?
   Both:

5. What are the areas of difference between the two of you?
   Both:

6. What are the areas of commonality or agreement between the two of you?
   Both:

7. As explicitly as possible, state your partner's behaviors that you find unacceptable in the conflict situation.
   Husband:
   Wife:

8. What events triggered the conflict?
   Both:

9. What are the things you yourself need to do to resolve the conflict?
   Husband:
   Wife:

10. What are some possible mutually desirable goals for the resolution of this conflict? (How would you like things to be different?)
    Both:

11. Identify possible solutions to the problem.
    Both:

12. What might be the outcome of implementing each possible solution identified in #11?
    Both:

13. What cooperative interaction and sharing of responsibilities will have to take place as a result of each possible solution should it be implemented?
    Both:

14. What solution would be the most constructive?
    Both:
    Implement that solution!

15. How will you know if the solution is effective and the conflict resolved?
    Both:

Logical consequences are more arranged or contrived. They are structured around the belief that individuals will not willingly do what they feel is not in their best interests. Partners are allowed to experience the consequences of their own actions (which their mates have more or less arranged). They are devised and applied so that the consequence has an understandable relationship to the partner's behavior. Choice is inherent in the nature and use of logical consequences. A partner should always give his or her mate a choice. the mate should be asked to choose between behaving in a positive, cooperative manner (and enjoy the positive consequences of doing so) or continuing with the destructive behavior (and thus suffer negative consequences).

Sara had been continuously arriving home late for dinner without calling and letting Joe know, despite his having asked her to call when such occasions should arise. As a result, Joe had to prepare a second meal for Sara when she did arrive. Joe offered Sara the option of calling so that he might delay dinner or the logical consequence of not having dinner prepared for her when she did arrive late, as it was creating a lot of extra work for him. After not calling a couple of times and either going without dinner or having to fix her own at the end of a long day at work, Sara soon became convinced of the advantages of calling Joe when she was going to be late. Joe's need to remind or coax Sara and engage in any upsettedness or quarrel over the situation was unnecessary.

Some couples initially may look upon logical consequences as retaliation with a new name. Retaliation, however, is an act in which a "superior" enforces his or her demands upon an "inferior." Retaliation is illogical and arbitrary rather than corrective or preventive. In a retaliatory action, Joe would have responded to Sara's unannounced lateness in a scolding, authoritarian way (e.g., "I've asked you a hundred times to call me when you're going to be late!") or in a way to "teach her a lesson" (e.g., "Tomorrow you'll just have to make your own dinner. I'm going out if you're not going to be here!"). By responding in a way that tied the consequence to the act in a logical manner, Joe was able to facilitate more constructive behavior on Sara's part through the reality of life, not the mandate of his authority.

Logical consequences will turn into retaliation if a partner takes a superior-inferior position. Utilizing logical consequences demands that a cooperative, mutually enhancing relationship be the focus of any efforts. Both partners have rights *and* responsibilities. Possible consequences are best communicated in an adult-to-adult manner, and clearly understood *before* they are applied. And logical consequences are best arranged to be as close as possible to what might be the natural consequences of a situation. Patience is critical, as it can take time for the use of consequences to take hold. Destructive behaviors that have been successfully achieving a sought-after goal will not always disappear immediately and may even be intensified in a last-ditch effort to succeed.

Encouragement

Encouragement focuses on building self-confidence and self-esteem. It entails searching intensely for strengths and assets and providing feedback regarding them. In utilizing encouragement, the focus is on helping one's partner to become more aware of and emphasize personal assets, at the same time diminishing the importance placed upon, or ignoring, deficits.

As discussed earlier, partners who exhibit destructive behaviors have been unable to achieve a sense of belonging and feelings of significance in their marriage through more constructive means. Therefore, the success of one partner in becoming empowered to facilitate a more satisfying relationship will depend largely upon the quality and quantity of encouragement or discouragement displayed. If a partner's actions contribute to discouraging his or her mate, the relationship is harmed. Conversely, by helping one's partner to overcome any feelings of discouragement, a mate can significantly contribute to the success and happiness of the marriage.

To become more encouraging, partners must first cease to be discouraging. Gordon (1970) identified a number of discouraging messages that individuals frequently send to each other, including:

1. Ordering, directing, or commanding: "Shut up."
2. Warning or threatening: "If you don't stop that, I'm leaving."
3. Moralizing or preaching: "You shouldn't talk like that in front of the children."
4. Giving quick solutions or advice: "Why don't you just call and say we're unable to come."
5. Teaching or lecturing: "You've got only one week left to pay that bill."
6. Judging, criticizing, or blaming: "That's a stupid thing to say."
7. Praising or agreeing when it ignores what a partner is actually feeling: "You're really OK, so don't feel so bad."
8. Labeling or name calling: "You've got no backbone."
9. Interpreting, analyzing, diagnosing: "You're just acting that way because you feel insecure in our relationship."
10. Reassuring, consoling, trying to make a partner's feelings go away: "Don't worry; everything will be fine."
11. Probing, questioning, interrogating, cross-examining: "Now tell me exactly what happened."
12. Using sarcasm, humor, and other such devices to distract a partner from his or her feelings or problems: "You're so cute when you get mad."

All of these messages convey the idea of "I'm superior to you" or "you're weak or inadequate in some way to have these feelings or problems."

Although many partners believe that offering criticism or informing their mates of their supposed lack of knowledge is their responsibility, this more than not results in mates becoming discouraged and demoralized and responding with destructive behaviors rather than being moved to function more effectively. Criticism implies finding fault, in which little is to be gained and much to be lost.

In recognizing how certain messages can detract from their good intentions, partners often do well to engage in some self-examination as they seek to become empowered to facilitate a more favorable marital relationship. This involves a determination concerning one's position toward his or her mate. Is that mate really respected as a potentially equal contributor to the marriage? Regardless of weaknesses or deficiencies in behaviors presently being exhibited, can the mate be accepted for his or her good qualities (even if minimally displayed) and potential for increasing them? The success of encouragement depends heavily upon the position that one's mate has individual value and importance as well as importance to the relationship. More specifically, encouragement entails:

1. Being positive. Expectations constitute a powerful force. By expecting a partner to succeed, a mate can provide a stimulus for this to actually come about.
2. Accepting one's partner's imperfections and shortcomings; separating the deed from the doer. Believing that one's mate has the potential to contribute and working to create opportunities for him or her to do so.
3. Focusing on strengths, assets, and contribution. Playing down mistakes and destructive behaviors communicates confidence that strengths and assets can be utilized.
4. Recognizing effort and improvement as well as final accomplishments. Encouragement implies recognition of a partner's efforts whether they end in success or failure.
5. Understanding the difference between encouraging and discouraging messages and behaviors and acting upon this understanding.

Encouragement is always appropriate, and the empowered partner should search for every opportunity to encourage his or her mate. Respect and trust can be shown toward one's partner even if that partner has not been so trustworthy. consider the alternative:

Linda was involved in an automobile accident. Should Chris make the situation worse by screaming harsh words or retaliating in some way? Or would refraining from criticism, commending what might be commendable, and ignoring what is annoying be more appropriate? By reacting so as to lessen, rather than contribute to discouragement and possible conflict, Chris' encouragement can only help Linda and strengthen their relationship.

Encouragement does not mean lavish praise or continual reminders. "I know you can do it" is more encouraging than "I know you can do *better*" (implying that what was done was not right). "If you would try *harder*" is less encouraging than, "Do you want to try it?" (implying that it can be done). Some additional examples of encouraging statements are:

> "I appreciated your helping me with the grocery shopping today."
> "You certainly worked hard washing the cars."
> "Why don't you try again? I'm sure it can be done." (after a partner attempts some task and fails)
> "I love all the nice things you did for me and the kids this week."

RESOLVING THE STUCK COUPLE'S DILEMMA

A common principle underlies each of the interventions presented in this chapter: the movement of one or both of the members of a couple from a position of helpless complaining that their partner contribute the bulk of effort to enhancing the marriage to a position in which each becomes individually empowered to initiate the effort. A new game is thus defined. The priority is no longer to achieve some hoped-for outcome. The new priority is to become individually empowered. Once empowered, one or both partners value the ability to initiate action rather than to wait for the other to do so.

To return to Table 5.1, if only one partner were to initiate cooperative effort, this would place the couple in Cell B or C. This situation is inevitably temporary. The symmetrical stalemate of Cell D is ended. The couple's expressed desire for mutual cooperation is now tested. One member of the couple has abandoned the demand that "the other has to act first," and the second member now faces a partner who has taken the initiative. If the second member of the couple does not rise to the occasion and accept the invitation to initiate mutually, the prognosis for the couple is poor. Clinical experience has shown that the asymmetry of Cells B and C is inherently unstable. If, on the other hand, the second member uses this opportunity to evolve from a waiting stance to one of initiating also, the symmetrical structure of a mutually enhancing, cooperative relationship is restored as both partners become positioned in Cell A.

One member of a couple often seems to occupy a "one-down" position in the marriage. While both partners play their parts in creating and maintaining the stalemate, the relationship as articulated by both frequently places one of them in a less powerful position. Aiming interventions at this person can be valuable. The counselor will be doubly motivated. The ethical motivation is to empower a person who feels disempowered, but the choice to aim intervention efforts at the one-down partner is also strategic. This partner usually is more desperate for change and typically feels there is little to lose. It is gratifying when the ethical choice and the efficacious choice are congruent (Fineberg & Walter, 1989).

Several reasons have been put forth why aiming interventions at the one-down partner seems to add to their impact. It has been suggested that if the one who has taken the less powerful position can become empowered, it is embarrassing for the apparently more powerful partner not to respond generously. Second, the newer the feeling of being empowered, the more gratifying it is to take the first step toward cooperative action. Finally, once the one-down partner has begun to feel empowered, that feeling becomes more desirable and gratifying than any given outcome (Fineberg & Walter, 1989).

If the one-up member of the couple cannot tolerate a more equitable distribution of power, or if the one-down partner cannot exchange familiar helplessness for the gratification of being empowered, the prognosis for the couple is poor. The approach offered in this chapter may not always bring a couple together to mutually enhance and contribute to their marriage; however, it will successfully test their overtly stated desire to do so.

CONCLUSION

Couples presenting for marital counseling tend to be stuck in a situation in which each partner waits for the other to change. Despite their overtly stated preference for mutual cooperation, this stalemate exists and is maintained by the attitudes and actions of both. Assisting the couple to move through their impasse of "stuckness" is no guarantee that the issues they raise can be successfully resolved, but dissolving the impasse represents a step that must inevitably happen before any movement toward a more satisfying marital relationship can occur. Typically, this breakthrough leads to rapid progress and closure of counseling efforts. Occasionally, it simply opens the way to begin to resolve a variety of issues. In either circumstance the stalemate is broken and the potential for progressive interactions is established.

REFERENCES

Adler, A. (1931). *What life should mean to you*. Boston: Little, Brown.

Campbell, A., Converse, P. E., & Rogers, W. L. (1976). *The quality of American life*. New York: Russell Sage Foundation.

Cherlin, A. J. (1981). *Marriage, divorce, remarriage*. Cambridge, MA: Harvard University Press.

Dinkmeyer, D., & McKay, G. (1976). *Parent's handbook: Systematic training for effective parenting*. Circle Pines, MN: American Guidance Service.

Dreikurs, R., Gould, S., & Corsini, R. J. (1974). *Family council*. Chicago: Henry Regnery, 1974.

Emery, R. (1982). Interparental conflict and the children of discord and divorce. *Psychological Bulletin, 92* 310–330.

Fineberg, D. E., & Walter, S. (1989). Transforming helplessness: An approach to the therapy of "stuck" couples. *Family Process*, 28, 291–299.

Freedman, J. (1978). *Happy people: What happiness is, who has it, and why.* New York: Harcourt Brace Jovanovich.

Gordon, T. (1970). *Parent effectiveness training.* New York: Plume Books.

Hetherington, M., Cox, M., & Cox, R. (1982). Effects of divorce on parents and children. In M. Lamb (Ed.), *Nontraditional families.* Hillsdale, NJ: Lawrence Erbaum.

Huber, C. H. (1981). An Adlerian approach to marital counseling. *Counseling & Human Development, 14*(3), 1–16.

Johnson, D. W. (1972). *Reaching out: Interpersonal effectiveness and self-actualization.* Englewood Cliffs, NJ: Prentice-Hall.

National Center for Health Statistics. (1985). Births, marriages, divorces, and deaths for November, 1982. DHHS Publ. No. (PHS) 83–1120., *Monthly Vital Statistics Report, 34*(5). Hyattsville, MD: Public Health Service.

Veroff, J., Kulka, R. A., & Douvan, E. (1981). *Mental health in America: Patterns of help seeking from 1957 to 1976.* New York: Basic Books.

Wamboldt, F. S., R Reiss, D. (1989). Defining a family heritage and a new relationship identity: Two central tasks in the making of marriage. *Family Process, 28,* 317–335.

Wamboldt, F. S., Wamboldt, M. Z., & Gurman, A. S. (1985). Marital and family therapy research: The meaning for the clinician. In L. L. Andreozzi (Ed.), *Integrating research and clinical practice.* Rockville, MD: Aspen.

RELATED READINGS

Bader, E., & Pearson, P. T. (1988). *In quest of the mythical mate: A developmental approach to diagnosis and treatment in couples therapy.* New York: Brunner/ Mazel.

Beavers, W. R. (1985). *Successful marriage: A family systems approach to couples therapy.* New York. W. W. Norton.

Bjorksten, O. J. W. (Ed.). (1985). *New clinical concepts in marital therapy.* Washington, DC: American Psychiatric Press.

Carlson, J., & Sperry, L. (1990). Psychoeducational strategies in marital therapy. *Innovations in Clinical Practice: A Source Book,* 9, 389–404.

Dinkmeyer, D., & Carlson, J. (1989). *Taking time for love: How to stay happily married.* New York: Prentice Hall.

Fredman, N., & Sherman, R. (1987). *Handbook of measurements for marriage and family therapy.* New York: Brunner/Mazel.

Glick, I. D., Clarkin, J. F., & Kessler, Dr. R. (1987). *Marital and family therapy* (3d ed.). Orlando, FL: Grune & Stratton.

Greenberg, L. S., & Johnson, S. M. (1988). *Emotionally focused therapy for couples.* New York: Guilford Press.

Gurman, A. S. (Ed.). (1985). *Casebook of marital therapy.* New York: Guilford Press.

Kaslow, F. W. (1988). *Couples therapy in a family contest: Perspective and retrospective.* Rockville, MD: Aspen.

Sperry, L., & Carlson, J. (1991). *Marital therapy: Integrating theory and technique.* Denver: Love Publishing.

6

Sexual Counseling

Ron J. Pion, Jack S. Annon, and Jon Carlson

Sex is good, but not as good as fresh sweet corn.
Garrison Keillor

Nearly 100% of the people in our society have been or will be involved in sexual behavior (Pion, 1975). The professional literature and public media give conclusive documentation of the confusion and distress among couples regarding their ability to fully utilize and express their sexual potential. The extent of these widespread problems would seem to mandate the development of diagnostic and therapeutic skills to meet clients' requests for assistance. Unfortunately, too few counselors have these skills and therefore do not feel comfortable working in the area of sexual counseling.

TYPES OF SEXUAL PROBLEMS

Sexual problems can be divided into two categories. *Primary* sexual problems arise directly from sex-related stimuli and occur only in sexual situations. *Secondary* sexual problems are only one manifestation of a larger personal or relationship dissatisfaction.

101

Classifying cases as secondary or primary helps determine the appropriate counseling strategy. Primary problems usually respond well to brief therapy. Secondary problems usually require intensive therapy.

BRIEF THERAPY

This chapter is concerned only with brief therapy. It describes a process that should be sufficient to alleviate many of the sexual problems that counselors encounter. It is based on psychological learning theory and can be used compatibly with all major intervention systems. Learning is emphasized as the means of changing both overt and covert sexual behavior. One to five visits of 30- to 60-minute duration are involved.

P-LI-SS-IT: The Four Levels of Intervention

Recently a treatment model has been developed to aid counselors in helping clients with sexual problems (Annon, 1974; Pion & Annon, 1975). As an aid to memory, it has been termed P-LI-SS-IT. The model provides for four levels of approach, with each letter or pair of letters designating a suggested method for handling the presenting sexual concerns. The four levels are: 1) *P*ermission, 2) *L*imited *I*nformation, 3) *S*pecific *S*uggestions, and 4) *I*ntensive *T*herapy.

To attempt to assess and treat each presenting concern in exactly the same way would be inappropriate. The model, both flexible and comprehensive, provides a framework for screening problems amenable to brief therapy approaches from among others requiring intensive therapy. The first three levels can be viewed as brief therapy, as contrasted with the fourth level, intensive therapy.

This model has a number of distinct advantages. It may be applied in a variety of settings and adapted to whatever client time is available. Theoretically, each descending level of approach requires increasing amounts of knowledge, training, and skill on the part of the counselor. Because each level requires increasing experience, the model allows professionals to gear their approach to their own level of competence. This also means that counselors now have a plan to aid them in determining when referral elsewhere is appropriate. Most important, the model provides a framework for discriminating between and among problems. How many levels of approach counselors will feel competent to use directly depends upon the amount of interest and time they are willing to devote to expanding their knowledge, training, and skill at each level.

PERMISSION: THE FIRST LEVEL OF TREATMENT

Sometimes, all that people want to know is whether they are "normal," "OK," not "perverted," "deviated," or "abnormal." They would like to find this out from someone with a professional background or from someone who is in a position of authority. Many times, clients are not bothered by their specific behavior but, rather, by the thought that something may be "wrong" or "bad" about what they are doing or not doing. Frequently, clients just want an interested professional as a sounding board for checking out their concerns. In these cases, the counselor will probably be able to tell them that they are not alone or unusual in their concerns and that many people share them. Reassurance of normality and permission to continue doing exactly what they have been doing are often sufficient to resolve what might eventually become a major problem.

Permission giving will certainly not solve all sexual problems, but it will resolve some. It has the advantages that it can be used in almost any setting at any time (given some measure of privacy) and the counselor faces only minimal preparation. Finally, it may be used to cover a number of areas of concern, such as thoughts, fantasies, dreams, and feelings (covert behaviors), as well as overt behaviors.

Concerns about sexual thoughts and fantasies are common. For example, both men and women periodically have sexual thoughts and fantasies about people other than their partners, about people of the same sex, or even about their own parents, brothers and sisters, sons or daughters, or friends. Letting the client know that this is not unusual may relieve some of the anxiety or guilt feelings about being "abnormal." Only when such thoughts or fantasies become persistent or begin to interfere directly in some way with other areas of functioning do they create a problem.

Permission giving also may be appropriate for handling dream concerns. Individuals may have occasional dreams involving sexual activity with a wide variety of persons other than their partners. At times, the dreams also may involve sexual activity with partners of the same sex even though the dreamer may never have had such actual experiences. Reassurance that the dreams are entirely within the normal range and are not unusual or indicative of "abnormality" is usually sufficient to relieve the anxiety or guilt associated with them. Often, permission giving is also sufficient to stop the recurring dream that was associated with the presenting anxiety.

Another presenting concern is in clients' responding with anxiety when they experience sexual arousal to what they consider inappropriate stimulation. Many of these concerns arise from failure to discriminate between arousal resulting from sexual thoughts and fantasies and arousal from direct tactile stimulation. For example, a mother who is breast feeding her baby might experience some degree of sexual arousal because of the direct tactile stimulation to her breasts. A father may experience an erection when playing with a young child on his lap. Reassuring clients that these are normal, involuntary responses to tactile stimulation may reduce unnecessary anxiety and prevent a minor happening from developing into a major concern. Similar permission giving for these feelings can apply to horseback and motorcycle riding, tree and rope climbing, the use of tampons, douches, and enemas, or any other circumstance that involves tactile stimulation of the breasts, genitals, or anal area.

Permission giving may be applied to a wide range of sexual behaviors that the counselor recognizes as common and normal but the client does not. Take the case of the couple who read in their favorite magazine that the average frequency of sexual intercourse for people of their age and education is two-and-a-half times a week. Their own frequency may be eight times a week or eight times a year, but now they begin to worry whether they are "normal," "oversexed," or "undersexed." A counselor's response that in essence gives them permission to continue with their own preferred frequency may be all that is necessary to relieve anxiety.

Many sexual concerns can be handled by giving the client permission to *not* engage in certain sexual behaviors unless he or she chooses to. An example might be the young woman who is receiving pressure from her partner to experience multiple orgasms or who has read or heard that every woman has the right to expect and demand them. Yet she is satisfied with the one orgasm that she experiences with her partner and does not really care whether she is multi-orgasmic or not. Giving this woman permission to not experience multiple orgasms may be helpful to her. Conversely, in the case of the woman who would really like to experience multiple orgasms but is fearful or hesitant that she might then become a "nymphomaniac," permission to be multi-orgasmic, if she chooses to, might be a more helpful approach.

Permission giving is most appropriate and helpful when used in direct relation to the client's goals. Keeping this in mind will enable the counselor to decide what form of permission giving will be the most beneficial for a particular client concern.

On the surface, the basic assumption underlying the permission-giving approach may seem to be that the counselor should sanction whatever sexual thought, fantasy, or behavior that a consenting adult wishes to privately engage in with other mutually consenting adults. In a general sense, this may be correct, but such an assumption has some definite limitations. Although an individual client ultimately has to decide upon his or her own behavior, a counselor's "blanket" permission giving may not be appropriate if the client is not making an informed choice. The counselor is responsible for informing the unaware client of the possible adverse consequences of engaging in certain thoughts, fantasies, or behaviors.

A number of popular books have "given permission" for the indiscriminate use of any fantasy a person may desire while engaging in masturbation or sexual behavior with a partner. Learning theory suggests, and clinical evidence substantiates, that systematically associating thoughts and fantasies with sexual activity is a powerful means of conditioning arousal to almost any stimulus (Annon, 1973). This has been used to therapeutic advantage. In certain circumstances, however, engaging in such activity by the uninformed may have undesired results. Informing clients of the possible consequences of their behavior and leaving the ultimate choice to them seems more appropriate than "blanket" permission giving.

The extent to which the counselor feels comfortable with and is willing to use the permission-giving approach generally depends upon his or her breadth of sexual knowledge, orientation, and value system. The more knowledge counselors have of sexual behavior in their own and other cultures, the more comfortable they feel in applying this level of treatment. Counselors' theoretical or professional orientation also may place limits on how appropriate permission giving may be for a particular thought, fantasy, dream, feeling, or behavior. Counselors with a psychoanalytic background may wish to withhold permission giving for recurrent sexual dreams, preferring to work through such material with the client. Obviously, that is the individual counselor's choice.

We do not wish to persuade professionals of any orientation to change their viewpoint to that of a learning-oriented approach. The counselor should use only those suggestions that he or she thinks are appropriate to his or her frame of reference. At the same time, we hope that counselors will be willing to experiment a little.

Ideally, counselors will try not to intentionally impose their personal value systems on their clients. In practice, however, this is sometimes difficult to achieve. Of course, the counselor should not give up his or her own value system. At times, the client's stated goals may come into direct conflict with the counselor's value system. When this happens, the counselor's responsibility is to clearly inform the client of this and refer him or her elsewhere.

A final important point is self-permission. Counselors should be able to give permission to themselves to not be experts. They must not be afraid to say they do not know the answer when they do not. No one person is an expert in this field. Theory, research, and practice in the sexual area are so far-ranging that no individual or group of individuals can be expected to know or keep abreast of even a sizable fraction of the information in this area. Counselors do what they can for their clients, based on their own knowledge and experience. In some cases, the most important thing a counselor has to offer is self—someone who will listen, who can communicate interest, understanding, and respect, and who will not label or judge the client.

If permission giving is not sufficient to resolve the client's concern and the counselor is not in an appropriate setting or does not have sufficient time or relevant knowledge and skills, the client should be referred elsewhere. On the other hand the counselor can combine permission giving with the next level of treatment - *Limited Information.*

LIMITED INFORMATION: THE SECOND LEVEL OF TREATMENT

In contrast to permission giving—basically telling the client that it is all right to continue doing what he or she has been doing—limited information means giving the client specific factual information directly relevant to his or her sexual concern. This may result in the client's continuing to do what he or she has been doing, or it may result in something different.

Limited information is usually given in conjunction with permission. Each may be used as a separate treatment level, but considerable overlap exists between the two.

Common Areas of Sexual Concerns. Providing limited information is an excellent method for dispelling sexual myths, whether they are specific ones such as those pertaining to genital size, or more general ones such as men and women differing markedly in their capacity to want and enjoy sexual relations and in their fundamental capacity for responsiveness to sexual stimulation.

A great deal of evidence indicates that men and women are far more similar than dissimilar to each other in their capacity for and experience of sexual desire, arousal, and orgasm. Numerous cross-cultural studies from fields such as anthropology and sociology consistently reveal that cultures that encourage women to be free in sexual expression produce sexually responsive women who are as uninhibited and responsive as males. Cultures that encourage and expect women to experience orgasm yield women who do experience orgasm. Other common sexual concerns are breast and genital shape and size, masturbation, intercourse during menstruation, oral-genital activities, sexual frequency and performance.

Limitations. The extent to which counselors are willing to use limited information in handling sexual concerns depends upon their breadth of knowledge in the sexual area. How counselors offer information to their clients depends upon the individual style with which they feel most comfortable and the manner of presentation they feel will be most helpful to their clients.

Whatever their style, counselors now have two strategies for approaching sexual concerns. As with permission giving, the degree to which counselors feel comfortable with and are willing to use the second level also depends upon their theoretical orientation and value system. The limitations imposed by the factors discussed in the first level of treatment apply here equally.

The additional use of this level of treatment may resolve some concerns that could not be handled by application of the first level of treatment alone. If giving limited information is not sufficient to resolve the client's sexual concern, the counselor has two additional options. He or she may refer the client for treatment elsewhere, or, with the appropriate setting, knowledge, skills, and experience, he or she may proceed to the third level of treatment—*Specific Suggestions.*

SPECIFIC SUGGESTIONS:
THE THIRD LEVEL OF TREATMENT

Before counselors can give specific suggestions to clients, they must first obtain specific information. The assumption here is that offering specific suggestions would not be therapeutically appropriate or helpful to the client without first obtaining information about the client and his or her unique set of circumstances. If the counselor were to immediately launch into a number of suggestions after hearing the client's initial *description of the problem* (not the "label" of the problem), the counselor may not only waste the client's time (e.g., offering suggestions the client has already tried) but may further compound the problem. By suggesting inappropriate and possibly useless treatment procedures based on insufficient data, the counselor may overlook other more necessary and appropriate treatment.

The Sexual Problem History. The counselor should elicit a sexual problem history. This is not to be confused with a comprehensive learning-about-sex history. The model proposed here assumes that a comprehensive learning history may not be relevant or necessary for instituting effective brief therapy. Application of the specific suggestion approach may resolve a number of problems that filtered through the first two levels of treatment, but, needless to say, it is not expected to successfully dispense with all such problems. If the third level of approach is not helpful to the client, a complete sexual history may be a necessary first step toward intensive therapy.

Guidelines for taking a sexual problem history, deemed necessary for a brief therapy approach to treatment, are:

1. Description of current problem.
2. Onset and course of problem.
    a. Onset (gradual or sudden, precipitating events, consequences).
    b. Course (changes over time: increase, decrease, or fluctuation in severity, frequency, intensity; functional relationships with other variables).
3. Client's concept of cause and continuation of the problem.
4. Past treatment and outcome.
    a. Medical evaluation (specialty, date, form of treatment, results, current medication for any reason).
    b. Other professional help (specialty, date, form of treatment, results).
    c. Self-treatment (type and results).
5. Current expectations and goals of treatment (concrete vs. general).

The proposed problem history is easily adapted to five minutes or several hours. Making up a form with the sexual problem history guidelines may be helpful. The counselor could use this as a general guide while interviewing or could write the client's responses directly on the form for future reference.

Either way, the form may help the counselor become comfortable and experienced with the guidelines until he or she no longer needs them as an aid to memory.

Self-Recorded Problem History. During the past few years considerable experience has been gained with the use of self-recorded (audio cassette) problem histories. In this method, the couple is requested, at the time of the first interview, to prepare a tape prior to the next visit. The purpose as explained to the client, is:

- To describe the problem(s) for which the person(s) is seeking help.
- To describe the possible influences that relate to or have preceded the onset of the problem.

The counselor provides a guideline outlining a satisfactory method of tape preparation, and the client is asked to read it in the office along with an introductory letter. In the letter, the client is told that the tape is a means of describing the problem and its history, that relistening to the tape after the therapy is over may help give the person a measure of self-growth and understanding, and that preparation of the tape at home can save treatment hours and thus lessen expenses. The client also is assured of confidentiality and maintenance of professional standards. We have been encouraged over time that permitting the client a greater amount of responsibility for history taking may actually facilitate the therapeutic process.

Once the counselor feels comfortable and at ease in obtaining the problem history from the client in whatever fashion, he or she is ready to offer specific suggestions. In contrast to permission giving and limited information, which generally do not require that clients take any active steps to change their behavior unless they choose to, specific suggestions are direct attempts to help clients alter their behavior to reach their stated goals.

Most of the suggestions that may be given can be used by a counselor who has only 10 to 30 minutes for a client interview. Furthermore, they may be used when the counselor is able to see the client on only one or several occasions at the most. Obviously, these are minimum time limits that may be expanded and adapted to the time available. This level of approach is intended for use within the brief therapy framework proposed. If the suggestions are not perceived as potentially helpful within a relatively brief time period, intensive therapy is probably more appropriate.

As with the previous levels of treatment, specific suggestions may be seen as a preventive measure as well as a treatment technique. For example, suggesting to a woman specific ways to avoid pain associated with genital intercourse may prevent her from experiencing vaginismus. Or a direct treatment approach to ejaculation problems may prevent the eventual occurrence of erection difficulties. This level of treatment may be combined easily and advantageously with the previous two levels.

Two common sayings have proven helpful when applying this third level of treatment. One that is particularly beneficial for clients with concerns about a particular feature of their body is: What you do with what you have rather than what you have is what counts! The second has even broader application. Many clients who have sexual concerns tend to see each forthcoming sexual event with their partner as the "final test." If the man once again ejaculates too soon or does not obtain an erection, he often feels as though he has lost his last chance. Women in search of orgasms report similar concerns. Thoughts such as, "Will it happen this time?" or "It's got to happen this time or I'll just die!" are not conducive to success in attaining those goals. Helping the client learn to say and believe that *there is always another day, another time, another occasion* can do a great deal to modify some of the self-defeating attitudes of clients.

This level of treatment is particularly effective for dealing with heterosexual problems involving arousal, erection, ejaculation, orgasm, or painful intercourse. The specific suggestions offered (redirection of attention, sensate focus techniques, interrupted stimulation, squeeze technique, vaginal muscle training, etc.) depend upon the information obtained in the sexual problem history. In general, suggestions might be considered as falling into three categories: 1) suggestions to the male, 2) suggestions to the female, and 3) suggestions to the couple.

Often the counselor sees a client who has no immediate partner available. In these cases a number of suggestions can be made for self-stimulation procedures. The counselor may encounter other situations in which a client is involved in a relationship with a second person who has a problem but who is not able or willing to come in for consultation. Assuming that the second person is open to suggestions, the client can pass along whatever suggestions he or she feels might be appropriate under the circumstances.

The most helpful suggestions are usually those that can be made to both partners together. Clients should be encouraged to have their partners come in with them. When the couple comes in together and is willing to cooperate with the treatment suggestions, the probability that mutual goals will be realized is much greater. Working with one person on a problem that involves two is always more difficult.

Limitations. Efficient use of this treatment level depends largely upon the counselor's breadth of knowledge in the behavioral and sexual areas, skill and experience, and awareness of relevant therapeutic suggestions. The limitations discussed under the other treatment levels apply here as well. For interested readers, a detailed description of the application of suggestions to the more prevalent heterosexual problems males and females encounter is available elsewhere (Annon, 1974).

Readings. Client readings might be specifically suggested. The counselor may use them as another means of providing permission or limited information pertaining to a certain sexual area or client concern. Readings may be used to supplement specific suggestions or to promote new client-initiated procedures. Because of time limitations either on the counselor's or the client's part, the counselor may suggest them in lieu of other specific suggestions. The counselor, of course, should not suggest any readings to clients unless he or she is well acquainted with the content and feels comfortable recommending them (Pion & Wagner, 1971). One helpful book for both client and counselor is *The Last Sex Manual* (Pion & Hopkins, 1978). This book includes the transcriptions of detailed tapes from clients who speak to readers before as well as after they have successfully resolved their sex problems. This constitutes good, practical help from people who learned to be sexually successful.

A number of sexual concerns may be treated successfully through the P-LI-SS-IT approach. Those that cannot be resolved will filter through. At this point, the counselor may refer the client for appropriate treatment elsewhere, or if he or she has the requisite time, knowledge, experience, and skills, he or she may proceed to the fourth level of treatment—*Intensive Therapy.*

INTENSIVE THERAPY:
THE FOURTH LEVEL OF TREATMENT

We will not describe or attempt to outline our intensive therapy approach to the treatment of persisting sexual problems. But for the counselor who already has received training for intensive therapy, this is the appropriate time to initiate such treatment. Readers may be interested in the detailed description of a psychological learning approach to intensive treatment available in Annon (1975).

We believe that involving a client in an expensive, long-term treatment program without first trying to resolve the problem from within a brief therapy approach may be unethical. A number of sexual concerns may be treated successfully by such an approach if counselors are willing to apply it. Specific suggestions that may work for one client will not always be effective with another. Or interpersonal conflict may prevent the suggestions from being carried through. When this happens, and when counselors believe they have done as much as they can from within the brief therapy approach, the time has come for highly individualized therapy.

In the model proposed here, intensive therapy does not mean an extended standardized program of treatment. By their nature, standardized programs are not of help to some people, and they may not be necessary. But many of the essential elements of some of the current standardized programs can be successfully utilized within a brief therapy approach.

In the P-LI-SS-IT model, intensive therapy is seen as highly individualized treatment that is necessary because standardized treatment was not successful in helping the client reach his or her goals. Within the present framework, intensive therapy means undertaking a careful initial assessment of the client's unique situation in order to devise a therapeutic program that is unique to the individual involved.

APPENDIX: How to Make the Tapes

Two 60-minute cassette tapes are provided. You will probably use only 30 minutes (side one) on each tape. If you feel you need more than the 30 minutes, feel free to turn the tape over and continue on side two. The tapes will be made at the beginning and at the end of therapy.

1. Read the instruction sheet for each tape before attempting to record. Please note that the questions listed are only *ideas of areas* you might want to think about while discussing your problems.

2. Do not identify yourself by name. The tapes will be numbered to ensure your privacy.

3. Use your own words, state the problem in a way that is comfortable for you. Pauses and hesitations are natural. It may help to make believe that you are telling a story, your story. The questions listed are suggestions to help you think about what concerns you and how you feel about those concerns. If you find the questions are not helpful to you, ignore them. We are most interested in your telling things the way you see them.

4. Couples, please note: Make you tapes *separately* and do not discuss the content until you come in. We want to be sure that each of you has an equal opportunity to freely discuss the problem from your viewpoint. This can be a good opportunity for you to state your feelings openly and honestly without fear of hurting your partner, because your partner will not hear the tapes.

5. After making the tape, listen to it to see if there are any additions you wish to make before returning the completed tape to us. Just add further comments to the end of your tape; there is no need to erase or redo any sections.

Remember, the tape is an addition to personal therapy sessions. During your sessions you and the therapist will have an opportunity for more in-depth discussion. The tapes are only a starting point.

Tape One

The purpose of this tape is: (a) to describe the problem(s) for which you are seeking help, and (b) to describe possible influences that may relate to or have preceded the stated problem.

People seek help for a variety of reasons. some of these include dissatisfaction with their relationship(s), communication problems, lack of physical responsiveness, and fears of being abnormal. We hope that the following list of suggested questions will be helpful to you in preparing your narrative (story) for the tape.

1. Describe, as best you can, the problem as you see it. Be as specific and descriptive as possible.
   a. Who has the problem? You? Your partner? Both?
   b. When and how often does the problem occur? Describe situations when it seems to be of most concern to you (or of least concern).
   c. How long has it been present? When did you first notice it?
2. How have you handled the problem before coming to us for help?
   a. What have you done about the problem?
   b. Have you sought other professional help? If so, where? What were the results?
3. Why are you coming for treatment now?
   a. Whose idea was it to come for treatment?
   b. How do you feel about coming?
   c. What do you want from the counseling program for yourself? Your partner?
   d. What do you want to increase or develop for yourself and/or your partner?
   e. How do you think the clinic might be helpful to you?
4. How did you learn about sex?
   a. Who taught you?
   b. What attitudes or actions did they encourage? Discourage?
   c. Possible sources of information include parents, other family members, friends, schools, books. Discuss the sources you feel were and are now the most influential in the development of your current problem.
5. Think about your early sexual experiences.
   a. What type of involvement were they?
   b. How did you feel about them?
   c. Examples might be child sex games, self-stimulation, opposite-sex encounters, same-sex encounters. Try to describe all the different types of experiences you've had.
   d. At what age(s) were you doing this (these) activity(ies)?
   e. Did anyone else know about your sexual activities? If so, what was their response? Encouragement? Discouragement?
   f. Under what circumstances did these activities take place (e.g., secret, openly, with others, alone, on dates, within marriage, outside marriage)?
   g. Do you think any of these prior experiences are connected to your current problem? If so, how?
   h. How often do you have sexual fantasies? Do they disturb you? Please describe them.
6. Are there other factors that you think may be adding to the stated problem (e.g., work, separation, children)?

7. Fantasize what the ideal sexual relationship would be for you.
   a. Where are you?
   b. What time is it?
   c. Do you have a partner? Who is he (she)?
   d. What is happening?
   e. How does it end?

Tape Two

The purpose of this tape is to evaluate the effectiveness of the entire therapy process in relation to your original problems.

We need your comments to help us evaluate the counseling program. Please be as descriptive as possible. Some people do not want to say what they think because they are afraid they will hurt the therapist's feelings. Don't worry! We welcome your honesty. Negative comments can be particularly helpful to us. Your comments and suggestions will be used in planning counseling sessions for others. Thank you for cooperating.

1. How was the therapy helpful or not helpful to you?
2. Were additional problems uncovered in the course of treatment? If so, were they handled to your satisfaction?
3. What were your expectations for treatment (what did you want to get out of it)? Were these expectations met? If not, how not? If so, what was most helpful?
4. What changes, if any, do you notice in your behavior toward your partner? In your partner's behavior toward you?
5. What changes, if any, in attitudes do you notice toward your partner? Toward yourself?
6. What changes, if any, in attitudes do you notice in your partner toward you? Toward himself (herself)?
7. What did you learn about yourself as a result of therapy? About your partner?
8. Discuss any exercises, reading, films that you experienced during therapy. Were these helpful to you?
9. How do you feel about making these tapes and their use? did they accomplish the stated goals? If not, how not? State reasons for and against their continued use. Make suggestions for changes, if any.
10. Additional comments and suggestions.

REFERENCES

Annon, J. S. (1973). The therapeutic use of masturbation in the treatment of sexual disorders. *Advances in behavior therapy* (Vol. 4). (pp. 199–215). New York: Academic Press.

114 *Strategies*

Annon, J. S. (1974). *The behavioral treatment of sexual problems: Vol. 1: Brief therapy.* Honolulu: Enabling Systems, Inc.

Annon, J. S. (1975). *The behavioral treatment of sexual problems: Vol. 2. Intensive therapy.* Honolulu: Enabling Systems, Inc.

Pion, R. J. (1975). Diagnosis and treatment of inadequate sexual response. In J. Sciarra (Ed.), *Gynecology and obstetrics* (Vol. 2.). Hagerstown, MD: Harper & Row.

Pion, R. J., & Annon, J. S. (1975). The office management of sexual problems: Brief therapy approaches. *Journal of Reproductive Medicine, 15*(4), 127–144.

Pion, R. J., & Hopkins, J. (1978). *The last sex manual.* New York: Wyden Press.

Pion, R. J., & Wagner, N. N. (1971). Diagnosis and treatment of inadequate sexual responses. In R. David (Ed.), *Davis' gynecology and obstetrics* (Vol. 2). Hagerstown, MD: Harper & Row.

RELATED READINGS

Dyk, P. A. H. (1990). Healthy family sexuality: Challenges of assessment. *Family Relations, 38,* 216–220.

Friedman, J. M., & Czekala, J. (1985). Advances in sex therapy techniques. *Innovations in Clinical Practice: A Source Book, 4,* 187-200.

Leiblum, S. R., & Rosen, R. C. (Eds.). (1989). *Principles and practice of sex therapy* (2nd ed.). New York: Guilford Press.

7

Family Mediation

Charles H. Huber, J. Barry Mascari,
and Aviva Sanders-Mascari

You're right from your side, I'm right from mine.
Bob Dylan

Mediation is a form of negotiation and conflict resolution in which the disputing parties are aided by a third party in making mutual decisions. The mediator does not exert decision-making power on the issue(s) in dispute. As such, family mediation maintains decision-making power with those it most directly affects—the family members themselves. It fosters a cooperative sharing of power that results in positively transformed rather than negatively severed relationships. The attraction of the mediation process for settling family disputes is obvious and is being applied to a wide range of issues throughout the family life cycle.

THEORETICAL FOUNDATIONS

Family mediation is a brief, cognitively oriented intervention that does not focus on the past to assign blame. Rather, it looks to the future to explore options for improved family interactions. As can be noted in Figure 7.1, mediation is particularly well suited as an intervention for family conflicts that might otherwise result in judicial or administrative proceedings. A num-

Mediation Along the Family Life Cycle

Pre-Marital Mediation
Mediators are helping couples draw up marriage agreements prior to the ceremony. This "ounce of prevention" can help ensure a more stable marriage.

Disabled and Handicapped
Stress often occurs in families caring for disabled or handicapped members. Counselors are using mediation to resolve some of the resulting conflicts.

Teenage Pregnancy
Struggles often arise over situations involving unmarried pregnant teenagers. Mediation can assist in resolving the conflicts between parents and child.

Homosexuals
Gay couples ending a relationship often have many of the same conflicts that divorcing couples do. The legal system does not necessarily provide a forum, so mediation can be valuable in resolving disputes.

Unmarried Cohabitants
At least one campus mediation service handles disputes between nonmarried couples who live together and seek a solution other than separation.

Teenagers and Parents
Numerous conflicts arise between parents and their adolescent children. Parent-teenager disputes often involve power struggles, and mediation can help restore relative peace to these households.

Runaways
Mediation is being used to bring together runaways and their families, and to resolve their conflicts out of court. Mediators are also helping to resolve family differences caused by juvenile drug abusers.

Relocation
New comprehensive relocation services use mediation to resolve the conflicts brought to the surface by a family move, such as problems related to dual careers, care of dependents, adolescent anxieties and emotional problems.

Domestic Violence
Mediation is helpful in the area of spouse abuse, particularly with first-time abusers.

Separation and Divorce
Property settlements and support payments are often the two areas of greatest contention in separation and divorce disputes. Mediation helps the couple to separate emotional issues from financial decisions.

Custody and Visitation
Mediation allows for more flexible and finely tailored child custody arrangements than those resulting from the adversarial process. Couples often reach cooperative joint custody agreements.

Retirement
Mediation services can help settle disputes at retirement time, such as when a husband might want to move to Florida just when his wife is embarking on a new career.

The Elderly vs. Their Middle-Aged Children
With the elderly population increasing, more and more conflicts are arising when older people can no longer care for themselves. Mediators help families to reach decisions about institutional versus home care.

Wills and Estate Planning
Mediation is useful when families disagree over estate plans. It also cuts costs when family members are contesting the execution of a relative's will.

Adapted from "Winning Through Mediation: Divorce Without Losers" by P. Vroom, D. Fassett, & R.A. Wakefield, 1982, *The Futurist, 16,* 28-34. Copyright© 1982 by World Future Society, Washington, DC. Reprinted by permission.

FIGURE 7.1
Some Issues in Family Mediation

ber of additional specific attractions are inherent in the process (Stahler, DuCette, & Povich, 1990):

1. It is a brief-oriented intervention.
2. It can thus be provided in a less costly manner (as compared to longer-term therapeutic efforts).
3. It requires a relatively short training period given the potential mediator's possessing basic facilitative skills.
4. It can make an immediate impact by targeting the manifest problems that might be particularly volatile within a family system.
5. It avoids the stigma frequently associated with psychotherapy.
6. It can be used in situations in which clients are unlikely to show up for counseling on a continual basis.

Conflict Resolution Versus Conflict Cessation

Mediation involves the resolution of conflict, not merely the cessation of it. Conflict cessation is frequently mistaken for conflict resolution.

Sarah, 15 years old and pregnant, has a strong personal conviction about abortion and believes it to be morally wrong. Her parents, actually more concerned about what the community would think of *them* as Sarah's condition became increasingly evident, provided her with numerous reasons why an abortion was the "best" alternative. Dependent and unassertive, Sarah followed their advice. Not really agreeing with that course of action, she later underwent a long period of therapy to deal with the guilt and depression she experienced as a result.

Without full and mutual participation in the decision-making process by all involved, actual resolution of a dispute may not be achieved. Some family members, like Sarah, are overwhelmed by others' seemingly more powerful position. Often, finding themselves in a disadvantageous position, individuals simply withdraw, but fully intend to resume the controversy when conditions are more favorable. Others respond by passively accepting whatever terms are thrust upon them, with absolutely no expection of complying with them. In none of these instances is resolution reached.

Decision making can be viewed as an unequal, superior-inferior relationship wherein one party (the superior) decides, while another (the inferior) is given little or no role in the process, only the outcome; or, alternatively, as a mutual venture in which all concerned contribute to the process and take responsibility in any outcome decided upon (Huber, 1981). Mediation seeks to make decision making "mutual" and its results mutually acceptable. This has a dramatic impact upon the way in which decisions are made and adhered to, as well as the emotional aftereffects experienced.

Coogler (1978) proposed that six conditions be present for true conflict resolution to occur:

1. The physical well-being of each party involved is maintained during negotiations and in the resolution reached.
2. Each party maintains its feelings of self-worth during the negotiating process and in the resolution itself.
3. All involved parties are respected and tolerated as persons, but with the understanding that this need not imply approval of others' morals or values.
4. All relevant facts, available options, and technical information are considered and used in reaching any resolution.
5. All parties consider the consequences of each available option before any resolution is agreed upon.
6. All parties agree to the resolution that is reached even though other choices were available.

The Structures of Family Mediation

Coogler further proposed that these six conditions suggest a specific structure that fosters resolving conflict rather than merely controlling or ending it. He identified coherent integration of three separate structures as being the essence of family mediation (Coogler, 1978); (a) the procedural structure, (b) the value structure, and (c) the psychological structure.

THE PROCEDURAL STRUCTURE

The procedural structure gives order to the mediation process. It presents all involved with a clear and common framework within which to function. It provides the means by which the factural and technical information needed for assessing alternatives becomes available to family members. The procedural structure identifies issues to be considered, schedules regular times for negotiations, establishes a neutral territory in which mediation is conducted, and gives the mediator the power to see that all parties follow agreed-to rules. Coogler (1978) cautioned that the procedural structure be kept simple so that family members need not devote excessive efforts to understanding it or, conversely, to be encouraged by its complexity and resulting confusion to manipulate it to their advantage.

THE VALUE STRUCTURE

The value structure establishes basic ethical standards of fairness to be followed during mediation. Family members should be told that these standards constitute the framework of an elementary sense of fairness. The standards cannot be expected to satisfy everyone's personal idiosyncratic conceptualizations of what is just. The intent is to project a common value structure that all concerned can comprehend and see as fairly applicable to them rather than to try to provide a procedure for meeting every test of fairness, which would be fruitless.

THE PSYCHOLOGICAL STRUCTURE

The psychological structure creates a setting wherein the physical and emotional needs of family members are met sufficiently so they can make optimal use of their decision-making capabilities. The mediator's understanding of group and family dynamics and accompanying skills for creating a favorable working environment provide the basis for the psychological structure. The procedural and value structures also contribute significantly to an appropriate psychological structure by creating a context that facilitates a fair and equitable resolution of conflict.

A Mediation Model

Gulliver (1979) proposed a cyclical and developmental model for understanding the process of mutual decision making in negotiated settlements. This model presents one concentrated focus that ties together the common threads used to define varying forms of interaction as being mediation. The cyclical aspects of Gulliver's model refer to the information sharing and learning that take place during the course of family mediation. The developmental aspects illustrate an overview of the family mediation process as it progresses from the time at which a disagreement becomes a dispute to its final outcome.

Family members come to mediation with often vague and inconsistent expectations that must be revised continually throughout the course of mediation eforts. Each member is expected to convey information about his or her demands, desires, strengths, and weaknesses, as well as to process similar forms of data from the other members and the mediator. Throughout this repetitive process of information exchange, family members and the mediator progressively adjust their expectations and preferences to make clearly understood and common choices. Thus, mediation is a dynamic interactive process that facilitates change through clarification and discovery (Girdner, 1983). This cycle repeats itself over and over as mediation proceeds from beginning to end.

A Typical Sequence of Mediation

When family members elect to come to mediation, they are mutually recognizing some dispute they need to work on together to resolve. Shortly, however, a shift from coordinated to antagonistic positions occurs as family members move from agreeing on mediation to disagreeing about the issues in dispute. This can involve disagreement about the issues themselves or the order in which they are to be considered. With the mediator's assistance the family members seek agreement regarding the boundaries of their dispute and the agenda to be followed. The mediator explains that his or her responsibility is to give them information about various options so they can make more informed decisions. The mediator stresses, however, that the final outcomes will be of their own making.

Agreement on the agenda normally is followed by an antagonistic phase in which family members communicate, often in rather extreme terms, their preferences and present positions. This is not a period during which solutions are considered but, rather, a phase in which symbolic issues and declarations are used to emphasize personally held positions. These can include open or veiled threats, or absolutistic statements about what one is willing to accept. In this phase the mediator's interventions are critically important. He or she must identify underlying overlapping interests and points of agreement. Otherwise family members may reach an impasse, refusing to move from an entrenched position.

For example, the mediator might acknowledge family members' mutual concern about constant arguing and fighting and ask them if they would like to know more about the potential future effects of their continuing conflict and possibly consider the types of arrangements that have created more cooperative circumstances for other families. In this manner the emphasis is shifted from individual personalities and positions to the shared problem. Specific potential outcomes are raised and discussed. As family members are helped to further clarify their preferences and positions, they revise them and begin brainstorming various possibilities. Family members are urged to consider options in terms of what they would perceive to be realistically workable for them. The mediator clarifies communication, identifies overlapping interests, and reinforces cooperative interactions.

Frequently, the mediator may have to refocus a problem. Before actual agreement can be reached, family members, with the mediator's assistance, must establish a range of acceptable outcomes, further clarify the more difficult issues, and examine possible trade-offs. During the final bargaining, the mediator proposes suggestions that would lead to an integrated outcome. A positive momentum evolves as successful coordination and agreements accumulate, leading family members to see that a mutually acceptable resolution is possible. The final agreement if followed by closure to the mediation process.

Throughout this process the mediator's role is that of "an advocate of the process of discussion and bargaining rather than an advocate of a particular settlement" (Trombetta, 1982, p. 69). The mediation process seeks to facilitate the orientation of family members and their efforts toward one another in arriving at a mutual solution. It helps them "achieve a new and shared perception of their relationship, a perception that will redirect their attitudes and dispositions toward one another" (Fuller, 1971, p. 325).

PREPARING TO MEDIATE: CHANGING HATS

Mediation is not psychotherapy. It may, of course, be therapeutic in many ways, but it should have no pretense of providing therapy. The mediator must learn to "change hats" from his or her primary function (e.g., as psychologist, counselor, family therapist, police officer) to that of mediator. Unlike clinical counseling or psychotherapy, *mediation is a nonexploratory process*. The mediator's role is not to change a family relationship but, rather, to help members resolve the concrete issues that have brought them to mediation (Vroom, 1983).

The mediator should keep in mind that his or her goal is to help family members reach *their* goals. Irrational beliefs, minor pathology or neurotic behavior may become obvious, but these must be left alone unless they are interfering in the mediation process. The subtle art of intervening in disruptive interchanges among family members as a mediator and not as, for example, a trained mental health professional often takes time to master. Without this competency, mediators can get lost in issues and never facilitate family members in achieving a solution.

Circumstances calling for therapeutic intervention are best approached through referral for concurrent treatment by a mental health professional. Thus, the mediator might share the following with the family members:

> My role is that of a mediator and not a therapist. It is my responsibility, however, to provide you with objective feedback that might be helpful to you during this mediation as well as in your future. For some reason, you all are having a great deal of difficulty objectively hearing what each other is saying. Emotions seem too often to be getting out of control. It might be best to seek the additional assistance of a mental health or family counselor.

Before seeking to mediate any family dispute, acquiring some formal training is advisable. The effective mediator must be competent in many skills. The mediator must be able to train and facilitate family members in negotiation—focusing, clarifying, bargaining, and compromising on important issues. Being able to create open, receptive communication channels is critical. Family members also must be aided in identifying general principles rather than simply specifying their demands.

Allowing family members to state fixed demands without understanding the general principles or underlying motives behind the demands results in "blind bargaining." In contrast, *principled negotiation* helps all sides see and understand others' positions and viewpoints and the real issues involved. These real issues are usually not what family members are actually disputing but, rather, an underlying principle of personal involvement on each participant's part—who is right, who is being treated unfairly, the desire to win, threats to personal status, prestige, or superiority (Huber, 1981). Increased give-and-take and real resolution can take place only if these principles are brought to awareness and considered. *Getting to Yes* (Fisher & Ury, 1982) is an excellent source explaining the key points of principled negotiation.

Family members are often heard to say, "Why do we need to mediate with you? It seems like a simple enough process." In a gentle way, family members should be told that if they had the skills to work out their differences on their own, they would not need formal mediation assistance. The mediator should stress to the family that mediation is not only an isolated problem-solving experience but also is a training program in which skills are being learned for future use. In one research investigation of family mediation efforts, the conclusion noted as most critical was "participants' increased confidence about their ability to solve problems given a new orientation for resolving future concerns on their own" (Pearson & Thoennes, 1982).

An initial contact with a family is not the time to consider "changing hats." Advanced preparation in both attitude and skills application is necessary before taking on the role of mediator. Readings, workshops, association with an experienced mentor, and participation in a peer supervision group are ideal ways of acquiring the knowledge base and mind set to facilitate the family mediation process.

THE MEDIATION PROCESS

The mediation process we follow in our work with families has 10 steps:

1. Referral.
2. Orientation and clarification.
3. Identification of principles and prioritization of demands.
4. Negotiations: initial demands.
5. Negotiations: early bargaining.
6. Negotiations: investigating options.
7. Negotiations: narrowing differences and trading.
8. Tentative agreement and revisions.
9. Memorandum of understanding.
10. Termination and follow-up.

Mediation is a fluid process, and the steps presented here can represent, but do not necessarily correspond to, specific sessions. Normally, more than one step of the process is accomplished during a session, depending upon the specific portion of the mediation involved. Also, the chronology of the process may be changed occasionally to meet the individual needs of certain families. Although a universal process of mediation can be described, the process should be applied idiosyncratically to individual families as it will be affected by the particular needs of a specific family (Haynes, 1982).

Referral

The typical mediation case is referred from the court, an involved community agency, a knowledgeable professional colleague, or a former client. Initial contact with a family is usually by telephone. The mediator should be prepared to provide a brief overview of mediation without going into great depth, especially if only one family member is initiating the contact. If this occurs, the mediator should request to speak to all involved parties before the intake meeting. In this way, the idea of mutuality and balance is established at the very onset (Haynes, 1982). An initial screening should be conducted by telephone so that a more relevant referral, if indicated, can be made immediately. If mediation appears appropriate, the first appointment is set.

Orientation and Clarification

Orientation and clarification take place in the initial intake session. The mediator's responsibility in this session focuses on a number of tasks: establishing his or her credibility, setting a positive tone, explaining the process and role of the mediator, clarifying family members' expectations, establishing empathy, and determining participants' readiness for mediation efforts (Haynes, 1981).

After sharing the scope, function, goals, and other pertinent details of the mediation process before it formally begins, the mediator should request that family members sign an *Engagement Letter* outlining the parameters of the process, as well as arrangements relating to fees, co-mediators, and the like. Copies should be distributed to all concerned parties to further ensure everyone's understanding of the process.

After introducing the Engagement Letter, the mediator must help family members become aware of the family issues that heretofore have gone unaddressed. This ability to help the family "focus" is an important skill that may enable family members to more correctly interpret their current conflict as a potential reflection or symptom of more serious dysfunction. Often, families come to mediation as a "premature referral." Too much dysfunction is present for mediation to effectively proceed. In cases like this, the mediator should recommend that the family seek therapeutic assistance either concurrent with, or prior to, beginning mediation efforts.

Engaging reluctant family members can create another issue that must be addressed in the intake session. The mediator must "sell" the positive and immediate, as well as the long-term problem-solving potential that mediation can have. Many persons entering mediation have a history of poor or ineffective experiences with professional "helpers." The family members have been termed resistant, blamed for lack of progress, or led to feel responsible and guilty for not achieving any concrete solutions to their problems. Providing a positive connotation through reframing the current conflict ("This crisis is a sure signal that your family wants positive change to take place") often helps to draw in all the family members.

Marie and her mother were reluctant to participate in mediation—very angry and hostile toward each other—knowing that nothing up to this time had worked for them. Both expected further failure and felt helpless. Getting basic information and identifying each party's beliefs about what was happening was impossible because the other openly disagreed and began yelling. The mediator met with each of them individually and suggested that the conflict and their responses to it were most helpful in calling attention to the problems at hand. The mediator also "joined" empathically with each of them, explaining that "it must be difficult to live with (Mom/Marie), and you have done an admirable job. . . ."

This family had experienced extreme conflict, and Marie had thrown scissors at her mother just prior to the session. Developing "ground rules" was imperative. Using the leverage of the juvenile justice system (and lock-up), a simple agreement for no violence, with built-in options such as punching the bed, was created. The mediator placed the demand for no violence, and the parties agreed. They were relieved of the sense of losing they would have felt from giving in to one another. The mediator accomplished this by going from room to room, meeting with Marie and her mother separately, shuttling information back and forth.

During the intake session the mediator also must elicit initial clarification of issues. The mediator should listen carefully to all the family members and actively question the relevant information presented. For example in working with Marie and her mother, the mother had a series of complaints about Marie coming home late, swearing, staying on the telephone, and other "smaller" issues. If the mediator were to similarly focus on these smaller events, the major issues would be missed. In this case, the major issues related to Marie's disregard of rules and basic challenges to her mother's power.

Successful orientation and clarification in the intake session will therefore establish:

— a win-win atmosphere with no "bad guy."
— an atmosphere of equality, but with a clear sense of the mediator's power to prevent imbalance in the participant's bargaining abilities.

— a sense that the mediator believes that each family member has valid, legitimate demands.

— the belief that resolution is possible.

— a clearer understanding of the major issues involved.

— a summary of agreements or beliefs common to all parties.

Identification of Principles and Prioritization of Demands

During the intake session, specific issues were identified. If these were to remain the focus of mediation, a stalemate would likely occur quickly. Basic principles underlying these issues must be brought to awareness if any movement is to occur when negotiations begin in the next step of the process. In addition, each family member must develop a sense of priorities. Frequently, family members employ a linear priority system in which every action carries the same weight.

If Marie came in late, played her stereo too loud, or visited a friend whom her mother disapproved of, Marie's mother would seek to ground Marie or even call the police. Whatever the offense, the mother's reaction was the same.

In identifying principles, the mediator seeks to facilitate family members' comprehension of their basic belief systems and the principles that guide them. Before beginning any in-depth discussions of demands, the mediator assists family members in formulating principled demands. Initial complaints are reconsidered with a goal of identifying general principles underlying

TABLE 7.1
The Formulation of Principled Demands

From Complaints	To Principles	To Demands
Mrs. S.: I want Marie to stop disobeying me. She totally disregards every rule I establish. I want her to come in early, clean her room, do what I say . . .	What is most important is that Marie is safe. Also, it is important that she know that I am her parent. Her room is not really that significant to me.	Marie should call me if she will be late. I want her to acknowledge that I am her parent and she must listen to me.
Marie: I hate my mother. All she wants to do is put restrictions on me and not allow me to grow up and have my own friends. I want to make my own rules.	I think I'm old enough to participate in making my own rules and should be allowed to pick my friends.	Mom should let me discuss rules instead of assuming that I have to agree with her because she is older and is my mother.

them, the result being more relevant, pointed demands. Table 7.1 illustrates this process as experienced in part by Marie and her mother.

When specific demands based on principles have been adequately identified, each party must rank them. This prioritization is done in private, although the mediator's assistance is strongly urged. The list of initial demands can be substantial. It may present a picture so imposing to other family members (in the upcoming step of the process) that they immediately feel a sense of defeat. The mediator might help by discussing with each family member the issues being prioritized, before their presentation, making sure that only major issues are noted, with a focus on underlying general principles.

Family members who have a prioritized list of principled demands will be better able to negotiate. They can enter negotiations with a clearer sense of what is important to them, what they *must* have to be satisfied, and what they are willing to give up. This knowledge encourages active participation and increases the probability that individual family members will be satisfied with their final agreement.

Negotiations: Initial Demands

"Negotiations" as an overall descriptor constitutes the next four steps of the mediation process, beginning with negotiations regarding initial demands. The various components are difficult to separate in terms of actual time and number of sessions. These portions of the process may repeat themselves throughout the entire process until the *Memorandum of Understanding* is firmly agreed to.

Before beginning each session—during the negotiations' portions of the process especially—the mediator must summarize and recap for family members the events of the preceding sessions and highlight any agreements made. Following this opening ritual, movement directly into specific negotiation concerns flows much easier.

"During our previous session, Mrs. S., you said that you wanted—from Marie, and you said you believed that. . . ." (Because an agreement was reached during that session, the mediator also highlights the points of agreement, providing a sense of positive movement and accomplishment.) "In addition, Marie acknowledged that she realizes that you (Mrs. S.) do worry about her, and she agreed with you that she will make a telephone call when she is going to be late."

In considering initial demands, each family member is given a limited time to present his or her list of demands that have been compiled privately (usually with the mediator's assistance) in the previous step. Even though each party knows his or her own priority order, the demands should be presented with equal importance. During this period, the mediator should request clarification of any demands that generate puzzled looks from fellow family members, prevent immediate discussion of any demand at this point in time, and block putdowns by one party toward another's demands. For reference purposes, the mediator might list the demands, in simplified form as they are presented, on a chalkboard or large newsprint so all can look at them simultaneously.

After the demands are presented and listed for all to see, the mediator should help family members take note of similar demands or common areas of concern. Different views about the same issue will present conflicts that must be addressed. By focusing on each family member's principles behind his or her demands, greater movement and flexibility can be attained. In the case of initial demands presented by Marie and her mother, the mediator rearranged the initial list of demands, placing similar issues across from each other to better focus on the degree of difference between Marie and her mother on the same issue. Relevant principles motivating Marie and her mother in their demands also were requested and noted at this time. This revised list is illustrated in Table 7.2.

TABLE 7.2
Initial Demands and Underlying Principles

Mrs. S.	Marie
• Stay away from "undesirable" friend. (An adult friend might sway your opinion/challenge my authority; *I* want to be your friend.)	• Visit friend Mom dislikes. (An adult friend can give me different ideas about areas I'm uncomfortable talking about with Mom.)
• Call if you are going to be late. (I worry that something might have happened to you.)	
• Follow *my* rules. (Mothers are supposed to be the ultimate authority; kids should listen.)	• Participate in making rules. (I'm old enough to have a say in rules that apply to me.)
• Keep your room clean. (Sloppy rooms are not good; you need to learn to be clean as a kid.)	
• No telephone calls after 10 p.m. (Late calls wake up the rest of the family.)	• Telephone use any time. (I like to talk to my friends about dates, etc. If I have to be in for curfew, at least I can use the phone.)
• Go to school every day and get good grades. (Marie oversleeps; if she keeps going this way, she won't amount to anything.)	• Stop being nagged about grades and school. (No matter what I do, it isn't good enough; I like school but hate to get up.)
• Come in at stated times: 9 p.m. weekdays and 10 p.m. weekends. (I'm responsible for your safety; something might happen at night. I worry.)	• Come in 10 p.m. weekdays and be allowed out later on weekends and special occasions. (When my brother was my age, he had later hours; my friends stay out until this time.)

In the case of parent-child conflicts, the process of identifying accompanying principles often has a remarkably positive effect on each party. Children, expecially, gain from hearing the beliefs their parents hold about issues or demands that have been longstanding areas of conflict. Frequently, this simple sharing in itself can unlock a diehard dispute by demystifying the importance of calling home or getting good grades in school.

After the initial list of demands has been prepared and recorded and has been arranged by the mediator, if appropriate, family members are ready to bargain based on the priorities individually established in the previous step of the mediation process.

Negotiations: Early Bargaining

Although family members are called upon to "bargain" daily, they surprisingly are often ill prepared to do so with each other. Children bargain with their friends over what games they will play and activities they will mutually participate in. Parents commonly bargain at the local fruit and vegetable stand or discuss what is a fair price for a used car in a give-and-take process similar to mediation. Yet, this procedure within the family is frequently "foreign."

At this point in the mediation, the mediator may have to demonstrate how to bargain. Especially in families with intense conflict or longstanding mistrust on the part of all parties, some "leading" must be done. Borrowing a technique from labor mediation, the mediator meets with each party separately. During these individually oriented sessions, the mediator plays each party off the other(s) by "speculating" about what the other side might accept, remembering, of course, not to influence family members toward a direction they truly may not want. The major function of this phase of the mediation process is to create enough movement and reference to specific principles so that family members will develop their own suggestions as to how and what they will proceed to bargain.

Negotiations: Investigating Options

All through the mediation process the mediator actually has been helping family members focus on potential options available to resolve their concerns. Now that family members have identified the items of most importance and the personal principles behind them, made their initial demands, and begun to consider how they will bargain, they have effectively narrowed their own options. They now are locked into working around specific problems and finding solutions that previously have eluded them. At this point, potential options are investigated in a way that will enable family members to narrow their differences and trade, using the options available to them.

A common deficiency among families in conflict is their failure to investigate or create various options for resolving mutual problems. One means mediators have for preparing family members to expand their outlook is to instill the belief that what has not worked in the past will not work now. Parents, in particular, hold on to methods that are ineffective or inappropriate with their children. The mediator can demonstrate through questioning that their present mode of interacting is not working; otherwise they would not be here. Staying with that mode will only continue to undermine cooperative family relationships and lead to further disagreements on additional issues.

New options for resolving differences must be developed and explored. If family members describe themselves as being stuck or continue to consider only one or two ideas, the mediator must tactfully probe these blockages. Questions that focus back on the principle of the demand often lead family members to their own discovery of new options; for example, "Are you telling me that his is the *only* way to solve this problem?" The mediator should encourage family members to create a long list of options, no matter how ridiculous. Brainstorming—simply listing potential options to be evaluated later—can be valuable in leading to mutually acceptable ideas.

Many times family members stop themselves from creating options, not because they do not exist or cannot be identified but, instead, because members would rather not see that these options exist. Confronting family members who withdraw into a "turtle-in-the shell" style of problem solving will encourage them to consider new options even if they don't like them. For example, with reference to Table 7.2, Marie's mother originally acted as if the only option available to prevent late-night calls from Marie's friends from interrupting the family's sleep was to make a rule: "No phone use after 10 p.m." The mother was unwilling to come up with alternative solutions. The mediator confronted her inflexible stance. The list eventually developed, as given in Table 7.3, might contain a number of presently unacceptable alternatives, but it did encourage the mother toward more creative thinking.

TABLE 7.3
Brainstorming Options

Problem	Current Option	Creative Options
Late telephone calls interrupt family's sleep	No phone use after 10 p.m.	1. Make only outgoing calls. 2. Put phone in Marie's room. 3. Get bell silencer on phone. 4. Store phone in insulated bag. 5. Remove phone from home. 6. Put light instead of bell on phone. 7. Buy family members head sets to block sound.

This creativity often is translated into a willingness to develop increased flexibility, and it frequently gives rise to humor stemming from the absurd possibilities available. Embroiled in conflict, many family members take everything, regardless of how insignificant or minor, seriously. Being able to laugh at what they previously saw as serious can indicate real progress.

When an impasse regarding options exists, the mediator can utilize self-disclosure and appropriately mention similar situations that he or she has worked with in the past: "One family I mediated with had a similar stalemate, and they came up with. . . ." Showing how other families have resolved their disputes makes family members feel that they are not alone. Framed properly, suggestions of this nature can facilitate identification with the case example and learning by modeling. If the mediator cannot think of a relevant previous example to propose, a hypothetical one created to fit the situation is appropriate.

Homework assignments can be another helpful tool for investigating options. Assigning family members the task of writing at least five options each for solving a given problem usually results in a list that did not exist before. If family members decide to work together to create options, this is most facilitative to the mediation. Other family members have consulted friends or other relatives in search of options. These interchanges, too, facilitate cooperative problem-solving interactions. The mediator must emphasize that homework is *required*. By forcing family members to consider doing something they may find distasteful, they are not choosing to do it; the mediator is "directing" them to do it. Participants may use this as an excuse to give up some of their responsibility. But they can regain it when they complete their assignment.

Negotiations: Narrowing Differences and Trading

Family members usually want to achieve their objectives without giving up anything. The work of previous steps of the process—setting priorities, early bargaining considerations, and investigating options—should have caused participants to begin to think that if any agreement is to be realized, they must give up some things or, at the very least, change their expectations. Now is the time to make these necessary concessions.

For example, parents often expect their children to change while they themselves refuse to give ground on issues. Gentle reminders such as, "You've been living in less than desirable conditions with your daughter, and I'm sure you're ready to try something new" can help create a more positive mind set. In more difficult cases, the mediator can meet individually with family members, encouraging movement by carrying options back and forth, suggesting a "deal" for them. Although this is a "gamey" technique, it is often quite successful.

With Marie and her mother, neither would budge unless the major objectives of both were met. It was suggested alternatively to both mother and daughter that if they were to accept one of the other's first-priority items, the other would be willing to give in on a demand.

Most trading is done, and resultant trade-offs made and accepted, in "package" form. In focusing on singular areas of disagreement, settling a dispute is often more difficult than considering total packages. The package that Marie and her mother arrived at is illustrated in Table 7.4

TABLE 7.4
A Trading Package

Mrs. S.'s Priorities	Marie's Priorities
1. Follow my rules.	1. Visit friend Mom dislikes.
2. Call if you'll be late.	2. Use telephone anytime.
3. Go to school every day.	3. Stop being nagged about school.
4. Don't be late; come in at stated times.	4. Revised curfew: weekends.

Concessions by Mrs. S.	Concessions by Marie
—Stay away from friend.	—Participate in making rules.
—Keep room clean.	—10 p.m. curfew weekdays.
—No telephone calls after 10 p.m.	
—10 p.m. curfew on weekends.	

Tentative Agreement and Revisions

Once family members agree to a tentative package, a rough draft of the areas of agreement can be set forth. Presenting the family members with a handwritten or typewritten draft on which they can make corrections or sign is preferable to simply summarizing the agreement by reading it to them. (Younger children, too, should be given a copy even though they may need the mediator's assistance in reviewing it.)

Having tangible evidence of their efforts to review and critique provides participants with a sense of accomplishment and power. They are now taking responsibility for refining what their agreement will actually be like. Any concerns raised in this step of the process are dealt with by recycling to relevant previous procedures. Once this step is completed, the formal Memorandum of Understanding can be prepared.

Memorandum of Understanding

Preparing a written document of what the family members have already agreed to is relatively easy. The Memorandum of Understanding should be written in simple, clear language and at a level that all family members can readily understand. They likely will have to refer to the agreement in the future and ought to be able to understand it completely without assistance. Incorporating the language the family members themselves have used to characterize their problems and solutions is usually best. This is especially important for keeping children involved in understanding and maintaining the agreement (Wixted, 1982). Also, by keeping language plain and simple and items behaviorally oriented, family members have a yardstick by which to measure compliance and, ultimately, the success of their agreement.

Although the mediator and the family members know that the document is an *agreement*, the mediator is advised to use the term "memorandum of understanding." Family members tend to see the final agreement more significantly when it has this formalized title. In addition, if the mediation is part of a court-sanctioned program or agency, this is the preferred descriptor for the document presented to a judge for approval.

Figure 7.2 gives an example of a Memorandum of Understanding. Note that a re-mediation clause is added to the basic agreement. This simple clause can prevent future disputes from adding to an already clogged court calendar, an overwhelmed social service agency client load, or most simply the already strained resources of a self-referred family. Reentry into mediation efforts forms a preventive first step.

MEMORANDUM OF UNDERSTANDING

This agreement by and between Mrs. S. and her daughter, Marie, was developed with full knowledge and participation by both of us on May 19, 1990. We have developed this agreement as outlined below to reduce conflict and continue to enjoy the good parts of our relationship. We agree to the following:

1. Marie will be allowed to choose and visit her own friends. Mrs. S's prior approval is required for overnight stays with friends.

2. Marie agrees to discourage her friends from calling her at home after 10 p.m. and before 7 a.m. She will be allowed to make outgoing calls during these times.

3. Marie agrees to call home if she will be late. If she does not call, her curfew will be shortened for the following night, at a ratio of two (2) minutes for every one (1) minute she was late.

4. Mrs. S. agrees not to be responsible for waking Marie up on school days and Marie will wake up on her own and attend school regularly.

5. The established curfew will be 9 p.m. weekdays and 11 p.m. weekends for Marie as long as she informs Mrs. S. of her destination.

6. A subsequent set of rules will be appended to this agreement.

In the event of any dispute arising out of this agreement, we agree that prior to directing the problem to the Court, we will first attempt to settle the dispute through the use of mediation services.

Signed this 19 Day of May, 1990.

_____   _____
                                         Aviva Sander-Mascari, Mediator

_____

cc: Juvenile Court Clerk
    Mrs. S.
    Marie
    File

FIGURE 7.2
Memorandum of Understanding

Termination and Follow-up

Family members who have signed the Memorandum of Understanding have worked out with the mediator and each other a most significant agreement: to seek new paths of conflict resolution. As noted earlier, the most important part of this process might simply be learning and experiencing the process itself. Agreements are only as good as the family members' willingness to adhere to them. The mediator should monitor agreements for a time, by telephone, brief follow-up "progress" sessions, or mail, as a gentle reminder that the mediator (and in relevant cases, the "system") is watching and really cares about the ultimate outcome of the mediation.

A CAVEAT: DIVORCE MEDIATION

One of the major areas of mediation practice is divorce mediation. All the components identified and discussed in this chapter are similar in divorce mediation, with one notable addition necessary. Mediators facilitating divorce mediations must have specific technical and legal knowledge and resources at their command to a degree not needed for most family mediation efforts. Consultation with attorneys, accountants, and similar professionals relevant to a divorce settlement are an integral part of the former. The interface of law and mediation, especially, must be clearly understood. State domestic relations laws must be fully comprehended because agreements a divorcing couple reaches through mediation eventually will be translated into a formal legal document drawn up by a relevant professional.

Readers who are interested in pursuing an investigation of divorce mediation are referred to *Structured Mediation in Divorce Settlements* (Coogler, 1978) and *Divorce Mediation: A Practical Guide for Therapists and Counselors* (Haynes, 1981). These are two seminal works on the intricacies of this process.

CONCLUSION

This chapter has offered family mediation as a useful approach for resolving many types of family disputes and thereby preventing the escalation of family conflict. Although the advantages of this approach have been asserted, it must not be perceived as a substitute for family therapy, or for more in-depth intervention procedures. It is not a panacea for preventing or resolving all family discord. Family mediation, however, does represent a brief intervention modality that should be employed in family circumstances calling for an impartial third party to assist in negotiating a fair agreement among family members, an agreement that offers the greatest probability of being adhered to.

REFERENCES

Coogler, O. J. (1978). *Structured mediation in divorce settlements.* Lexington, MA: Lexington Books.

Fisher, R., & Ury, W. (1982). *Getting to yes.* Boston, MA: Houghton-Mifflin.

Fuller, L. (1971). Mediation: Its forms and functions. *Southern California Law Review, 44.* 305–339.

Girdner, L. K. (March, 1983). *Adjudication and mediation: A comparison of custody decision-making processes involving third parties.* Paper presented at National Conference on Peacemaking and Conflict Resolution, Athens, GA.

Gulliver, P. H. (1979). *Disputes and negotiations: A cross-cultural perspective.* New York: Academic Press.

Haynes, J. (1981). *Divorce mediation: A practical guide for therapists and counselors.* New York: Springer.

Haynes, J. (1982). A conceptual model of the process of family mediation: Implications for training. *American Journal of Family Therapy, 10,* 5–16.

Huber, C. H. (1982). An Adlerian approach to marital counseling. *Counseling & Human Development, 14*(3), 1–16.

Pearson, J., & Thoennes, N. (1982). Divorce mediation: Strengths and weaknesses over time. In H. Davidson, L. Ray, & R. Horowitz (Eds.), *Alternative means of family dispute resolution.* Washington, DC: American Bar Association.

Stahler, G. J., DuCette, J. P., & Povich, E. (1990). Using mediation to prevent child maltreatment: An exploratory study. *Family Relations, 39,* 317–322.

Trombetta, D. (1982). Custody evaluation and custody mediation: A comparison of two dispute interventions. *Journal of Divorce, 6,* 65–75.

Vroom, P. (1983). The anomalous profession: some bumpy going for the divorce mediation movement. *Family Therapy Networker, 7,* 38–42.

Wixted, S. (1982). The children's hearings project: A mediation program for children and families. In H. Davidson, L. Ray, & R. Horowitz (Eds.), *Alternative means of family dispute resolution.* Washington, DC: American Bar Association.

RELATED READINGS

Blades, J. (1985). *Family mediation: Cooperative divorce settlement.* Englewood Cliffs, NJ: Prentice Hall.

Folberg, J., & Milne, A. (1988). *Divorce mediation: Theory and practice.* New York: Guilford Press.

Haynes, J. M., & Haynes, G. L. (1989). *Mediating divorce: Casebook of strategies for successful family negotiations.* San Francisco: Jossey-Bass.

Marlow, L, & Sauber, S. R. (1990). *The handbook of divorce mediation.* New York: Plenum.

Milne, A. L. (1986). Divorce mediation: A process of self-definition and self-determination. In N. S. Jacobson & A. S. Gurman (Eds.), *Clinical handbook of marital therapy* (pp. 197–216). New York: Guilford Press.

Robin, A. L., & Foster, S. L. (1989). *Negotiating parent-adolescent conflicts: A behavioral-family systems approach.* New York: Guilford Press.

Shaw, M. L., & Phear, W. P. (1989). *Parent-child mediation.* New York: Institute of Judicial Administration.

8

Parenting

Jon Carlson and Brenda Rifkin Faiber

One of the most visible effects of a child's presence in the household is to turn the worthy parents into complete idiots when, without him, they would perhaps have remained mere imbeciles.
Georges Courteline (1917)

With few exceptions, the family—and, in particular, the parents—exert the most significant influence on an individual's development. In today's stressful and changed world, however, most parents are having difficulty with leading a mentally and physically healthy life and specifically with rearing children. The reasons are multifold and complex but are not the purpose of this chapter. We do know that this situation need not continue, because parents *can* learn appropriate and effective procedures for rearing children in today's complex times.

Many counselors are willing to help fill this void in effective living and already possess the teaching and consulting skills necessary (Dinkmeyer, Carlson, & Dinkmeyer, 1991), but they are not sure just what parents need to know. The parenting skills we have found to be necessary, after training thousands of parents, fall into the following seven categories:

1. Understanding human behavior.
2. What we really want for our children.
3. Understanding human personality development.
4. Motivation and encouragement.

5. Discipline/logical and natural consequences and choice-making.
6. Communication.
7. Family meetings.

To help parents learn new and more effective parenting skills, they need to understand why their children act as they do. Children behave in similar ways but *for different reasons* and, therefore, each child must be dealt with individually. Parents have a lot of good solutions to child management problems, but they frequently are unsuccessful because they do not understand why children behave as they do. Frequently, parents support the behavior they are trying to remove.

For example, the parent who tries to talk to a child who is misbehaving to seek attention is giving attention to the child. The parent who argues with the child who is misbehaving to seek power is demonstrating to the child how important power is. Because all situations cannot be prepared for, parents need to learn how to understand behavior and to be able to handle new problems. It is important to give parents this skill rather than just a series of magical solutions. As the old adage goes: "Give a man a fish and you feed him for a day. Teach a man to fish and you feed him for a lifetime."

All behavior has a purpose or is directed toward the achievement of a goal. Children, as well as adults, have needs, the most important of which is a sense of belonging and the feeling of significance or importance, whether in the family, the peer group, or the community. To find our place in life, we will behave (or misbehave) in ways to achieve these goals. Because all behavior is goal-directed, a transaction that involves two pieces or more of behavior by an individual will reflect movement toward the goal. Therefore, by using the ABC system of understanding human behavior (Dinkmeyer & Carlson, 1973), the goal can be accurately identified in a short time. The procedure involves:

A. Observing what the child or person does.
B. Identifying what the reactor (parent or teacher) does and how he or she feels.
C. Recording the consequences of the transaction or how the person responds to B.

After observing several situations, a pattern in the behavior will emerge and the goal or purpose of the person's behavior can be seen.

The socioteleological or Adlerian approach to understanding human behavior (Adler, 1957; Dreikurs, 1950; Dinkmeyer, Dinkmeyer, & Sperry, 1987), proposes that children misbehave to reach one of four basic goals:

Goal 1. *Attention.* The child believes "I am important only when people notice me or are in my service" or "I'm not outstanding but *at least* I will not be overlooked if I can obtain special attention, fuss, or service."

Goal 2. *Power.* "I count in life when people do just what I want" or "I may not be a winner but *at least* I can show people they cannot defeat me or stop me from doing what I want or make me do what they want."

Goal 3. *Revenge.* The discouraged child who seeks this goal believes "I count or I'm special only when I hurt" or "People do not care for me, but *at least* I can do things to strike back when I am hurt."

Goal 4. *Inadequacy.* The child who seeks this goal has given up on life and feels "I do not count, so why bother?" or "I will not be able to measure up, but *at least* if I do nothing, people will leave me alone."

Table 8.1 uses the ABC system as a framework to identify the four goals of misbehavior. The understanding and facilitation of healthy or productive behavior can be seen in Table 8.2. Once an individual's goal and purposes are discovered, appropriate modification plans can be developed. Modification programs have three fundamental aspects: (a) removing unwanted and inappropriate goals and their corresponding behavior, (b) encouraging and developing already existing goals and behavior, and (c) initiating new behavioral responses and healthy goals. Most people concentrate on eliminating existing behaviors; yet, developing appropriate goals and responses will yield greater gains.

In helping parents understand human behavior, providing them with a series of principles or rules of behavior is helpful. These may serve as guidelines for parents when situations become overly complex and the ABCs become clouded and not as easy to identify:

1. *All behavior has a purpose and is goal-directed.* Every behavior is done to reach a goal, and this goal is what causes the act. The individual's actions, displayed through his or her interactions with others, reveal the purpose. The consequence then becomes the cause of behavior.

2. *Behavior is best understood in terms of its unity or pattern.* The individual approaches the world and its challenges with all he or she has—foot, fist, ear, purpose, value. A person responds to any stimuli as a total being with thoughts, actions, feelings, and so on. These are all part of a meaningful pattern. Therefore, to understand the individual, we must perceive the pattern and help him or her in relation to it. To be special, to control, to be right, to get even, to be served are examples of patterns that reflect the individual's unity, as exemplified in Table 8.2.

3. *Each individual is striving for significance.* We all have hopes and aspirations that we are attempting to achieve in order to be "important," "successful," or "special." This striving for significance becomes the motivating force behind human activity. Although all humans do not seek to be significant in the same way, they do seek a sense of importance. The way in which an individual seeks significance will reveal his or her self-concept.

TABLE 8.1
ABC SYSTEM

Goal of misbehavior	"A" What the child does	"B" What the teacher/ parent do and how they feel	"C" What the child does as the consequence	What the child is saying	Some corrective measures
Attention	Active and passive activities that may appear constructive, destructive	Annoyed; wants to remind, coax; delighted with "good" child	Temporarily stops disturbing action when given attention	"I count only when I'm being noticed or served"	-Ignore -Answer or do the unexpected -Give attention at pleasant times
Power	Active and passive activities only destructive in nature	Provoked, angry; generally wants power challenged ("I'll make him do it", "You can't get away with it")	Intensifies action when reprimanded; child wants to win, be boss	"I count only when I am dominating, when you do what I want you to"	-Extricate self -Act, not talk -Be friendly -Establish equality -Redirect child's efforts into constructive channels
Revenge	More severe active and passive activities	Hurt, mad ("How could he do this to me?")	Wants to get even; makes self disliked; intensifies action in a hurtful fashion	"I can't be liked; I don't have power, but I'll count if I can hurt others as I feel hurt by life."	-Extricate self -Win child -Maintain order with minimum restraint -Avoid retaliations -Take time and effort to help child
Inadequacy	Passive activities that defy involvement	Despair ("I give up")	No reprimand, therefore, no reactions; feels there is no use to try; passive	"I can't do anything right, so I won't try to do anything at all; I'm no good"	-Encourage-ment (may take long) -Faith in child's ability

By Jon Carlson, modified from "Children's Mistaken Goals" Chart by Nancy Pearcy of Corvallis, OR.

4. *All behavior has social meaning.* People are primarily social beings and seek human relationships. Therefore, human behavior is best understood in terms of its social context and its distinct interpersonal relationships. The significance of behavior is in terms of our interactions and transac-

TABLE 8.2
Goals of positive behavior

Child's Belief	Goal	Behavior	How to Encourage Positive Behavior
I belong by contributing	Attention Involvement Contribution	Helps Volunteers	Let child know the contribution counts and that you appreciate it
I can decide and be responsible for my behavior	Power Autonomy Responsibility for own behavior	Shows self-discipline Does own work Is resourceful	Encourage child's decision making Let child experience both positive and negative outcomes Express confidence in the child
I'm interested in cooperating	Justice Fairness	Returns kindness for hurt Ignores belittling comments	Let child know you appreciate his or her interest in cooperating
I can decide to withdraw from conflict	Withdrawal from conflict Refusal to fight Acceptance of others' opinions	Ignores provocations Withdraws from power contest to decide own behavior	Recognize child's effort to act maturely

From D. Dinkmeyer & G. McKay, *Systematic Training for Effective Parenting* (Circle Pines, NY: American Guidance Service, 1989).

tions with others and the subsequent consequences. Social striving, then, is of primary, not secondary, importance.

5. *The individual's beliefs determine behavior.* We are not concerned with how the event appears externally but instead seek out the meaning the event possesses for the individual. This principle refers to the necessity of understanding the individual's private logic. As Adler (1957) stated, "A perception is never to be compared to a photographic image, because something of the peculiar and individual quality of the person is inextricably bound up with it" (p. 49.). For example, the sun represents something very different to the farmer, the poet, the sunbather, the albino, the Inca, and the physicist. People have the creative capacity to interpret and explain their experiences to fit their own lifestyle.

6. *Belonging is a basic need.* Individuals can be actualized only to the extent that they find their place and belong to someone. When an individual doubts he or she will be accepted or feels he or she will not belong, anxieties and apprehension arise. In understanding individuals, identifying the source(s) of their acceptance and identity are often helpful.

7. *The basic need is to actualize human potential.* Human needs arrange themselves in a hierarchy, as Maslow (1970) rates them, beginning with the most immediate: physiological, safety, belonging, love, self-esteem, and self-actualization. This allows us to understand that individuals must deal first with their lower hierarchic needs before they can become fully functioning persons.

WHAT DO WE REALLY WANT FOR OUR CHILDREN

Parents should have a clear idea of what characteristics and behaviors they want their children to acquire. Most people have a good and clear idea of what they do not want their children to do (e.g., swear, smoke, pick their noses, bite fingers, touch windows with their hands) but are vague about what they want their children to be like. Following are some of the positive characteristics of a mentally healthy or socially and emotionally well adjusted individual. Once a parent has a clear idea of the desired traits, these characteristics can be facilitated or attended to. According to Dewey (1972), p. 68), a healthy individual:

1. Respects the rights of others.
2. Is tolerant of others.
3. Is interested in others.
4. Cooperates with others.
5. Encourages others.
6. Is courageous.
7. Has a true sense of his/her own worth.
8. Has a feeling of belonging.
9. Has socially acceptable goals.
10. Puts forth genuine effort.
11. Meets the needs of the situation.
12. Is willing to share rather than being concerned with "How much can I get?"
13. Thinks of "we" rather than just "I."

These characteristics are the criteria for social-emotional maturation, or what Adler (1957) called "social interest."

The elimination of negative behaviors, or remediation, has dominated psychology since its inception. If mental health and productive people are going to inhabit this planet, an educational or educational or preventive philosophy is needed. Mental health and positive personality development no longer can be left to chance but must be developed deliberately. Only through helping parents develop clear ideas of what constitutes *health* (not just absence of illness) can we reach this plateau. More information on these ideas can be found in Dyer's (1985) *What Do You Really Want for Your Children?*

UNDERSTANDING HUMAN PERSONALITY DEVELOPMENT

The personality, or *lifestyle*, of an individual evolves from a combination of the following five components:

1. Family atmosphere and values.
2. Sex roles.
3. Family constellation.
4. Methods of child rearing.
5. Heredity.

The family and especially the parents have the most significant influence on the children's personality development. The family is the arena in which love, trust, acceptance, and actualization are cultivated. The child's position in the family constellation and his or her relationship with siblings also exert a tremendous impact. If this structure is unhealthy, a negative and harmful influence, characterized by fear and atypical growth, results. It is in the family that the culture and the values, beliefs, and mores of society are transmitted to the individual.

Family Atmosphere

The child's first exposure to life is within the family environment. Here the child is introduced to values, beliefs, and feelings. The child observes relationships within the family and sees this as a way of communicating with others. If a child sees the mother and father fighting or one of them using some type of power to gain control, the child incorporates this into his or her own behavior. Children choose the behaviors that they feel will be most effective.

Families that emphasize working together for mutual interest often influence this attitude in children. Children usually familiarize themselves with the same interests that parents have, because of their exposure to them. If a family is interested in outdoor sports and music, the child probably will develop similar interests. The children's patterns of behavior are not carbon copies of the family patterns, though. Children accept or reject what they want. Usually, however, family members show similar traits.

Sex Roles

Sex roles also influence personality development. The child usually is exposed to a male and female role through the parents. From these models children learn what it is like to be a man or woman. This not only involves learning what the same sex does but also involves learning what the opposite sex does and one's relationship to them. Here the child learns about intimacy and how to deal with the same and the opposite sex. Children are free to interpret what they see and to accept or reject what they feel is or is not feasible.

Family Constellation

Each child has a unique position in the family structure. The ordinal position (firstborn, second, middle, youngest, only child) determines certain characteristic attitudes and traits.

The oldest child usually strives to be number one in all areas because this is the way he or she entered into the world. This child is also an only child for a while and feels dethroned when another child enters the family structure. When the oldest no longer can be number one, he or she may give up completely. If this child can no longer be the best in a useful way, he or she may revert to being the worst, which is another way of being first.

The secondborn child usually feels that he or she has to compete with the firstborn. This child might feel inferior and might compensate for this by overtaking the firstborn. If the competition between the two is strong, the second usually strives to become what the first is not. The two will excel in different areas and give up in the areas in which they feel they cannot be successful.

The middle child usually feels "squeezed out." Children in this position usually view life as unfair and full of injustice and give up. Or they may choose to compete and have more success than the other two siblings. They then will overcome big rivals and be number one.

The youngest child sees himself or herself as the baby. These children sometimes are spoiled and feel entitled to special attention. They always have to get their own way and frequently go through life feeling inadequate. Sometimes they take on the characteristics of being the cutest or most charming.

Only children usually grow up in an adult world and become very grown-up at an early age. They typically feel they can take adult roles and are special. They always want to be catered to and, in some instances, never actually grow up. Frequently they have a difficult time developing feelings.

The number of children in the family and the sexual distribution in the family constellation are additional factors. Birth order should never be looked upon as the only determining factor in a child's personality development. The way in which children perceive their environment, along with their creative and intellectual capacity, also influences their development.

Method of Child Rearing

The type of child rearing philosophy has a definite effect upon the personality development of the child. The child who is reared in an autocratic family learns that being the boss is best ("I don't count unless I have power") and other beliefs that reflect the feeling of "I'm not OK." The child who is reared in a laissez faire environment lives in confusion and frequently lacks the confidence and security that results from stability. The child reared in a democratic family learns to value self and others. An environment that stresses social equality breeds children who become responsible adults.

Lifestyle or personality can be influenced by how the child is actually reared in the family environment. Dinkmeyer and McKay (1989) suggest the following principles to help parents establish democratic child management procedures:

1. The parent should understand the child and the purpose of his or her behavior or misbehavior.
2. The relationship between parent and child always should be one of mutual respect.
3. Parents should be both firm and kind. The firmness indicates respect for themselves, and the kindness shows respect for the child.
4. Children should be valued as they are. Their assets and strengths should be discussed, valued, and emphasized. A parent should spend more time encouraging than correcting. One positive statement a day is a good motto.
5. Parents should have the courage to live with their own inadequacies. They should accept themselves as well as the child.
6. Parents must act more and talk less. Natural and logical consequences that teach respect for order should replace reward and punishment.
7. If a poor or ineffectual relationship exists, parents must have the patience and take the time to make corrective efforts. Developing human relationships that are mutually satisfying require awareness but are worth the effort.

Parents play a large part in the formation of a child's personality. If they approach a child negatively, children will carry this with them. But if parents respect children and give them positive reinforcement and encouragement throughout their formative years, the children will attain healthy positions in life.

Heredity

To assess the effect that heredity plays on personality development is impossible. In most instances there is little anyone can do about hereditary characteristics, but people can choose what the *believe* about the characteristics. Not all muscular people feel strong, or short people inferior, or intelligent people capable. Parents should help children develop healthy beliefs about both exceptional and limiting characteristics.

ENCOURAGEMENT

Encouragement is one of the most important skills for improving all relationships, including that of parent and child, and for building healthy behavior. Encouragement is the process of finding the assets and strengths of an individual to build self-concept and feelings of worth. Instead of criticism and high expectations, the individual is accepted for what he or she can do. Parents often set goals that are beyond the child's capabilities.

When using encouragement, a feeling of success has to be built in the child. Giving the child a feeling of independence and responsibility helps instill a positive self-image. Children need to possess courage to face new challenges and tasks. The first step in the encouragement process is for parents to take the attitude and visualize the child in terms of what the child is able to do and not what he or she *should* be doing. Parents can develop a list of the child's assets and the manner in which they encourage each. This can be a most helpful (and insightful) procedure.

The child with a feeling of inadequacy needs encouragement the most. Encouragement should be used whenever the child attempts and achieves even the smallest success. This becomes a difficult task because (a) we are not accustomed to seeing the positive or noticing slight improvement (the converse, however, is not true), and (b) discouraged children usually reject any attempts to initiate their OKness, because it does not fit their self-concepts. The individual's rejection will change 180 degrees with a *persistent* positive approach over time. Individuals who feel inadequate eventually will build courage when they discover that they can be successful at what they try.

Matthew is a small child who feels that he is not able to achieve. He comes home from school with a spelling paper that has 15 correct and 5 wrong. How would you respond? It is not important to worry about or dwell on the five mistakes but, rather, to encourage Matthew about the 15 correct responses: "Wow, 75%—that's 3 out of every 4 right. I sure wish I could do that well in the stock market!" or "I really like the thoughtfulness with which you prepared your paper. Each word is clearly written and easy to read."

It is important to focus on the positive, or where the individual actually is, and not the negative, or where he or she is not. When the focus is on individuals' ability, it leads to individuals' believing in themselves.

Encouragement works best when it is used at the appropriate time and focuses on specific assets and strengths. The language is used in encouraging children has to be thought out carefully. Our opinions and values must not be included. The following show encouragement (Dinkmeyer & McKay, 1989):

Phrases that demonstrate acceptance
"I like the way you handled that."

"How do you feel about ____?"

"I'm glad you're pleased with what you did."

"Since you aren't satisfied, what do you think you can do so that you'll be pleased with it?"

Phrases that show faith

"You'll make it."

"I have faith in you."

"I'm sure you will be able to handle it."

"That's a difficult one, but I'm sure you'll be able to do it."

Phrases that focus on contribution, assets, and strength

"Thanks, you really helped me a lot."

"I appreciate what you did."

"I need your help with this."

"Looks like you're really proud of that."

Phrases that recognize effort and improvement

"It looks like you really worked hard on that."

"Look at the progress you've made." (be sure to tell how)

"You may not feel you've reached your goal, but look how far you've come."

More information on encouragement may be found in *The Encouragement Book* (Dinkmeyer & Losoncy, 1980).

DISCIPLINE AND CHOICE MAKING

For many years parents have used reward and punishment to discipline children. The word "discipline" has been used synonymously with "to punish," "hurt," or "take away." Yet, discipline is actually a term that refers to *teaching* children how to act appropriately or to learn social and emotional maturity. Learning theory expounds that children learn best in situations in which threat and anxiety are minimized, the material has meaning, and appropriate behavior and responses are acknowledged or encouraged.

Traditional procedures of reward and punishment do not meet these conditions and actually have many disadvantages. For example, when using this method, the responsibility for the child's behavior is placed upon the parents. The child is not allowed to make decisions and choices and to become independent. Also, positive behaviors tend to occur only when an authority figure (parent or another adult) is around to give out rewards. Children perform in a positive manner only when there is something in it for them.

To help reinstate discipline to a functional and meaningful level, the concepts of natural and logical consequences have merit. *Natural consequences* are the laws or discipline of the natural world. If an animal moves when a predator is near, death is the probable outcome. If a fish swims close to shore in a small pool and the tide goes out, the fish frequently dies. If lions do not hunt, they do not eat, and go hungry. These same rules apply to people. If you touch a hot stove, you get burned; if you run down a hill too fast, you fall down; if you put your shoes on the wrong feet, you develop sore feet. Natural consequences are excellent teaching devices, as they allow the child to learn from the natural order of events. Individuals see that the responsibility for the behavior is their own.

If we were not civilized people, natural consequences could govern all of our events just as they do in the natural world. But, being civilized, we are not willing to allow people, from direct experience, to kill or be killed from fast automobile driving, to hurt or abuse others through physical fighting, or to understand the danger of playing in the street. Therefore, we have developed a series of contrived or *logical consequences* to be used when there are no natural consequences or when danger is too great. They allow children to experience in a meaningful fashion the logical nature and reality of the social order.

Our laws, for instance, are based on this idea. If people drive too fast, the natural consequence might be their own or someone else's death or injury; therefore, we use the logical consequence of losing the privilege to drive. If people fight with other people, the logical consequence is to put them in jail, away from others. These procedures are most effective when the individual sees the consequence as logical and sees that rights and respect have not been violated.

The advantages of logical consequences over punishment are that:

1. The power of authority is taken away.
2. The consequences are logically related to the misbehavior.
3. No moral judgments are placed upon the individual's action.
4. Concern is only with what will happen in the present, not what happened in the past.
5. The tone of voice used when stating the logical consequence is friendly, not threatening.

Keeping these points in mind, we must remember that nonverbal communication enters into the picture as well. When stating logical consequences, the child will perceive an angry look as a threat. This is contrary to the purpose of logical consequences, which is to give the child the opportunity to make reasonable decisions and to learn from mistakes or unpleasant consequences. When a child repeatedly faces unpleasant consequences, eventually he or she will learn more appropriate behavior to avoid the consequences.

When implementing logical consequences as a form of discipline, timing is an important factor. Letting the anger and hostilities "cool off" before dealing with the misbehavior is more effective. This maintains the positive and friendly relationship. If the child is being disruptive and it is not feasible to wait until later, the logical consequences should be established immediately, but with a positive and friendly attitude.

According to Dinkmeyer and McKay (1989), the following basic principles should be used as guidelines in implementing logical consequences.

1. Understand the child's goals, behavior, and emotions.
2. As parents, be both firm and kind.
3. Don't be a "good" mother.
4. Become more consistent in your actions.
5. Separate the deed from the doer.
6. Encourage independence.
7. Avoid pity.
8. Refuse to become overconcerned about what others think.
9. Recognize who owns the problem.
10. Let all children share the responsibility.

Keeping these basic principles in mind, effective consequences involve *giving the child a choice*. The parents propose the course of action they feel is right and then allow the child to make a free choice. This procedure is effective only when the child is held responsible for the consequences of his or her action. The child is given the responsibility. For example: "I'm sorry, but I'm trying to watch TV. You may settle down and watch the program with us or leave the room. You decide."

Sometimes logical consequences involve stating your intentions and letting the child decide how to respond: "I don't feel that it's my responsibility to make your bed when there are clothes all over it. From now on I'll make the bed when your clothes are in the proper place."

Once the child has made the choice, parents must accept his or her decision and let the child try again. At this point the child may test the parents. If you let the child try again and the misbehavior recurs, you might set longer time limits before the child is allowed to try again. Eventually, if children feel the consequence is logical, they will change their behavior.

In sum, natural and logical consequences are better and more effective alternatives than reward and punishment. Consequences are most effective when employed in a friendly and respectful manner. Their purpose is to give the child more and more responsibility and encourage independence, which should produce a healthier, stronger person. Communication is an underlying agent of change when using logical and natural consequences. Change cannot take place without effective communication.

COMMUNICATION

Communication is the most important element in any relationship. To open up effective communication channels with children, parents must take the time to listen and learn to communicate clearly. This lack is probably the biggest downfall in family relationship. According to Gordon (1975), nine of 10 parents (conservatively) miscommunicate or communicate in destructive ways to children and youth. Very rarely do parents and children communicate effectively.

The most important point to keep in mind in communicating is *mutual respect*. This means accepting children's feelings without transmitting rejection toward them. Even though we may not agree with what they are saying, we can show them that we accept what they are saying. Acceptance is transmitted to children by the parent's attitude, choice of words, and tone, not through the content of the response. Eye contact and facial expressions also play an important role. People communicate more through nonverbal than through verbal behavior. Therefore, we must show children, by physically attending, that they and their message are valued. This involves looking at the child, facing the child directly, and following the statements with interest. Parents need to acquire four major skills of communication:

1. Reflective listening
2. Problem solving
3. Problem ownership
4. I-messages

Reflective Listening

Reflective listening is the process in which the feelings and facts of the child's message are restated to clarify the message for both parties. In this way, parents can accurately understand how the child feels and what he or she means. It also helps convey to the child that we understand what they have said.

Reflective responses may be subtractive or interchangeable. *Subtractive responses* indicate that we have not heard or understood what has been said. It means that we really have not listened and do not understand the message and are actually taking away from what the child really means. *Interchangeable responses* are statements that indicate to the other person that we have clearly understood the feeling and meaning of their original statement. It can be looked upon as "feedback."

Reflective listening requires accuracy of interchangeable responses. Being sensitive to the feelings that are being stated and the ability to express these are musts. At all times these restatements must be nonjudgmental—not initiating any new ideas or thoughts but, rather, clarifying those of the child. This keeps the communication channels open and encourages the child to continue talking. An example of reflective listening is:

> Child: "I don't want to play with Mark any more. He's always unfair and quits when he can't get his way."

Parent: "You sound upset with Mark because of the way he plays, and you don't enjoy playing with him any more."

Problem Solving

Once effective listening and reflective responding are established, problem-solving procedures have to be developed. When a child has a problem, a parent can help the child to explore the alternatives or possible solutions. Frequently in problem-solving situations, one party loses. this need not be the case. Gordon (1970) has developed a procedure that he calls the "no lose" method, which utilizes the following six steps:

1. Define the problem in terms of needs (not competing solutions).
2. Generate possible solutions (no evaluation allowed at this step).
3. Evaluate and test the various solutions.
4. Decide on a mutually acceptable solution.
5. Implement the solution.
6. Evaluate the solution.

Problem Ownership

The above techniques—reflective listening and exploring alternatives—are helpful when a child realizes that he or she has a problem or owns the problem. In many situations the parents and not the child are the ones who are experiencing difficulty or own the problem. Determining whether the problem is the child's, the parents', or the relationship's is essential (Gordon, 1975, p. 269):

1. The child owns the problem when the child is troubled, needful, disturbed, bothered, upset, unhappy, frustrated, and so on, because he or she is having some problems with his or her own behavior.
2. The adult owns the problem when the adult is troubled, needful, disturbed, bothered, frustrated, upset, or unhappy because the child's behavior is causing the adult a problem.
3. The relationship is the problem when the adult and the child find themselves in a disagreement or a conflict, involving a clash between the needs of each.

I-Messages

If the parents own the problem, they should clearly share with the child how they feel about the situation and why they feel that way. This is done most effectively with I-messages as opposed to You-messages. You-messages usually are ineffective because they are used for criticism or blame. You-messages are never very well received, whereas I-messages are frequently valuable in bringing about behavioral change and seldom jeopardize the parent-child relationship.

An I-message tells the child exactly how the adult feels about the behavior. The child is not being blamed, just told how the parent feels: "I can't hear what my friend is saying on the telephone when there is so much noise." The tone of voice is important. If this statement is said in a hostile way, the child will look at it as blame or criticism, whereas the child will listen to and respect a friendly tone.

The I-message has three components:

1. I feel . . .
2. when . . . (a nonjudgmental statement of what is happening)
3. because . . . (just what its effect is upon you).

If parents take the time to use I-messages, communication will improve. There is also a better chance of changing the child's behavior without hassles. If children feel the respect, they will be eager to listen, whereas, with criticism, yelling, and judgmental statements, they just turn off.

Parents must take the time to listen to children as well as to talk to them in a friendly manner. Parents must be sensitive to a child's feelings and make sure they understand the message the child is trying to convey. Sometimes alternatives should be set up and explored with the child. I-messages should be substituted for you-messages. If all of these communication skills are applied properly, the child-parent relationship will become a pleasant experience.

FAMILY MEETINGS

The last of the necessary parenting skills is that used in the family meeting. The family meeting is an integral part of a good, healthy family atmosphere. It allows all members of the family to come together and air their views democratically. It can be viewed as the governing body of the family.

The family meeting is a regularly scheduled meeting, usually held once a week for an hour or so, to deal with all family business. All family members are encouraged to attend, but attendance is not mandatory. A member can choose to attend or not to attend, but decisions (as in a democracy) are made about absent members. Each member takes a turn at being the leader of the meeting, and each has one vote. The family meetings deal with responsibilities and chores of the household, family activities and vacations, problems, and anything else that a family member wishes to bring up.

Few people have any idea how to run or coordinate a healthy family environment. The family meeting can fill this void by providing for family decision making, communication, and problem solving. In these meetings, discipline, conflicts, and family planning can take place. Each member has an equal voice, and each must be respected and listened to. Many families keep an agenda and minutes and run a structured meeting. The minutes can be kept to serve as a "family history." Other families prefer flexible and loosely run sessions. Each family can decide on the specifics to fit the family lifestyle.

An emergency meeting can be called if enough of the members think it is warranted. This usually occurs when a crisis arises or plans cannot be carried through. Many times problems come up that cannot wait until the next regularly scheduled meeting, and an emergency session is therefore encouraged.

The usual family meetings should be scheduled at times of least interference and fewest interruptions. Mealtimes, for example, are not suggested because too many other things are going on at this time.

The family meeting has many benefits for the family. It increases honesty, sharing, and expressing feelings in a nonthreatening manner. Each family member has an equal input, which lends itself to a more harmonious family atmosphere. If all members of the family can participate in setting up rules and regulations, the family is bound to be happier.

REFERENCES

Adler, A. (1957). *Understanding human behavior*. New York: Fawcett.

Dewey, E. (1972). Understanding children's behavior. *Counseling Psychologist, 3*(2).

Dinkmeyer, D., & Carlson, J. (1973, April). Consequences--Cues to understanding. *Elementary School Journal*, pp. 399–404.

Dinkmeyer, D., Carlson, J., & Dinkmeyer, D., Jr. (1991). *Consulting in the schools: A systems approach*. Muncie, IN: Accelerated Development.

Dinkmeyer, D., Dinkmeyer, D. Jr., & Sperry, L. (1987). *Adlerian counseling and psychotherapy*. Columbus, OH: Charles Merrill.

Dinkmeyer, D., & Losoncy, L. E. (1980). *The encouragement book*. New York: Prentice Hall.

Dinkmeyer, D., & McKay, G. (1989). *Systematic training for effective parenting*. Circle Pines, MN: American Guidance Service.

Dreikurs, R. (1950). *Fundamentals of Adlerian psychology*. New York: Greenberg.

Dyer, W. (1985). *What do you really want for your children?* New York: William Morrow.

Gordon, T. (1970). *Parent effectiveness training*. New York: Peter Wyden.

Gordon, T. (1975). Training parents and teachers in new ways of talking to kids. In D. Dinkmeyer & J. Carlson (Eds.), *Consultation: A book of readings* (pp. 268–275). New York: John Wiley.

Maslow, A. (1970). *Motivation and personality* (2d ed.). New York: Harper & Row.

RELATED READINGS

Arnold, L. D. (1985). *Parents, children, and change*. Lexington, MA: D. C. Heath.

Dinkmeyer, D., McKay, G. D., & Dinkmeyer, J. S. (1989). *Parenting young children*. Circle Pines, MN: American Guidance Service.

Firestone, R. (1990). *Compassionate child-rearing: An in-depth approach to optimal parenting.* New York: Insight Books.

Lancaster, J. B. (Ed.). (1987). *Parenting across the life span.* New York: A. de Gruyter.

Weissbourd, B. (1986). Parent education and support. In *The prevention of mental-emotional disabilities: Resource papers to the report of the National Mental Health Association Commission on the Prevention of Mental-Emotional Disabilities.* Alexandria, VA: National Mental Health Association.

Three

Issues and Challenges

All families are affected by the stresses and challenges of life. No system, no matter how stable, can avoid every crisis or withstand every pressure. The key to healthy functioning can be found not in the family unit's ability to remain trouble-free but, rather, in its ability to cope with the kinds of chronic and acute stressors that affect us all.

If family members experience a certain situation as a crisis, it is because their usual ways of coping with one another and with the world at large are not working. If they learn from the crisis and develop an improved repertoire of behaviors, they can surmount the immediate problem and prevent future difficulties. Similarly, families can overcome chronic, long-term difficulties through a process of learning new coping styles and reorganizing family structures.

Family counseling strategies enhance this learning process. Regardless of the specific focus of the intervention or the tool being used, the family counselor's role is to encourage the healthy development of the family and each of its members. Healthy development is never defined in terms of some idealized picture of the "perfect family." Rather, it is defined in terms of the goals and resources of the specific system being addressed. Each family unit has problems and chal-

153

lenges that must be overcome in the interest of meeting its unique goals. Effective family counseling depends on the counselor's awareness of the scope of possibilities for family organization and of the need to respond to each family's needs at the point of intervention.

The chapters that make up this section describe counseling interventions designed to help families respond to specific issues and challenges. Some of the challenges described, such as the issues surrounding alcoholism or abuse, are clearly problematic and require interventions designed to prevent the victimization of children and their families. Other issues, such as single parenthood and remarriage, reflect the reality that today's families vary widely in their structures and that counseling interventions must accept—even embrace—this heterogeneity. Each chapter shares a concern with designing concrete, growth-oriented methods that respond to families' most pressing needs.

In "Counseling Single-Parent Families," Leroy Baruth and Margaret Burggraf make clear the scope of possibilities for modern family organization through their overview of the needs of five types of single parents: widowed, divorced, separated, never married, and adopting. The family-focused strategies they describe involve building communication systems, each of which can be addressed, at least in part, through the vehicle of the parent study group. Baruth and Burggraf also discuss the effects of the single-parent home on children, presenting a number of practical guidelines that can help educators work more effectively with this large and still-growing population.

Another rapidly-growing segment of our society, the "remarriage family," is described by Richard Hayes and Bree Hayes. Pointing out that the nuclear family of mom, dad, and their children living together in bliss remains "the standard but not the norm," Hayes and Hayes discuss the possibility of developing new traditions and more realistic standards for modern families. They review the special concerns that parents, stepparents, and their children face and provide clear suggestions for counselors to follow as they attempt to help blended families acomplish their developmental tasks.

The difference between an unrealistic picture of homogeneity and the reality of the diverse modern family is also emphasized by Betty Newlon and Miguel Arciniega in their chapter, "Counseling Minority Families: An Adlerian Perspective." In their discussion of situations in which the client family is culturally different from that of the counselor, Newlon and Arciniega point out that the counselor must have cultural information and awareness. The basic premises of Adlerian psychology, including the notion that behavior is best understood in a social context, contribute to the counselor's ability to serve minority families.

Changing demographics also have brought major changes in the average age of our clientele. Every year brings an increase in the number of elderly persons in the population and in the projected length of the individual's lifespan. Although the counseling strategies Douglas Gross describes in his chapter, "Counseling the

Elderly," focus on the individual, Gross leaves little doubt that issues related to aging have a major impact on family dynamics.

Clearly, today's families are in the throes of change. That fact alone would make family counseling a challenging endeavor. In addition, however, most counselors now find themselves working with people who are feeling the effects of pressing—even life-threatening—problems. In "Counseling and Child Abuse: A Developmental Perspective, Judith Cooney outlines the developmental effects of emotional, physical, and sexual abuse and emphasizes the need for counselors to be aware of their responsibilities in this area and to act as advocates on behalf of children. "Counseling Children of Alcoholics: Overcoming the Effects of the Alcoholic System" also addresses the special needs of children who are being asked to pay the price for adult dysfunction. In this chapter, Judith Lewis suggests strategies for working with children still in the alcoholic home and with adult sons and daughters of alcoholic parents. Finally, Loretta Bradley and Mary Ostrovsky address the tragic situation of families affected by the AIDS diagnosis of one of their members. Using case illustrations, the authors discuss the responses of family members to AIDS and suggest potential counseling strategies for dealing with this emerging issue.

As "Counseling Families Affected by AIDS" makes apparent, many of today's families face struggles and crises that were unknown in the past. In fact, as individuals, the social units we identify as our "families" may be chosen rather than biologically determined, and may bear little similarity to the customary structures of the past. One important point that Bradley and Ostrovsky make—and that all of the chapters in this section support—is that the days of the "Ozzie and Harriet syndrome" are over.

9

Counseling
Single-Parent Families

Leroy G. Baruth and Margaret Z. Burggraf

Kids' needs are best met by grown-ups whose needs are met.
Jean Illsley Clark

In the near future more than 50% of the children in the United States are expected to be in single-parent families. This is an awesome projection with serious implications for school counselors and others engaged in human services. The five basic types of single parents are: widowed, divorced, separated, never married, and adopting parent.

THE ADOPTING PARENT

Probably the newest development in single parenthood has been the decision to allow nonmarried individuals to adopt children. Adopting parents are usually highly motivated to be good parents, and they provide well for their children. Unlike most other single-parent situations, this new situation tends to be viewed as a welcome relief to the child, who often has been in a children's home or in foster care for several years. The biggest plus in the adopting parent situation is that the individual freely chooses to become a single parent.

157

THE DIVORCED PARENT

Currently, about 45% of single-parent families are a result of divorce, compared to only 32% in 1980. Most cases of divorce are characterized by adequate warning or even preparation that a one-parent family will develop. During this period a separation may be involved. Children frequently are involved in quarrels, discrimination, and accusations of the parents. The divorced single parent and the children are likely to have many feelings including frustration, failure, guilt, and ambivalence.

Divorced parents' sense of frustration may come from their confusion about their new status in society, their loneliness and fears, and their resentment about not being able to "walk away from it all." Children and parent alike hope to end the frequent sense of incompleteness that frustrates them. This is why children often encourage their single parent to remarry (possibly before the parent is psychologically ready).

Both the single parent and the children frequently view the ending of a marriage as a personal failure. The parents' feelings often center on the original selection of the marriage partner. The children's sense of failure seems to relate to their inability to prevent the family breakup. These children are likely to express doubts about their personal worth.

In parents, feelings of guilt resulting from the perceived failure may be compounded by new feelings of guilt that the children's needs are being neglected. In children, guilt might stem from their perception that they have caused deterioration of the marriage.

The single parent may feel ambivalent about the children, depending on the current mood. If the parent is tired after a long day, he or she may feel shackled and resentful about the children's presence. If things are going well in the parent's life, he or she may feel privileged to share in the children's experiences.

After the divorce is finalized, the children are faced with difficulties involving the absent parent's visitation, dual loyalties, and frequently *two* families, if a parent remarries. Financial arrangements between parents frequently cause intense conflict. Most often, the problems center on the children. The parent with custody often feels burdened by the primary responsibility for the children and resents the other parent's apparent freedom. Eventually, even in middle-income families, child support tends to become a problem, and the parents often "bargain" with the child's visitation rights.

THE NEVER-MARRIED PARENT

Ever increasing numbers of never-married women are deciding to keep their child. The percentage of never-married mothers has doubled, from 8% of all single parents in 1970 to more than 17% in the early 1980's. In the past, society tended to reject these parents, but this seems to be changing. The stereotype of the never-married mother being a young teenager victimized by an older man is not supported by the data. In reality, the largest percentage of unmarried mothers is between 20 and 24 years in age, and the second largest percentage is 25-29 years in age. Because these women are more likely to be better educated and self-supporting, they tend to merge into the mainstream of society, especially if they live in a large urban community.

Children of an unmarried mother typically do not miss their father in the way other children do because, in most instances, they do not know him. As the children grow older, they commonly show an increasing interest in the father and his whereabouts.

When money is a problem for never-married mothers, they are at a decided disadvantage when compared to other single parents. No widow's pension or alimony payments are forthcoming. In fact, child support is rare.

In recent years counseling for unmarried fathers has increased. Engulfed with guilt feelings and unsure of their responsibilities, these men are seeking help. Their role as the father of a child born to a never-married mother, however, is still ill defined.

THE WIDOWED PARENT

The percentage of all single parents who are widowed fell from 22% in 1970 to 11% in the early 1980's. This change, however, is a result of the significant increase in number of single parents who are divorced and the group of never-married parents, rather than a decline in the actual number of widowed single parents.

Typically, a parent is unprepared for a spouse's death. The children, too, are not prepared. The family has a great deal of adjusting to do in terms of the financial, social, and emotional problems thrust upon them by the loss of one parent. Usually a period of grief and mourning is followed by acceptance of the reality that this is now a one-parent family, with its economic and social changes, which may seem frightening. Loneliness will probably emerge as the parent's single most distressing consequence.

The situation caused by the death of a spouse is made more complex in that the children are likely to fear losing the remaining parent. They think, "One parent is gone. How do I know something won't happen to the other one?" The child's world has been shaken; it has become less secure. Open discussion of this fear and reassurance do help, but time and experience are the best remedies. Coming to believe that the remaining parent can leave and will return, that the leaving is not permanent, takes time.

The children also may feel anger toward the deceased parent. Particularly if the parent had a prolonged illness that deprived the children of both parents' attention, the child may say, "I'm glad he (she) is gone." Or the children may become angry with their new life and their "different" status and blame the deceased parent.

One final consideration that is evident to the remaining parent and the children is the change in financial status. The family unit can only hope that the father, if he was the breadwinner, provided an adequate will or life insurance policy. Unlike the divorced parent, no monthly support check can be hoped for otherwise. In most cases, a single-parent mother must go to work regardless of whether she had been working previously.

THE SEPARATED PARENT

Although the percentage of parents who are single as a result of parental separation dropped from 37% in 1970 to 28% in the early 1980's, the actual numbers continue to increase. Many of the considerations that apply to divorced parents also apply to separated parents, with some noteworthy exceptions. Separated parents are in a vacuum as far as our society is concerned. In their social life most separated parents (especially mothers) feel uncomfortable because they are neither single nor married, and yet are not legally free to marry again.

Children are usually unprepared for a separation when it occurs. Although they are almost always aware of tension at home, children do not usually have the benefit of discussions and explanations before the separation. Most children are affected negatively by a separation. Their unresolved questions and attitudes about the absent parent can transfer to problems at school and in other settings. Many of these children feel humiliated at being abandoned by their parent. Most children do not know the reasons for the separation. This adds to their anxieties, and they can become easily upset when asked about their absent parent. They often feel responsible or at fault.

A special type of separation involves a parent who is away for extended periods of time while the marriage remains intact. An example is presented in *The Great Santini* by Pat Conroy, who describes a family in which the father, a marine officer, is frequently away for long periods, and is more recently represented by parents overseas in the Persian Gulf region. Family interactions change dramatically when the children and one parent are left to carry on until the other parent's return.

Many other circumstances cause family members to be apart (e.g., serving time in prison, recuperating from a serious illness, being confined in a mental institution). Little material has been written on the problems of this type of family. In many ways the situation is similar to that of other single-parent families, but with one major exception: They usually do not suffer financial worries to the same extent.

GENERAL EFFECTS ON THE CHILDREN

Marino and McCowan (1976) reported four major differences in one-parent and two-parent homes:

1. Single parents attempt to assume the roles and responsibilities of both parents, which may affect the emotional and intellectual development of their children.
2. Financial stress may result in less time and energy being devoted to the children.
3. The child may assume increased responsibility at home because of the parent's employment.
4. Child-care services are frequently necessary, which, in addition to the financial obligation, can adversely affect the child.

These differences can impact the child's sex role development, intellectual development, academic achievement, and social development.

The child's age is a critical variable in determining the effect of parental loss. Wallerstein and Kelley (1977) found that preschool children react with denial and often assume that they had a part in causing the divorce. Children who were 7 and 8 were sad and were less able to use denial as a coping mechanism. Typically, 9- and 10-year-olds felt shame and anger. Herzog and Saudia (1968) reported that when a child is 18-24 months of age, he or she may have recurring nightmares about monsters (indicating misplaced aggression and vulnerability). In 2 1/2- and 4 1/2-year olds, hyperactivity and aggression were observed; stories about stern, male authority figures were reported. At age 5 and older, the youngsters experienced depression, sadness, withdrawal—turning aggression inward, believing they were to blame.

During the first year after their parents' divorce, some children play less maturely and less imaginatively. Adverse effects usually disappear for girls after two years; effects are more enduring and intense for boys. Hetherington et al. (1976) noted that both male and female children were more independent, sought more help, acted out more, and were less cooperative during the early stages of adjusting to the single-parent family. Benedek and Benedek (1979) reported that children had academic difficulties during the first 18 months after the parents' divorce or emotional breakup.

Kalter (1977) studied the presenting symptoms of single-parent families and found that children of divorce had a higher rate of occurrence of antisocial, delinquent problems (specifically drug taking and sexual behavior among the adolescent female group) than did children of married parents. He also found that children 12 years and older were more likely to show overt aggression toward their parent which resulted in referral for counseling.

The research by Raschke and Raschke (1977) found a negative impact of parental conflict—verbal, physical, or both—on a child's self-concept. A child's perceived parental happiness, however, had a positive correlation with the child's self-concept. The family structure made no difference in this particular study.

Not all research on single-parent families has negative findings. Nye (1957) demonstrated that children of divorced or separated parents were better adjusted than children from intact but unhappy homes. When parents experience unresolvable marital discord, divorce may be the best solution for the children.

HELPING STRATEGIES

Single parents can do several things to help the family adjust to the situation. Helping professionals should be able to provide some practical suggestions, such as those that follow.

The most basic strategy needed is to implement a communication system in the family. This system can take many forms, but probably the most widely used was developed by Rudolph Dreikurs (Dreikurs, Gould, & Corsine, 1974). The family council is a way of facilitating a more harmonious family relationship by using a democratic method to solve daily problems and plan activities. This is a structure that encourages developing responsibility in children, as well as allowing the peaceful resolution of situations that might otherwise cause much conflict among family members. The family as a group becomes the governing body, making appropriate decisions that affect everyone in the group. Meetings should be scheduled regularly (usually once a week), and everyone should be encouraged to participate.

Once the communication system is in place, the family can begin addressing some real issues. A primary issue, according to Mendes (1979), is the feeling of personal worth. This feeling of worth comes from being able to make positive contributions. When the single parent and the children all work together to help the family run smoothly, everyone feels important. The logistics of "who does what" can be worked out at the family council meeting.

Single-parent families commonly have financial difficulty. This can create guilt feelings on the part of the single parent and resentment by the children. The best strategy is to meet this issue "head-on." Single parents should discuss budget issues with the children. For example, the budget could be discussed at a family council meeting. The single parent could explain where most of the money goes (e.g., housing, food, utilities, clothes). Any money remaining could be the focus of discussion. How does the family want to spend the money? By handling the financial problem in this fashion, the single parent does not have to feel guilty, because the children soon realize what might be realistic to ask the parent for and what might be beyond the family budget. Resentment the children feel will usually dissipate because they have been involved in the process of deciding how all the money should be spent.

Another helping strategy is to encourage single parents to plan, in conjunction with their children, numerous recreational activities. Families that have fun together will develop a positive regard for each other. Many free or inexpensive activities are available in almost every community. City parks offer a wide assortment of options from tennis to picnics. Libraries, museums, and other public attractions are usually free or minimally priced. The actual activity is not as important as the fact that the family is doing something together.

Establishment of a support system can be extremely important to single-parent families. This can be an informal network with other single parents or a formal group that meets regularly. Parents Without Partners, Inc. (PWP) is a national organization with more than 1,000 chapters. PWP has been successful because it provides a support group and planned activities for both the parent and the children. Many churches and community organizations are also providing support groups. An extra benefit from belonging to a support group is that it offers an opportunity to be of help to others.

GUIDELINES FOR EDUCATORS

Counselors and other individuals in the school setting have a special opportunity to directly and indirectly help children in single-parent families. First, counselors can look for behavioral patterns that give clues as to how the child is feeling. These observations should be frequent and in several types of situations. Any deviation from a child's past behavior should be especially noted. Observational information will be helpful as opportunities are provided for the child to work through feelings or if the counselor is called upon to share important insights with other professionals if the child is referred.

Second, curriculum activities such as painting, working with clay, drawing pictures, and dancing or movement can be used to help younger children recognize and acceptably express feelings and resolve conflict. Topics such as different types of family systems may be discussed so children learn that being in a single-parent family is acceptable. Books and discussions can be used to provide information about one-parent families in general and to promote peer acceptance and support for the child. Establishing discussion groups for parents and counseling for children, conducted by trained leaders, should be supported.

Third, the child's school environment should be made as stable as possible, and expectations for the child should remain consistent. Overprotecting the child should be avoided and, even though the child might have problems, he or she should not be allowed to disrupt others. Caringly but firmly setting reasonable, consistent limits for the child's behavior is important. Every effort should be made to communicate to the child that he or she is worthwhile, but that specific disruptive behavior is not acceptable. Also, school personnel should avoid becoming parent figures. The child must not be led to feel, at the end of the school year, that another adult has deserted him or her by being promoted to a new grade level with new teachers.

Fourth, feelings and values educators have about single-parent families should be examined, because they affect the interactions with children and parents. Terms such as "broken homes," which indicate that something is wrong, should be avoided. An effort should be made to help each child experience positive growth even in this crisis situation. A child in a healthy single-parent family often will develop better than in a conflict-ridden two-parent family.

Fifth, because becoming a single parent is usually a stressful experience, communication with the parent should be as supportive and positive as possible. Parents must be shown that school personnel are concerned and care about them. Parents should be encouraged to be as open and honest as possible with the child. Parents may be told that their child might experience a behavioral change but that this is normal and that they should not become alarmed unless the behavior persists. Parents should be encouraged to establish a meaningful personal life both as single parents and as persons of value apart from their children. This will help the parent to not overprotect the children but instead allow them to become independent and responsible.

Finally, if a parent or child seems to be having an unusual amount of difficulty in coping with the situation, educators should not hesitate to suggest professional help. Numerous community agencies, ministers, psychologists, and other helping professionals are trained in this regard.

Concerns of single parents in one school district (Henderson, 1981) centered on their children's education being free of societal stereotypes traditionally bestowed on single-parent families. The schools responded by having single parents do inservice presentations for administrators, librarians, and PTO presidents of the district. Parents shared identification lists of the noncustodial parents so that the school could keep each parent informed. National and local statistics on single-parent families were presented. Local community groups and agencies that were assisting single-parent families were discussed as potential referral sources.

Workshops were incorporated into faculty meetings, led by the school counselor and four single parents (a custodial father, a noncustodial father, a custodial mother, and a widow). Discussion groups of six to 10 teachers aired their ideas and beliefs about single-parent families. Societal myths regarding single-parent families initiated the discussion. Some of these myths are (Henderson, 1981):

- The structure of the family unit has more effect on the child's well-being than the emotional climate of the home.
- Having divorced parents means that the child has only one parent.
- The single parent's life-style is detrimental to the development of a child's morality.
- One can always identify a child from a broken home.
- To grow up properly, a child must have both a male and female role model present in the home. (p. 126)

Also as a result of single parents' expressed needs in this district, support groups for parents and their children were established. The children met in daytime groups, and the parents met at night. The structure was:

Meeting 1	Communication rules defined; initial sharing of experiences.
Meetings 2-5	Members share information on tasks and roles in new family structure.
Meetings 6-7	Validation of new roles.
Meeting 8	Termination. (p 127)

Palker (1980) suggested the following guidelines for working with children who have single parents:

- Change mother-daughter/father-son school functions to parent-child activities.
- Do not assume that all children have two parents or are living with two parents. Recognize single-parent families as families.
- Look for behavior changes indicating that a child may be going through a rough time. Listen to a child's signals and clues.
- Encourage both parents to continue their interest in their child's education; foster that interest by making school records available to both custodial and noncustodial parents; schedule conferences and other parent activities so working single parents can attend.
- Help single parents form a discussion group connected with the school (perhaps the group could be led by single-parent teachers).
- Read books written on children of single-parent families; suggest books to parents; make children's literature on the subject available in the classroom and school library.
- Have parents and counselors work together to form discussion groups for children of single parents.
- Contact the local mental health association to arrange a speaker who will talk to teachers and parents about the effects on children of parental death or divorce.
- Encourage depressed and withdrawn children to get involved in after-school activities to become more sociable and to get their minds off their problems for a while.
- Take time to listen. Take the student aside and let him or her talk about what's bothering him or her. Provide a supportive, conflict-free setting.
- Consult parents and work closely with them. Parents are concerned. Together, parents and teachers may agree the child should see the school psychologist or counselor or that after-school activities might help the child to be more sociable. Parents may decide to seek help for themselves, and the best way to help kids is to help their parents.
- Learn how to cope with the child by nurturing, listening, supporting. Also allow the child to experience the pain until a degree of resolution is reached; don't take away the pain, but allow it to run its course. In this way, the healing occurs over time and is permanent, not temporary and subject to festering. Accept that the child's adjustment takes time and that it is painful and frightening.
- Do not expect children to react in a predetermined way; expectations are often self-fulfilling. Educators must be informed as to what *might* happen in order to better understand and comfort the child, but one should not assume that a child's work or behavior will be impaired by a departed parent.

SINGLE-PARENT STUDY GROUPS

An excellent way to help single parents with their child-rearing responsibilities and also serve as a support group is to establish study groups. The purpose is to provide information that single parents need to develop a constructive relationship with their children. Usually a resource book is used to stimulate group discussion. Many study groups are using *A Single Parent's Survival Guide: How to Raise the Children* (Baruth, 1979) and the *Study Group Leaders Manual* designed to accompany it.*

Individuals beginning study groups for single parents usually have many questions. Some of the questions most frequently posed, and some of the answers, are:

Q. How are single parents contacted to inform them of the study group program?

A. Basically, the approach used to notify parents depends on the setting in which the groups will be conducted. In a school setting, the most expedient method is to send a notice home with the students, giving the basic information and establishing a time and place for an organizational meeting. If the group is to be in a church setting, announcements regarding the group can be included in the weekly bulletin. Other effective methods include TV and radio public service announcements, the local newspaper, and communications by and with agencies and civic groups.

Q. How many single parents should make up a study group?

A. The number of parents in a group varies considerably; however, no more than 8–12 is recommended. This allows ample opportunity for everyone to participate in the discussion. Often, no more than three to five parents are interested, but they can comprise an effective group.

Q. When, where, and how often should a study group meet?

A. Generally, the group should meet at a mutually convenient time for the participants. Because most single parents work, the best time is usually in the evening. Often, providing child-care services during the meeting time will increase attendance. The "where" should be some neutral place such as a school, church, or civic area. Meetings are best held somewhere other than participants' homes, because host parents sometimes tend to get involved in "one-upmanship." The "how often" is usually once a week for 10 weeks. Each meeting lasts approximately 2 hours. The 10 sessions can be held in 6 or 7 weeks, but they should not be extended beyond 10 weeks. If parents wish to continue beyond this period, an advanced group can be formed.

---

*Both the book and the manual are available from the Alfred Adler Institute, 159 North Dearborn St., Chicago, IL 60601.

Q. How long after its inception are new members accepted into the group?

A. Parents interested in joining a group are usually not accepted after the second meeting. By keeping a list of interested parents, they can be contacted when a new group is being organized. Settings in which more than one group is being conducted usually stagger the starting dates so that interested parents have to wait only a few weeks to join a new group.

Q. What qualifications are required to become a group leader?

A. Leadership for this particular type of group has no specific requirements. But the best training is to first participate in a group, then serve as a co-leader, and finally assume leadership of a group. As the study group program expands in the community, former participants might be recruited for leadership roles.

Q. Do the groups have to be highly structured?

A. No. For beginning group leaders, however, structured groups are strongly recommended. Until leaders gain confidence in what they are doing, groups should not drift too far from the prepared syllabus. Table 9.1 contains the outline from the *Study Group Leaders Manual* designed to accompany *A Single Parent's survival Guide: How to raise the Children* (Baruth, 1979). Gradually, as the leader gains experience, more flexibility can be incorporated into the group.

Q. Are parent study groups really helpful?

A. Probably the best way to answer this question is to mention the reaction of parents who have participated in these groups. Agati and Iovino (1974) reported that when they implemented the groups in Derry, New Hampshire, 103 parents participated and 44 parents were placed on a waiting list. Only 7 parents withdrew from their group, which suggests that the program met a need for most of the parents. This conclusion is further supported by the fact that 90% of the parents in the group expressed an interest in continuing the program.

Unfortunately, most evaluation data are subjective in nature. The absence of hard data, however, does not mean that the study groups are ineffective, but only emphasizes the need for research in this area. In one of the few research studies available, Hereford (1963) found that parental attitudes toward child-rearing can be changed through participation in a 10-week study group.

LITERATURE AS A SOURCE OF HELP

People involved in the helping professions are increasingly realizing that they can use written material for therapeutic purposes. This process of using books for therapeutic (rather than instructional) purposes is known as *bibliother-*

TABLE 9.1
Outline for Single Parents Study Group

Session	Topics for Discussion	Experiential Exercises or Demonstrations	Handouts	Home Activities	Reading Assignments
1	-Group organization	– Let Me In – Single Parents —Who Am I?	– Group Outline chart – Could You Just Listen?	Have fun with each child	Chapter 1
2	– Ex–spouse – Attitudes toward single parents – Priorities	– The Myth of the Broken Family	– Grandparents of Divorce and Remarriage – Your Family Has Changed	Treat yourself	Chapter 2, Pages 10–13
3.	– Hectic schedules – Family Constellation	– My Family Constellation – Family Constellation and My Children	– Did You Hug Your Child Today?	Become aware of family constellation	Chapter 2, Pages 14–16
4	– Goal–oriented behavior – Dating	– The Four Goals of Misbehavior	– Child's Mistaken Goals – Blank Goal Chart	Identify children's strengths	Chapter 3
5	– Goal–oriented behavior – Superparenting – Self–encouragement	– Superparent and Single, Too – Love Cups	– Encouragement/ Discouragement	Practice self– encouragement	Chapter 5
6	–Encouragement – The Language of Encouragement	– I'm Good At . . . – Good Girl! Good Boy! – Encouragement for Us	– Retraining and Rethinking Take Time— Be Patient	Practice encouraging remarks	Chapter 3, Pages 20–23 Chapter 4
7	– Natural and logical consequences – Family communication and sharing responsibility	– Natural and Logical Consequences – Are Your Children Part of the Family?	– Sharing Responsibility	Conduct a family meeting	Chapter 5, to Page 43
8	– Family meetings – Summarizing Child–rearing Techniques	– Withdraw from the Power Struggle – This is How It *Should* Be – I'll Be Good If . . .	– Developmental Tasks of Children		Pages 44–53
9	– Summarizing Child–rearing techniques	– The Superior Parent – Mistakes Feel Miserable Already – Problem Solving, Step by Step	– The Binuclear Family	Implementing the next step	
10	– Summarizing child–rearing techniques – Evaluation – Termination – Resources		– Etiquette Lesson		Chapter 6

From L. G. Baruth, *A Single Parent's Survival Guide: How to Raise the Children* (Dubuque, IA: Kendall/Hunt, 1979).

apy. Both adults and children can benefit when written materials are used in conjunction with therapy. According to Cionciolo (1965, p.897), "Books can provide a source of psychological relief from the various pressures and concerns that stem from the things that happen to children." Bibliotherapy can be used to solve actual, existing problems and pressures, or it may be used to help make a satisfactory adjustment to some trying situation in the future.

The underlying assumption of bibliotherapy is that when people read, they bring their own needs and problems to the reading experience. They interpret the author's words in light of their own experiences. Through identification with characters in literature, readers can attain a better understanding of themselves. Counselors can use bibliotherapy to help individuals deal with social, emotional, and psychological problems (Baruth & Phillips, 1976).

Historically, counselors have tended to overlook the enormous possibilities of using bibliotherapy. This could be in part a result of the lack of understanding regarding the bibliotherapeutic process. This process has three stages: identification, catharsis, and insight. First, the individual identifies with a character in the book. In a hypothetical situation in which Tom, whose parents have recently divorced, was asked by his counselor to read a relevant book, Tom might be able to relate to the boy in the book and the problems arising from the divorce. As a result of Tom's identification with the boy in the story, he might be able to experience a release of emotion or psychological tension—catharsis. As a result of releasing this tension, Tom might be better able to achieve additional insights into his problem (usually with the counselor's help).

Complementing the process are several important tenets regarding the use of bibliotherapy. Moses and Zaccaria (1969) have summarized eight basic principles, of which a modification follows:

1. Bibliotherapy is supplemental and should be used with other types of helping relationships. Books should be recommended to individuals as an aid to counseling rather than as a substitute for counseling.
2. The most favorable time for introducing bibliotherapy is when a working relationship involving mutual trust has been developed, the individual's problem has been described and explored, and the individual is exhibiting personal involvement in solving the problem.
3. Bibliotherapy is more useful and effective with individuals of average and above-average reading ability than those of lesser ability, because these individuals are more likely to feel comfortable in reading. Parents can be encouraged to read aloud to children under age 12. If more than one child is involved, the adult should choose a book geared to the interest level of the oldest, stopping to explain difficult passages to the younger one(s) when necessary. Even if parents think 10 or 11 years of age is too old to be read to, they should try it. Most of these children love the warmth of parental closeness and the sound of their voice just as

much as the younger children do. In addition, it encourages the parent and children to discuss the meaning of the story and how their own feelings relate to it.

4. Counselors should be familiar with the material to be used: type of literature, level of difficulty, plot, characters, length, and readability.

5. Individuals with certain physical handicaps may require special types of reading materials. In suggesting material for visually handicapped children, for example, the counselor should be aware of size of type, spacing between the lines, and type design. If "talking books" are available in the community, they could be used in counseling visually handicapped individuals (and possibly the normally sighted but below-average reader).

6. Whenever possible, counselors should suggest a number of alternative selections from which the individual can choose the actual piece of literature to read.

7. After the person has read the material, a follow-up counseling session should always take place, in which the counselor brings up topics such as the individual's reaction to the literature, amendment or disagreement with the decisions or behavior of characters in the book, and insights gained from the reading.

8. Undoubtedly, bibliotherapy cannot be used with all persons, in all settings, and for all purposes. Counselors are urged to use good judgment in applying bibliotherapy if they decide to add it to their arsenal of helping techniques.

The value of literature as a means of coping with crisis situations has long been recognized—but neglected by many counselors. Although bibliotherapy is not without limitations, it has significant potential that should be explored by those working in the helping professions.

WHAT ABOUT REMARRIAGE?

A high percentage of single parents remarry. Therefore, counselors and other helping professionals should have some understanding of the remarriage developmental sequence. Whiteside (1982) divided the sequence followed by divorced individuals into five stages:

1. Married family (usually with children).
2. A period of parting that includes marital separation, divorce, and establishment of two separate households.
3. A courting period with plans for remarriage.
4. Early remarriage.
5. Established remarriage.

Several areas from the first marriage are important to examine. One is the length of the first marriage. Parents who are older or who were married the longest generally have the most difficulty, with changes in self-concept and identity in the post-divorce period. Because the children are older, however, they have an advantage in being able to separate themselves from their parents' difficulties. These children usually better understand the complexities of the situation and maintain a significant relationship with the noncustodial parent.

Another important area involves the role each parent played in the first marriage. For example, Hetherington, Cox, and Cox (1976) found that fathers in marriages where rigid male-female role segregation existed in terms of child-rearing and household responsibilities were much more disorganized immediately after the divorce than were men who had shared the household and child-rearing responsibilities.

Also the degree to which the child has been drawn into the original marital conflict will determine, to a large extent, the child's ability to adjust to the separation and divorce. In this regard, Ackerman(1966) stated that when a family has a disturbed child, a marital disturbance always accompanies it. Conversely, when a marital disturbance exists, the children do not necessarily become disturbed.

These areas illustrate some of the ways in which knowledge of the first marriage is important. It helps in understanding how the family will be affected by the separation, handle the feelings of loss, and adjust to life in a single-parent family.

The parting stage is one in which all family members go through a process, similar to mourning, in which they deal with the loss of an important, intimate relationship and begin to develop a new, more distant relationship with the same person. The feelings the adults experience during this period are different from the feelings their children experience. Adults are placed in a dilemma, with the need to maintain emotional distance for an effective marital separation and yet maintain enough positive feeling to continue a cooperative co-parenting relationship. This process of parting takes a long time. Weiss (1975) estimated at least two to four years. This process has no shortcuts, and both parents and children need all the support they can get.

During the courting stage, an intimate relationship with a new partner is a major influence in developing feelings of worth and self-confidence. And if a commitment to marry follows, another period of adjustment and change in family relationships begins. The transition from a single-parent family to a remarried family requires a great deal of preparation. The kind of issues that have to be dealt with have been discussed by Messinger (1976). She found that couples contemplating remarriage begin with a combination of hopeful idealism and pragmatic realism. They are hoping to avoid the mistakes they made in the past and supporting each other in a much more satisfying way. They feel they have learned a great deal about themselves and are aware of the potential problems in an intimate relationship. They are aware of the realities of parenting even though they tend to be overprotective of their children. No matter how prepared the couple may be, however, when two families are joined together, the process is difficult.

The early remarriage stage begins with the wedding and requires accomplishment of several tasks paramount to success of this new marriage. The husband-wife relationship must be established; stepparenting relationships must be strengthened and clearly defined; positive relationships must be developed among step- and half-siblings; and relationships must be defined regarding the children and their noncustodial parents. This period is crucial to success of the marriage and requires a great deal of commitment, understanding, patience, and hard work.

The last stage, established remarriage, usually begins about three years after the marriage and is generally characterized by much more of a sense of stability and clarity about the couple relationship than existed in the previous marriage. Thus, families are confronted with the normal developmental changes that occur in other families, such as special problems of adolescence, marriage of one of the siblings, or children having difficulty at school. Sometimes these problems are more complex to resolve because they might involve not only the stepfamily but also the noncustodial parent. Couples who have been described as successful with remarriage usually have been open about their feelings, clear about role relationships and ground rules of the family, and supportive of the special relationship of the biological parent and child. Also, they often have established regular times for family meetings in which all members have important input in running the household.

REFERENCES

Ackerman, N. W. (1966). *Treating the troubled family.* New York: Basic Books.

Agati, G., & Iovino, J. (1974). Implementation of a parent counseling program. *School Counselor, 22,* 126–129.

Baruth, L. G. (1979). *A single parent's survival guide: How to raise the children.* Dubuque, IA: Kendall/Hunt.

Baruth, L. G., & Phillips, M. W. (1976). Bibliotherapy and the school counselor. *School Counselor, 23*(3), 191–199.

Benedek, R., & Benedek, E. (1979). Children of divorce: Can we meet their needs? *Journal of Social Issues, 35*(4), 155.

Cionciolo, P. J. (1965). Children's literature on affect coping behavior. *Personal & Guidance Journal, 43,* 897–903.

Dreikurs, R., Gould, R., & Corsini, R., (1974). *Family council: The Dreikurs technique.* Chicago: Henry Regnery Co.

Henderson, A. (1981, Nov.). Designing school guidance programs for single-parent families. *School Counselor,* pp. 124–132.

Hereford, C. (1963). *Changing parental attitudes through group discussions.* Austin: University of Texas Press.

Herzog, E., & Saudia, C. (1968). Fatherless homes: A review of research. *Children, 15*(5), 177–182.

Hetherington, E. M., Cox, M., & Cox, R. (1976). Divorced fathers. *Family Coordinator, 25,* 417–428.

Kalter, N. (1977). Children of divorce in an outpatient psychiatric population. *American Journal of Orthopsychiatry*, 47(1), 40–51.

Marino, C., & McCowan, R. (1976). The effects of parent absence on children. *Child Study Journal*, 6(3).

Mendes, H. A., (1979, May). Single-parent families: A typology of life-styles. *Social Work*, pp. 193–200.

Messinger, L., (1976). Remarriage between divorced people with children from previous marriages: A proposal for preparation for remarriage. *Journal of Marriage & Family Counseling*, 2, 193–200.

Moses, H. S., & Zaccaria, J. S. (1969). Bibliotherapy in an educational context: Rationale and principles. *High School Journal*, *52*, 401–411.

Nye, I. (1957). Child adjustment in broken and unhappy homes. *Marriage & Family Living*, *19*, 355–361.

Palker, P. (1980, Sept.). *Teacher,* pp. 51–54.

Raschke, H., & Raschke, V. (1977). Family conflict and children's self-concepts: A comparison of intact and single-parent families. *Journal of Marriage & the Family*, pp. 367–374.

Wallerstein, J., & Kelley, J. (1977). The effects of parental divorce. In A. Skolnick & J. Skolnick (Eds.). *Family in transition*. Boston: Little, Brown.

Weiss, R. S. (1975). *Marital separation*, New York; Basic Books.

Whiteside, M. F. (1982). Remarriage: A family development process, *Journal of Marital & Family Therapy*, 8(2), 54–68.

RELATED READINGS

Barnes, A. S. (1987). *Single parents in black America*. Bristol, IN: Wyndham Hall.

Baruth, L. G. (1982). Educators and children of divorce. In L. W. Abromczyk (Ed.), *Issues of children and youth*, (pp. 149–152). Columbia, SC: University of South Carolina Center for Child and Family Studies.

Baruth, L. G., & Jones, M. D. (1975). Initiating child study groups for parents. *School counselor*, *23*(2), 121–126.

Fireside, B. J. (1981). Books to help kids get it together when their world has fallen apart. *Single Parent*, *24*(10), 25–27.

Garfinkel, I., & McLanahan, S. S. (1986). *Single mothers and their children: A new American dilemma*. Washington, DC: Urban Institute Press.

Kamerman, S. B., & Kahn, A. J. (1988). *Mothers alone: Strategies for a time of change*. Dover, MA: Auburn House Publishing Co.

Lash, M., Loughridge, S. I., & Fassler, D. (1990). *My kind of family: A book for kids in single-parent homes*. Burlington, VT: Waterfront Books.

Lindblad-Goldberg, M. (1989). Successful minority single-parent families. In L. Combrinck-Graham (Ed.), *Children in family contexts: perspectives on treatment* (pp. 116–134). New York: Guilford Press.

Mulroy, E. A. (Ed.). (1988). *Women as single parents: Confronting institutional barriers in the courts, the workplace, and the housing market*. Dover, MA: Auburn House Publishing Co.

10

Counseling
Remarriage Families

Richard L. Hayes and Bree A. Hayes

It wasn't exactly a divorce—I was traded.
Tim Conway

One of every three children under the age of 18 in the United States spends a portion of his or her life living with a single parent (Glick, 1979). Given that 80% of divorced persons remarry within 4 to 5 years, and that 60% of them have children, single-parent and remarriage families comprise nearly 45% of all families (Visher & Visher, 1982). As a consequence of these changes, more people are expected to be living in a second marriage than in a first marriage by the end of this century (Duberman, 1975). Recognizing that these figures represent large amounts of loss and pain—much of which will go unresolved—one can easily understand why 40% of second marriages end in divorce in the first 4 years, with the likelihood of another divorce increasing when children from a previous marriage are present (Becker, Landes, & Michael, 1977).

This statistical picture suggests that most of us will have close contact with people who have divorced (at least once) *and* remarried. Moreover, these people are likely to be living with children other than their own or with a person some of whose children will be living with someone else. Yet, despite the prevalence of this family structure, the portrait of the American family continues to present mom, dad, and *their* children as living together in marital bliss. One might say that the nuclear family remains the standard but not the norm.

What will be required during the final decade of this century is to develop new traditions that set more realistic standards for families to follow. Counselors can play an important role in the development of these new traditions.

WHAT DO WE MEAN BY REMARRIAGE FAMILIES?

Despite calls from some researchers for counselors to broaden their views of acceptable family structures (Ahrons, 1981), the rapid increase in families resulting from the merger of two preexisting families has left the profession without a common vocabulary to describe the phenomenon. Traditionally, these families had been called *stepfamilies*, but many writers have abandoned the term in reaction to its long historical use as what Bernard (1956) has called a "smear word." *Blended, recoupled, reconstituted, merged, reorganized,* and *restructured* have emerged as more sympathetic and descriptive titles.

Although the term *restructured* captures an essential element of these families, it describes single-parent families as well. We use the term *remarriage family* here to refer to families that are formed as the result of a marriage between two partners, at least one of whom has been previously married. This type of family is considered a specific type of restructured family. Even though remarriage families may and do arise without children, the concern here will be with remarriage families that include at least one child from the outset.

A PRESENT BORN OF THE PAST

To point out that one must have been married before one can be remarried may seem so obvious as to be unworthy of mention. Nonetheless, critical to understanding the remarriage family is to recognize its origins in the losses of prior marital relationships. Unresolved losses play significant roles in the lives of remarriage family members and can profoundly limit subsequent developmental progress (Hayes, 1984). Members of remarriage families each must resolve the losses associated with dissolution of previous family structures as a prelude to creating a successful remarriage family.

Parents must resolve the losses associated not only with the old marriage but also with the *expectations* for marriage, and then with the passing of their single-parent status. As Garfield (1980) pointed out, those who divorce must attend to a number of developmental tasks in dealing with resolution of loss. These include self-acceptance, acceptance of new roles and responsibilities, renegotiating roles and relationships with family and friends, and transforming the relationship with the former spouse.

Unlike death or abandonment, only the relationship—not the person—is lost through divorce. Often, former spouses continue to influence the lives of those who remarry, especially when children are involved. Spouses who have resolved former marital losses seem better prepared for remarriage than those who have not (Messinger, Walker, & Freeman, 1978).

Counselors working with remarriage families must evaluate the extent to which unresolved mourning is exerting an influence on the current situation. Clients then must be encouraged to work through rather than around previous losses and to accept the reality of former losses. Bowlby (1980) noted that widowed spouses were healthier if they continued to speak with their spouses in fantasy rather than to let go of the relationship. This method for resolving mourning suggests that remarriage clients may do better to transform existing relationships to more productive ones rather than to deny the loss, especially when those former spouses are living and in frequent contact with the client. Because clients may be reluctant to raise these issues in front of the current spouse, counselors should be sensitive to and aware of the need to schedule some sessions with spouses individually.

As complicated as divorce and remarriage seem to an adult, to the child these changes present "a cognitive puzzle [that brings] dissonance and inconsistency to the child's social and affective world. To deal with loss and to rearrange the disrupted perceptions demand time and energy that must be withdrawn from the work of the schoolroom and from social interaction with peers" (Hess & Camara, 1980, p. 82). The cycle of attachments and losses that attends the history of a remarriage family disrupts the child's normal developmental progress. Familiar schemes of family and the social order must be reconstructed as the child attempts to form workable solutions to the problem of forming attachments to many different people.

In working with families, Huntington(1982) encouraged counselors to consider a number of transactional factors associated with attachment, divorce, and remarriage (pp. 27–28).

1. For the child:
    • the child's cognitive and emotional assimilation and understanding of the divorce and the subsequent remarriage.
    • personality traits, flexibility, temperament, tolerance for stress, handling of affect, adaptive behaviors, and areas of competence.
    • developmental level and prior developmental tasks accomplished.
    • the gender of the child and siblings.
2. For the parent:
    • each parent's emotional health or relative narcissistic injury.
    • the effects of being a single parent; in terms of the economy; on discipline and order; emotionally; and practically, in terms of child-care arrangements and the like.
    • the remaining bonds with the ex-spouse; the desire to continue the battle or to resolve it.

- remarriage and the quality of that new relationship; the dynamics are very different for the cases in which both parents remain single, either custodial parent remarries, or both remarry.
3. For the parent-child relationship:
  - quality of total family interrelationships, prior to and after divorce.
  - parental needs for the child for emotional support.
  - loyalty conflicts.
  - custody and visitation battles and agreements.
  - the effects of parental absence directly on the child, and indirectly via the impact on the remaining parent.
4. For the context:
  - the life event changes that coincide with divorce.
  - outside supports and support networks—social groups, extended family, and so on.
  - economic realities.
  - prior and current levels of discord—conflict prior to and after divorce.
  - the changes over time; divorce does not set people in concrete—the outcome is not predetermined.

MYTHS AND EXPECTATIONS

Myths are powerful half-truths that crystalize our thinking and actions around important social issues, the most important of which may be the family (see Capaldi & McRae. 1979; Coleman & Ganong, 1985; Einstein, 1982; Lewis, 1980; Schulman, 1972; Visher & Visher, 1979). Early in their lives children are introduced to the folklore about stepfamilies as hostile environments. Taking heed of the warning to avoid these entanglements, children are sent happily to bed, secure in the knowledge that they are safe in the care of their natural and biological parents. As Mead (cited in Thies, 1977) noted, "Each American child learns, early and in terror, that his whole security depends on that single set of parents" (p. 60).

This notion—that to love anyone else as your mother or father means that you are being disloyal to them—has been called the *loyalty myth* (Lewis, 1980). Not infrequently children in remarriage families believe, and often rightfully, that their biological parent will be angry or hurt if the children express any affection toward the stepparent. The frightening experiences of Snow White, Cinderella, and Hansel and Gretel serve as cogent reminders of the importance attached to keeping the family intact and avoiding contact with persons who would presume to take the place of one's parents.

The term *step* actually comes from the Anglo-Saxon *aste-pan*, "to deprive," from which came *stepchild*, "a bereaved child or orphan" (Simon, 1964, p. 19). Despite their prevalence, remarriage families continue to be the object of popular derision, viewed as led by parents who have deprived their children of a *normal* family life and who are somehow *out of step* with the natural order of things.

The myth of the *wicked stepparent* is balanced by the myth of *instant love.* Because two adults love one another and choose to become marriage partners is no guarantee that they will love each other's children or that the children will love them in return. Yet this expectation, perhaps more than any other, is the source of a substantial amount of the stress generated in remarriage families. More to the point is the realization that love takes time to grow and must be nurtured. Parents and children do have a right to expect that they will be treated with respect; they must not expect, however, that this will be easy or instantaneous.

The modern antidote to the fairy tale presentation is the equally engaging myth that remarriage families are really no different than nuclear families. Television's "Brady Bunch" blissfully combined a father and this three sons with a mother and her three daughters with the housekeeper Alice. Together they encountered the problems common to original families but met few of the problems that remarriage families encounter.

The major difference between original and remarriage families is in the structure of their relationships (Capaldi & McRae, 1979; Jones, 1978; Kompara, 1980; Nelson & Nelson, 1982). Consider that two people can have one relationship with each other. Add another person, and three people now have a system characterized by three relationships (see Figure 10.1). It is little wonder that a new baby in the home creates stress in a previously stabilized relationship. Add another child, and the number of relationships doubles to six—confirming many parents' observation that two children are far more work than they had originally anticipated. Using the formula $[n^2-n]/2 = R$ (where n equals the number of people and R equals the number of relationships between them), the Brady Bunch, with its 9 members (including Alice), has 36 relationships ([81-9]/2) with which to contend.

FIGURE 10.1
Relationships Between Family Members
in Selected Family Structures

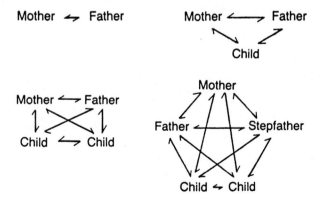

Beyond the obvious note that members of remarriage families are not nec-essarily related biologically, stress is created by the division of loyalties between separate but related nuclear families (Ahrons & Perlmutter, 1982). The presence of other parents and grandparents, as well as stepgrandparents, and unresolved feelings from the past, continue to remind family members of their previous fam-ily history. Add these members to the 9, and the number swells to 19, if all parents and grandparents are living, neither absent spouse remarries or has children, and Alice's parents stay out of the family. (Actually we never heard about these peo-ple on "The Brady Bunch.") The number of relationships that this is not-so-un-usual remarriage family must form is an overwhelming 171!

Remarriage families, at least at first, have a family but no history. More than any single thing remarriage families need, but don't yet have, is time together. Clearly, love is not something that stepparents ought to expect instantly.

A final myth that characterizes the expectations of remarriage families is the *take away myth* (Lewis, 1980), so-called because those who accept it believe that the stepparent will take away the love of the child or the parent. So, too, the cus-todial parent may see the continued involvement of absent parents with their chil-dren as undermining the stepparent's relationship with the children. Of course, love is not a fixed pie to be divided among those who want a share, but the sig-nificance of a myth is its power to shape the believer's reality.

CONCERNS OF REMARRIAGE FAMILIES

In our experience in working with remarriage families, not the least impor-tant of which has been our own, we have found a set of concerns that arise recur-rently in our discussions. These concerns, which have been described in varying detail by other authors (Brady & Ambler, 1982; Crohn, Sager, Brown, Rodstein, & Walker, 1982; Skeen, Covi, & Robinson, 1985; Visher & Visher, 1978), can be grouped under four general categories: roles and relationships, feelings and fantasies, rules and regulations, and external forces.

Roles and Relationships

The instability of remarriage families is exacerbated by the lack of positive, institutionalized roles for each of the members to play. Because more than half of remarriage families formed after divorce include stepfathers (Rallings, 1976), the task of dealing with the spouse's children more often falls to men than to women. Socialized to be in charge, men find themselves in the awkward position of en-forcing discipline when they have no apparent authority. In remarriage families wherein stepfathers set consistent limits, however, and when the mother wel-comed his support, the stepchildren (especially boys) generally functioned better than did children in single-parent families or conflicted, nondivorced families (Hetherington, Cox, & Cox, 1982). Stern (cited in Skeen, Covi, & Robinson,

1985) suggested that "stepfathers are more likely to be successful disciplinarians when taking a slow, gentle, flexible approach and develop a friendship to foster the child's participation, instead of trying to control the child through authoritarian means" (p. 122).

Women, on the other hand, have been socialized toward fulfilling the needs of others as their primary obligation in life. Placed in the role of stepmother, the woman often tries to take on the burdens of the entire family and finds herself rearing his children. Duberman (1975) reported that women were far less likely than men to achieve a good relationship with their stepchildren. Although reports are mixed on whether older or younger women have less difficulty as stepmothers, there is agreement that younger children have better relationships with their stepmothers than do adolescents (Draughton, 1975; Duberman, 1973; Wallerstein & Kelly, 1980). In general, the younger the child is at the time of divorce, the more likely the child is to accept the stepparent (Hetherington et al., 1982; Santrock, 1972; Wallerstein & Kelly, 1980).

A final difficulty that stepparents encounter is their ambiguous legal status. Although stepparents are considered in loco parentis—and thereby have all the rights, duties, and obligations of the biological paren -their assumption of the role is voluntary and may be terminated at will (Walc, _981). As well, the rights of the stepparent toward the stepchild, regardless of whether that parent provides support for the child, are unclear and vary from one court ruling to another (Kargman, 1983).

Sibling rivalries are typical in any family. In families with a common history, territorial battles often are resolved on the basis of privilege of age. In remarriage families, however, each dispute provides an occasion for rekindling old memories.

After an extensive review of the literature, Skeen, Covi, and Robinson (1985) concluded that "stepsibling relationships are crucial to the success of stepfamilies . . . [and although] in most cases the presence of stepsiblings makes the marriage much more complex . . . , the better the relationships between stepsiblings, the better the total family integration" (p. 122). In addition, when couples choose to have children of their own following the remarriage, relationships among all the children are more likely to be harmonious, although some children from former marriages may feel left out of the new relationship (Brooks, cited in Skeen, Covi, & Robinson, 1985, p. 122). As remarriage families grow in their relationships with one another, the children report feelings of divided loyalties—uncomfortable feelings that often are vented as anger directed at the stepparent (Einstein, 1982)—as each move toward the "new" family threatens to separate them from the "old."

Perlmutter, Engel, and Sage (1982) have suggested that sexual boundaries loosen in remarriage families. Without the usual time to develop deeper parent-child relationships, and devoid of the customary biological and legal prescriptions against sexual contact, stepfamilies become stimulating places sexually, especially for adolescents (Visher & Visher, 1979). "In biological families, children often consider their parents as nonsexual beings" (Visher & Visher, 1982, p. 117), whereas in remarriage families sexual desires can be heightened, increasing anxiety and disrupting already fragile relationships. Anger may mask attempts to cope with the situation, further compounding the difficulties in developing meaningful relationships. Although sexual abuse by males accounts for more than 80% of reported cases (Berliner, cited in Skeen, Covi, & Robinson, 1985), no clear data support the notion that stepfathers are any more or less involved in incestuous relationships with their stepdaughters than are biological parents (Meiselman, 1978).

Feelings and Fantasies

As noted earlier, myths play an important role in the lives of remarriage families, especially to the extent to which those families are dysfunctional. Because the remarriage family begins with children and without a history, these myths provide an instant history that projects at least a sort of reality to which the members can react. The inevitable disappointments that result are a direct consequence of the experience of the remarriage family to live up (or down) to the various members' expectations. For example, the wicked stepmother turns out to be less wicked and more likeable (if not loveable) than the children expect, and the stepmother comes to grips with the reality that she is less perfect and her stepchildren less adoring than she had thought they might be.

The consequences of members' failed expectations are feelings of disappointment. Some turn this feeling outward in anger or resentment directed at any convenient target. Disappointment turned inward becomes guilt. Although these expectations remain unidentified, they continue to go unmet and set up a recurring cycle of guilt and resentment (Einstein, 1982).

Rules and Regulations

Stepparents appear to take one of three approaches to the discipline issue (Capaldi & McRae, 1979; Skeen, Covi, & Robinson, 1985). Some remain inattentive and disengaged from the relationship, giving the natural parent little support or encouragement. Others become actively involved, tending to be overly restrictive—especially stepfathers with stepsons. And some remain tentative, as if "walking on eggs," paralyzed by the anticipation of feeling guilty if they do or don't this or that just right.

Of course, none of these strategies is particularly successful, because each acts to inhibit the development of an open and trusting relationship between the stepparent and the stepchild. Instead, the struggle degenerates into a series of contests in which neither participant emerges with the respect each attempts to get from the other. Remarriage couples do not have the luxury of time to develop shared ideas on discipline as they did in their original families before the children were born. Because these couples must develop a relationship with each other and with their children at the same time, Capaldi and McRae (1979) advocate a cooperative approach to discipline that acknowledges the rights of all parties.

External Forces

Because parents divorce each other and not their children (Duncan & Duncan, 1979), the degree to which the absent parent accepts the fact of the remarriage family has a significant impact on its chances for success. Research indicates that the greater the amount of contact is between the absent parent and the child, the less is the disruption in the parent-child relationship, and thus less stress in the remarriage family (Greif, 1982). The more limited the contact between absent parents and their children is, the more precious that time becomes, such that both parties are reluctant to say goodbye as they court one another to extend the visit.

Despite the "common assumption that diminishing a child's relationship with a biological parent promotes the development of a relationship with the same-sexed parent, . . . children often feel as though an unequal distribution of their time with each parent is reflective of their having been made to choose the stepparent over the absent biological parent" (Greif, 1982, p. 53). Instead, Greif suggested that shared parenting after divorce may protect the remarriage family system by decreasing the experience of loss, blunting the potential for conflicting loyalties, and mitigating competition between adults.

Beyond the instability introduced by the relative involvement of the absent parent in the affairs of the remarriage family, people whom Bohannan (1970) called *quasi-kin* are present. These relatives of relatives, so to speak, create an extended network of additional expectations that complicate an already ambiguous social structure. As Clingempeel (cited in Skeen, Covi, & Robinson, 1985) reported, people from remarriage families in which only the wife had children from a previous marriage showed higher marital quality than did people from more complex families. Further, people who maintained only moderate, as opposed to high or low, contact with quasi-kin showed better marital quality.

Given that the predominant proportion of children affected by divorce and remarriage is of school age, the school, its policies, and the people who work there have a substantial effect on the success of remarriage families. Visher and Visher (1979) believe that effect is largely negative, serving to reinforce stereotypes and exacerbate conflicts in the family. In particular, the school's role in observing customs such as Mother's Day or Father's Day, holding father-son banquets, limiting seating at school functions or graduations to selected family members, and sending notices and report cards to only one set of parents all serve to increase stress and miscommunication between parents.

DEVELOPMENTAL TASKS OF REMARRIAGE FAMILIES

More than anything, remarriage families seem to be characterized by a greater reliance on fantasy and hopes in their interactions (Schulman, 1972), greater expectations for themselves and acknowledgment by their stepchildren (Visher & Visher, 1979), and the lack of a commonly shared history (Goldner, 1982) than is the case with natural parents in original families. Because remarriage families start with children and yet have had no time to build a history, the family must deal with the tasks required of more mature families while possessing the skills of a family just starting out. Because they lack a common set of experiences, remarriage families hold limited or unrealistic expectations that paralyze them into inaction or galvanize them into a reaction against people or events they little understand.

Developmental tasks that are important for remarriage families to accomplish include clarifying roles and developing realistic expectations, setting reasonable limits and establishing a pattern of appropriate discipline, and liberalizing the boundaries between families by acknowledging the nature of shifting alliances. Most important the family must begin to shape its own traditions and to acknowledge the development of its own history. Turnbull and Turnbull (1983) suggested 10 guidelines that parents in remarriage families might following resolving some of their inevitable conflicts:

1. Provide neutral territory.
2. Don't try to fit a preconceived role.
3. Set limits and enforce them.
4. Allow an outlet for feelings by the children for natural parents.
5. Expect ambivalence.
6. Avoid mealtime misery.
7. Don't expect love.
8. Don't take all the responsibility. The child has some, too.
9. Be patient.
10. Maintain the primacy of the marital relationship.

WHAT CAN COUNSELORS DO?

Counselors working with remarriage families can help by:

— encouraging family members to relinquish myths they may hold about the remarriage family.
— helping members to understand the entire family system, its differences from their past families, and the involvement of nonfamily members in the system.
— teaching members more effective communication skills.
— helping members, especially children, to mourn the loss of previous relationships and encouraging the development of new relationships.
— providing a forum in which members can work out their relationships

with one another and with quasi-kin, especially the absent parent.
— offering structured programs of parent training and lists of readings that family members can use as self-instructional devices.
— informing members of the latest research findings and clinical evidence that may be helpful to them in the reorganization process.
— identifying the tasks of parenting and the relationships that are necessary to enact those roles.
— running groups for remarriage parents in the community or for stepchildren in the schools.

These questions by Kirby (1979) are offered for remarriage families:

- What evidence is present to indicate that each family member will feel secure in the merged family?
- What are illustrations of how the merged family will gain strength from the usual cultural conditions imposed?
- Under what conditions have the merged family members demonstrated open family discussions?
- When have we as parents cooperatively reinforced predictable consequences in the children?
- What are our attitudes toward seeking professional help in working with the children?
- What are the role expectations of the various merged family members?

THE FUTURE FOR REMARRIAGE FAMILIES

Remarriage is coming to be recognized as a normal developmental phase in an increasingly complex family life cycle (Goldner, 1982). As such, remarriage families represent a normal adaptation to changing social conditions. Recognizing that more complex internal organizations are better able to withstand the threats posed to them by outside forces, remarriage families may provide just the family structure necessary to prepare members for survival in the multicultural, interdependent, global society of the future. Indeed, its differences from the nuclear family of recent American tradition may be the very strength of the remarriage family.

Certainly, members of remarriage families have made notable contributions to our history. Unlike the remarriage families of fable, those of George Washington, Abraham Lincoln, Nancy Reagan, and Jacqueline Onassis are all reported to have been nurturing environments that encouraged greatness in their members. In a nation where some fear that the family may be failing, it just may be that the society around it fails to appreciate the vitality of the family's evolution in this period of transition.

REFERENCES

Ahrons, C. R. (1981). The continuing coparental relationship between divorced spouses. *American Journal of Orthopsychiatry, 51*, 415–428.

Ahrons, C. R., & Perlmutter, M. S. (1982). The relationship between former spouses: A fundamental subsystem in the remarriage family. In L. Messinger (Ed.), *Therapy with remarriage families* (pp. 31–17). Rockville, MD: Aspen Systems Corp.

Becker, G. S., Landes, E. M., & Michael, R. T. (1977). An economic analysis of marital instability. *Journal of Political Economy, 85*, 1141–1187.

Bernard, J. (1956). *Remarriage: A study of marriage.* New York: Dryden.

Bohannan, P. (Ed) (1970). *Divorce and after.* New York; Doubleday.

Bowlby, J. (1980). *Attachment and loss*(Vol. 3). New York: Basic Books.

Brady, C. A., & Ambler, J. (1982). Use of group educational techniques with remarried couples. In L. Messinger (Ed.), *Therapy with remarriage families* (pp. 145–157). Rockville, MD: Aspen Systems Corp.

Capaldi, F., & McRae, B. (1979). *Stepfamilies: A cooperative responsibility.* New York: New Viewpoints/Vision Books.

Coleman, M., & Ganong, L. (1985). Remarriage myths: Implications for the helping professions. *Journal of Counseling & Development, 64*, 116–120.

Crohn, H., Sager, C., Brown, H., Rodstein, E., & Walker, L. (1982). A basis for understanding and treating the remarried family. In L. Messinger (Ed.), *Therapy with remarriage families* (pp. 159–186). Rockville, MD: Aspen Systems Corp.

Draughton, M. (1975). Step-mother's model of identification in relation to mourning in the child. *Psychological Reports, 36*, 183–189.

Duberman, L. (1973). Step-kin relationships. *Journal of Marriage & The Family, 35*, 283–292.

Duberman, L. (1975). *The reconstituted family: A study of remarried couples and their children.* Chicago: Nelson-Hall.

Duncan, T. R., & Duncan, D. (1979). *You're divorced, but your children aren't.* Englewood Cliffs, NJ: Prentice Hall.

Einstein, E. (1982). *The stepfamily.* New York; Macmillan.

Garfield, R. (1980). The decision to remarry. *Journal of Divorce, 4*, 1–10.

Glick, P. C. (1979). Children of divorced parents in demographic perspective. *Journal of Social Issues, 35*, 170–182.

Goldner, V. (1982). Remarriage family: Structure, system, future. In L. Messinger (Ed.). *Therapy with remarriage families* (pp. 187–206). Rockville, MD: Aspen Systems Corp.

Greif, J. B. (1982). The father-child relationship subsequent to divorce. In L. Messinger (Ed.). *Therapy with remarriage families* (pp. 47–57). Rockville, MD: Aspen Systems Corp.

Hayes, R. (1984, November). Coping with loss: A developmental approach to helping children and youth. *Counseling & Human Development, 17*(3), 1–12.

Hess, R., & Camara, K. A. (1980). Post-divorce relationships as mediating factors in the consequences of divorce for children. *Journal of Social Issues, 35*(4), 79–96.

Hetherington, E. M., Cox, M., & Cox, R. (1982). Effects of divorce on parents and children. In M. E. Lamb (Ed.), *Non-traditional families* (pp. 233–288). Hillside, NJ: Erlbaum.

Huntington, D. S. (1982). Attachment loss and divorce: A reconsideration of the concepts. In L. Messinger (Ed.), *Therapy with remarriage families* (pp. 17–29). Rockville, MD. Aspen Systems Corp.

Jones, S. M. (1978). Divorce and remarriage: A new beginning; a new set of problems. *Journal of Divorce, 2,* 217–227.

Kargman, M. W. (1983). Stepchild support obligations of stepparents. *Family Relations, 32,* 321–328.

Kirby, J. (1979). *Second family.* Muncie, IN: Accelerated Development.

Kompara, D. R. (1980). difficulties in the socialization process of stepparenting. *Family Relations, 29,* 69–73.

Lewis, H. C. (1980). *All about families: The second time around.* Atlanta, GA: Peachtree Publishers.

Meiselman, K. (1978). *Incest.* San Francisco: Jossey-Bass.

Messinger, L., Walker, K. N., & Freeman, S. J. (1978). Preparation for remarriage following divorce. *American Journal of Orthopsychiatry, 48,* 263–272.

Nelson, M., & Nelson, G. (1982). Problems of equity in a reconstituted family: A social exchange analysis. *Family Relations, 31,* 223–231.

Perlmutter, L. H., Engel, T., & Sage, C. J. (1982). The incest taboo: Loosened sexual boundaries in remarried families. *Journal of Sex & Marital Therapy, 8,* 83–96.

Rallings, E. M. (1976). The special role of stepfather. *Family Coordinator, 25,* 445–449.

Santrock, J. W. (1972). The relations of type and onset of father absence to cognitive development. *Child Development, 43,* 455–469.

Schulman, G. L. (1972). Myths that intrude on the adaptation of the stepfamily. *Social Casework, 53,* 131–139.

Simon, A. W. (1964). *Stepchild in the family.* New York: Odyssey Press.

Skeen, P., Covi, R., & Robinson, B. (1985). Stepfamilies: A review of the literature with suggestions for practitioners. *Journal of Counseling & Development, 64,* 121–125.

Thies, J. M. (1977, Summer). Beyond divorce: The impact of remarriage on children. *Journal of Clinical Child Psychology, 6,* 59–61.

Turnbull, S. K., & Turnbull, J. M. (1983, April). To dream the impossible dream: An agenda for discussion with stepparents. *Family Relations,* 227–230.

Visher, E. B., & Visher, J. S. (1978). Major areas of difficulty for stepparent couples. *International Journal of Family Counseling, 6,* 70–80.

Visher, E. B., & Visher, J. S. (1979). *Stepfamilies: A guide to working with stepparents and stepchildren.* New York: Brunner/Mazel.

Visher, E. B., & Visher, J. S. (1982). Stepfamilies in the 1980s. In L. Messinger (Ed.), *Therapy with remarriage families* (pp. 105–119). Rockville, MD: Aspen Systems Corp.

Wald, E. (1981). *The Remarried family: Challenge and promise.* New York: Family Service Association of America.

Wallerstein, J. S., & Kelly, J. B. (1980). *Surviving the break-up: How children actually cope with divorce.* New York: Basic Books.

RELATED READINGS

Coleman, M., & Ganong, L. (1987). An evaluation of the stepfamily self-help literature for children and adolescents. *Family Relations, 36,* 61–65.

Glassman, B. (1988). *Everything you need to know about stepfamilies.* New York: Rosen Publishing Group.

Hansen, J. D. (1982). *Therapy with remarried families.* Rockville, MD: Aspen.

Hetherington, E. M., & Arasteh, J. D. (Eds.). (1988). *Impact of divorce, single parenting, and stepparenting on children.* Hillsdale, NJ: Lawrence Erlbaum Associates.

Leslie, L. A., & Epstein, N. (1988). Cognitive-behavioral treatment of remarried families. In N. Epstein, S. E. Schlesinger, & W. Dryden (Eds.), *Cognitive-behavioral therapy with families* (pp. 151–182). New York: Brunner/Mazel.

Pasley, K., & Ihinger-Tallman, M. (1987). *Remarriage and stepparenting: Current research and theory.* New York: Guilford Press.

Pill, C. J. (1990). Stepfamilies: Redefining the family. *Family Relations, 39,* 186–193.

Sager, C. J. (1986). Therapy with remarried couples. In N. S. Jacobson & A. S. Gurman (Eds.), *Clinical handbook of marital therapy* (pp. 321–344). New York: Guilford Press.

Whiteside, M. F. (1989). Remarried systems. In L. Combrinck-Graham (Ed.), *Children in family contexts: Perspectives on treatment*(pp. 135–160). New York: Guilford Press.

11

Counseling Minority Families: An Adlerian Perspective

Betty J. Newlon and Miguel Arciniega

American Muse, whose strong and diverse heart
So many men have tried to understand
But only made it smaller with their art,
Because you are as various as your land.
                                        Stephen Vincent Benet

Complex societies such as the United States contain many ethnic and regional subcultures rather than one homogeneous culture. The most readily identifiable minority groups in America are Asian Americans, Americans of African descent, Hispanic Americans, and Native Americans. These groups have all experienced exclusionist legislation and discriminatory practices. Groups that have come from other countries and cultures, either voluntarily or by force, have been thrust into a culture that routinely has subordinated non-white peoples.

Each minority group has a unique cultural heritage that makes it distinct from other groups. Cultural distinction, however, often has been erroneously interpreted as evidence of cultural conformity. This frequently has led to a monolithic view of minority group attitudes and behaviors. Clearly, uniformity of attitudes and behaviors is no more true for minority individuals than it is for members of the dominant culture. Not only do intragroup differences exist, but individuals' attitudes and behaviors also can fluctuate greatly as their identification with one culture or another changes.

Until the mid 1960s the counseling profession demonstrated little interest in or concern for the status of racial, ethnic, or other minority groups. With its traditional focus on the needs of the "average" student, counseling and guidance tended to overlook the special needs of students and their families. By virtue of their skin color, physical characteristics, or socioeconomic status, these groups were simply seen as disadvantaged in a world designed for white, middle class people.

When working with minority clients, nonminority counselors cannot operate without cultural information. They must understand the culture of the clients they are serving, including the history, beliefs, values, and behaviors, in an interacting holistic sense. Counselors need to develop an awareness not only of the cultural factors and their effect on the client but also of the effects of the client's interaction with the dominant culture. Rather than demanding that the client adapt to the counselor's culture, the counselor should adjust to and work within the client's culture. This means that counselors must recognize that their own values have been shaped by a particular cultural environment, and that this environment may be significantly different from the client's cultural environment.

Crosscultural counseling not only can be effective for resolving client difficulties, but it also can serve as a forum for unique learning experiences, with benefits to both client and counselor that may not be possible in intracultural counseling. Although cultural differences do result in unique experiences for both the client and the counselor, our experiences as human beings are remarkably similar.

MINORITY CULTURE: DEFINITIONS AND CHARACTERISTICS

To understand the concept of minority cultures, we might examine the definition of the words that in many cases dictate the affective semantic mind-set. *Minor* is defined by *Webster's New Collegiate Dictionary* as "inferior in importance, size, or degree; comparatively unimportant." One of the definitions of *minority* is, "A part of a population differing from others in some characteristics and often subjected to differential treatment." These definitions, set by the majority society, have psychological implications for minority members.

These definitions permeate our major institutions, particularly education. They victimize individuals from a minority culture by assuming that minorities are inferior, and they thus encourage, consciously or unconsciously, negative treatment by either patronization or oppression. These institutional mind-sets affect minority members' self-esteem, identity, and sense of belonging.

To develop and maintain their sense of identity and self-worth, minority cultures operate from a psychologically cohesive family/group structure that reinforces their sense of who they are. The history of the family is tied to the history of the cultural group and to the interactional history of the group with the majority society. Because most identifiable cultural minorities have experienced oppression, the psychological tendency is to band together closely within the family and cultural group, to ensure survival (Arciniega, Casaus, & Castillo, 1982). The sense of self and "others" becomes both distinct and interwoven with the majority culture.

The process of *acculturation* for minority cultures is a reality that affects both the evolving culture and the minority individual. Although the acculturation that takes place in all American minorities is a generic process, its effects on distinct cultural groups and individuals are unique. This is manifested by the extent of cultural variability within all minority groups. No single, static definition for all minority groups exists. Each culture has its own unique means of integration, and each minority individual has his or her own interpretation of the cultural variables.

When minority cultures come in contact with the majority culture, the beliefs and value systems do not become more entrenched, nor are they supplanted; instead, they are added to the culture of origin in a synthesizing, creative manner. The acculturation process is unique for each individual, resulting in much intra-cultural variability. Acculturation involves an integration of selected beliefs and views often dictated by environment, socioeconomic status, and education.

Because the majority culture historically has viewed minority cultures as inferior, it has labeled problems that occur "minority problems" rather than problems of interacting cultures. Gordon (1958) indicated that, although individuals may become superficially acculturated to the majority culture, they do not totally assimilate but retain much of their own ethnic group identity. This has become more evident since the 1960s and 1970s, when all cultural groups exhibited a resurgence of ethnic pride.

If counselors are to work more effectively with American minorities, they must adopt a broader world view encompassing the interactive process of majority/minority cultures. Counselors must understand not only the world view, culture of origin, and process of the client's cultural variability but also the significant family, cultural, and institutional systems in the client's life. Even more important, counselors should be aware of the minority individual's *interpretation* of his or her subjective world.

CULTURAL GROUPS

Within the confines of this chapter, we have not attempted to provide a comprehensive analysis of the history, psychology, sociology, values, and beliefs of all minority groups. Rather, we are presenting an overview of information and cultural considerations specific to four minority groups: African Americans, Hispanics, Asians, and Native Americans.

African Americans

The African American population constitutes the largest identifiable minority group in the United States. With a population estimated at 26 million, a median age of 24.9 years, and a median income of $12,000 (United States Department of Commerce, 1980), the majority of African Americans are economically poor in relation to the total population and historically have been poor because of racial discrimination.

To understand the African American experience before initiating intervention approaches, counselors have to understand the history. This history includes historical figures; omissions and bias of books; the social, political, and economic climate; and the dynamics of the evolution of the militant movement of the 1960s and 1970s.

Counselors must recognize that (a) no prescriptive approaches can be applied in dealing with African American clients, and (b) the myth that the problems of these clients are their own sole responsibility is indeed a myth. Counselors must incorporate a systemic view into their experience if they are to understand the interrelationship of the individual's history with self, family, institutions, and economic and political factors. As with all groups, cultural stereotyping is endemic. Counselors must exercise caution to separate the culture of poverty from the culture of the group itself.

The following *general* characteristics manifested by African American clients may help counselors develop a systemic view (Vacc & Wittmer, 1980).

1. One of the defining characteristics of African American, as contrasted with Caucasian, people is the differential access to the resources of society.
2. Several forces keep the African American cultural system intact; one is the group of internal factors operating within the African American community to maintain cohesiveness.
3. Older African Americans are treated with respect—often addressed as "uncle" or "aunt."
4. Turning the head and putting the hand over the mouth when laughing, or averting the eyes and perhaps even the face when speaking to elders or other respected persons are considered marks of respect.
5. The African American mother must prepare her child to take on appropriate sex and age roles as well as the racial role.
6. The African ethos is "survival of the tribe" and "oneness with nature." The cultural values associated with this world view are cooperation, interdependence, and collective responsibility.
7. A strong achievement orientation is a strength of African American families.
8. The church offers a kind of extended family fellowship, providing significant adults to relate to the children, as well as materials and human resources for the family.

Although these characteristics are general, counselors should understand the progression of ramifications: African American clients may come from situations in which they feel powerless, hostile, and lacking specific direction. The systems and institutions that influence problems for these clients are often insensitive and unresponsive to change. Therefore, African American clients want concrete responses from the counselor much like they would receive from respected family members or friends.

Hispanic Americans

According to the Bureau of Census (United States Department of Commerce, 1980), the Hispanic population in the United States was approximately 14.6 million, with a median age of 23.2 years. The standard of living for Hispanics is well below the national average. The median family income for Hispanics in 1980 was $14,700, compared to $20,840 for Caucasian families. By the year 2000, Hispanics are expected to constitute the largest minority group in the United States.

The various Hispanic groups in the United States have distinct differences as well as similarities. The similarities include language, values, and some traditions, but major historical differences are present among as well as within the various groups. For example, the history of the Mexican American is tied to the history of the land; Mexicans were already in the Southwest when the Anglo Americans arrived in the East. Other Hispanic groups, such as Cubans, appeared in the United States later, for political or economic reasons.

Most Hispanics have chosen to remain identified with their own ethnic group rather than to be categorized under the aggregate Hispanic/Latino label. To understand the diversity of Hispanics, each group must be examined historically.

When the Spanish explorers came to the North American continent in the early 16th century, they intermarried with the Indians and produced the Mestizo. The Puerto Ricans also intermarried with many of the native peoples. In Cuba, some cultural fusion occurred with imported African slaves while some Spanish colonists maintained their European lineage. The same phenomenon is true for many of the Central and South American countries. Thus, the population labeled Hispanic is heterogeneous and diverse.

Because of this complexity, common characteristics of Hispanic American clients are difficult to determine. The following are shared by *most* Hispanics (Ruiz & Padilla, 1977):

1. More than 50% of Hispanics report that Spanish is their native language.
2. The extended family structure is still an important factor in Hispanic clients' backgrounds.
3. The concept of respect is a value, particularly for authority figures.
4. Unwavering love and respect for the mother, who serves as a unifying force in the family, is a prominent feature.
5. Formalized kinships, such as the compadrazgo "godfather" system, operate in varying degrees.
6. Loyalty to the family takes precedence over loyalty to social institutions.
7. Sex roles traditionally have been more rigid, but this is currently undergoing some change.

8. The concept of "personalismo" for personal contact is a preferred relating style.

In attempting to understand these characteristics, counselors must recognize how the concept of acculturation affects each member. Rather than assume that the above characteristics are static, each client must be taken individually and the heterogeneity of the Hispanic population kept in mind.

Asian Americans

The Asian American population in the United States consists of people from China, Japan, Korea, Malaysia, the Philippines, Samoa, and Viet Nam. The largest numbers are from Japan and China. The Bureau of The Census (United States Department of Commerce, 1980) reported that approximately 3.7 million Asian Americans are living in the United States, with a median age of 28.6 years. Atkinson, Morten, and Sue (1983) reported that Chinese, Japanese, and Filipinos exceed the median income of $22,000 and complete a higher number of education grades than other ethnic groups. Those authors contend, however, that under closer analysis the reports are skewed: The higher incomes do not take into account the number of wage earners in one family, and the extraordinarily high educational level of some Asian Americans cancels out a large number who remain uneducated.

Like the Hispanics, the diversity among Asian American groups is vast. Each group has its own cultural norms, values, language, and traditions. The focus of this discussion is primarily on Chinese and Japanese Americans, who comprise the largest Asian population in the United States, the Japanese being the larger of the two (Sue, 1973). The majority live in the western United States and Hawaii, with a significant number in New York.

The first Asian American group to immigrate to the United States was the Chinese, in the 1840s. The immigration resulted from the discovery of gold in California, and many Chinese came with the idea of returning home once they made their fortune. These Chinese immigrants who came to work as laborers in the gold mines and the railroads were subject to massive acts of discrimination (Sue, 1973).

Japanese immigration began in the late 1800s. The Japanese filled a demand for cheap agricultural labor and were not treated with the same anti-Oriental disrespect that the Chinese were. The Japanese people's success in agriculture, however, antagonized the white citizens, contributing to the threat of "yellow peril." Acts of racism toward Asians increased and were fanned by the press. By World War II, sending more than 110,000 Japanese to relocation camps had become relatively easy (Daniels, 1971).

The Chinese and Japanese cultures have many similar values and traditions. It is not surprising, then, that scholars have found similar psychological characteristics for these Asian Americans. Following is a synthesized list of some of the psychological characteristics of Japanese and Chinese Americans (Atkinson, Morten, & Sue, 1983):

1. Chinese and Japanese people feel a great sense of obligation toward the family and parents.
2. Family expectations of obedience produce problems when exposed to white values.
3. Asian Americans tend to evaluate ideas on the basis of practical application. Consequently, they tend to be more intolerant of ambiguities.
4. Asian Americans seem to be more obedient, conservative, conforming, and inhibited than their white counterparts.
5. They tend to exhibit the cultural values of emotional restraint, dependence on family, and formality in interpersonal relations.
6. Asian Americans generally feel more comfortable in structured situations.
7. They are more reluctant to self-disclose than are their white counterparts.
8. Because of their minority status and potential discrimination from white society, Asian Americans may be suspicious of nongroup members.
9. Asian Americans seem to have a need to feel guilty and accept personal blame when things go wrong.
10. Asian Americans seem to be less verbal about their feelings with nongroup members.

Though this list is limited, it does provide some information regarding Asian Americans. Again, counselors must exercise caution. All characteristics described in the list do not apply to all individuals. The list is intended as a starting place, a structure for beginning to understand the cultural characteristics of Asian Americans.

Native Americans

For the first time since the period of European colonization, the Native American population in the United States has topped 1 million. Of the current 1.4 million Native Americans (United States Department of Commerce, 1980), approximately 600,000 live on or near reservations. Richardson (1981) reported the following: Their average annual income is $1,500, much less than for all other groups; their life expectancy is 44 years of age, with a median age of 23; 50% of school children do not complete high school; and their suicide rate is 100 times that of the white population.

One of the most neglected areas in counseling literature has been the Native American client. What literature exists has been largely limited to historical or philosophical treatises. This neglect may be attributed to several causes:

- The monolithic tradition of Western training is prevalent in most counselor training institutions, leaving little room for other world views.
- Little adequate information is available on the psychology of the Native American. More important, counselors and psychologists are lacking to assist in interpreting counseling information.
- The number of tribes, more than 200, each with its own language and customs, increases the complexity of developing this counseling area.

Of all the minority groups, counselors have the most difficulty working with Native Americans, partially because of the strong stereotypes that exist. Western modes of counseling are not compatible with the traditional Indian cultures. Further, many Native Americans have become bicultural or have acculturated within the dominant society. The process of acculturation is a major counseling factor with all minority groups, and counselors will encounter Indian clients on all points of the acculturation continuum.

Although the statistics are appalling, they do not dampen the optimism inherent in this group in spite of all the obstacles they have encountered. To gain some understanding of the Native American family, the cultural origin must be examined. The following list is compiled from the values and traits found in traditional Native American cultures and provides some basic guidelines and information potentially helpful to counseling (Vacc & Wittmer, 1980):

1. The concept of sharing is a major value in family life.
2. Time is secondary to people and is seen more as a natural phenomenon.
3. Nature is part of living and is part of happenings such as death, birth, and accidents.
4. Acceptance of life is a style of being in harmony with the world.
5. Family, including extended family, is of major importance, and the tribe and family to which one belongs provide significant meaning.
6. The basic worth of the individual is in terms of his or her family and tribe. Individual responsibility is only a part of the total responsibility concept.
7. Harmony and cooperative behavior are valued and encouraged.
8. Tradition is important; it adds to the quality of life in the here-and-now.
9. Assertive or aggressive behavior is seen as an impingement on others' dignity.
10. Respect for elders is valued, and the elders play an important part in family life.

Native American history is replete with failures of intervention programs. So before giving any consideration to a counseling approach in working with Native Americans, counselors must develop an understanding of the culture itself; what occurred between Native American cultures and United States society; and, more important, what effect culture, history, economics, and politics have had on the

Native American. Counselors also must be aware of the institutional mind-set that has permeated the literature about Native American problems.

As with all minority groups, a generic understanding of Native American cultures is essential. Of equal importance is learning about the differences that exist between each member, family, and tribe. Counseling as it is now in the United States has not worked with traditional Native American cultures. Therefore, counseling will have to assume a contextual frame of reference compatible with the view of the individual and family. The concept of family counseling as we know it in the institutional sense is not presently a viable approach for the traditional Native American. Only through increased awareness of cultural influences and expanded education for counselors can family counseling with Native Americans become a reality.

FAMILY CONSIDERATIONS

The single most important influence in a person's life is the family. Each family has a unique set of cultural values and mores and socializes the children in its own cultural milieu. This applies equally to cultural minority individuals in the United States, who are still reared to identify with family, community, and cultural group during the formative years of their personhood.

Recently, counseling has begun to focus on the *family systems approach* when working with individuals. The family in its sociocultural context, including the systems that affect development, is recognized as being important. To effectively counsel minority families, the basic tenets of this approach must be accepted.

Basic Tenets of Family Systems Approach

- Most important, all people are of equal worth, not the same, but equal in value.
- The concept of counseling is broadened to include a world view rather than the traditional monolithic view.
- No single approach encompasses all sociocultural considerations. Thus, counseling minority families has no prescriptive approach.

Most traditional family counseling interventions are based on the premise that viewing an individual's problem outside the context of interactions within the family is not desirable. These interventions share the ideology that change can best be realized and maintained if modification of the beliefs, attitudes, and behaviors of significant persons or institutions occurs simultaneously with modification of the beliefs, attitudes, and behaviors of the so-called problem individual (Okun & Rappaport, 1980). The modification required is usually in the direction of majority culture beliefs.

ADLERIAN PSYCHOLOGY AND
CROSSCULTURAL PLURALISTIC COUNSELING

The underlying assumption in most counseling approaches requires a "fixing" of the family interpersonal systems. Little note is taken of how external systems operate on the family, and of the subsequent cultural interpretations. Of the various counseling theories, Adlerian psychology seems to come closest to providing a belief system plus a rationale for behavior that encompass the sociocultural factors necessary to understand minority families.

In Adlerian psychology all problems are seen as social problems, and counselors assign equal importance to the relationships between people, groups, and institutions, including how the individual's family views these problems (Manaster & Corsini, 1982). The goal of family counseling is to teach family members how to deal effectively with one another, how to live together as social equals, and how to contribute to the greater community and society.

The family counseling process is seen as a mutually educational process. Dysfunctional behavior is viewed as a lack of information, rather than as pathology, on the part of the family. By providing opportunities for insight and action-oriented information, the counselor can assist the family in learning to operate more effectively. The counselor and the family are involved in a mutually beneficial, egalitarian process in which the counselor and the families assume a posture of mutual learning (Christensen & Schramski, 1983).

Counselors must gain some understanding of systems interaction with minorities in order to impart information about systemic problems. With this information, the family can arrive at decisions more effectively and with a greater degree of comprehension. An awareness of how the dominant social system prescribes the same goals for all people, without consideration of distinctiveness or location of the individual and groups within the social structure, must be imparted to the families.

The fact that counselors are trained in institutions that are usually microcosms of the dominant group presents a problem. Counselors usually are trained to see maladaptive behavior from one perspective—the dominant one. Thus, counselors inadvertently may seek to help a minority family move toward a dominant normative tractive response that would be ultimately detrimental. Rather, counselors should strive to be advocates for minority families in interpreting and managing the system. In doing this, counselors must integrate information regarding sociocultural variables, racism, and economic and acculturation factors when counseling minority families. This has been identified by LeVine and Padilla (1980) as *crosscultural pluralistic counseling*. The pluralistic family counselor considers all facets of the client's personal history, family history, and social and cultural orientation.

To work effectively with minority families, counselors must heed the systems that most influence the individual. Because the family is the single most important influence in a person's life, counselors must develop an understanding of the family and cultural group, and of the interacting impact of social institutions. Understanding alone, however, cannot effect change. Successful intervention with families requires a concrete belief system that is realistic and pragmatic. The following premises, derived from Adlerian psychology, represent this belief system and include crosscultural applications (Arciniega & Newlon, 1981).

1. *Behavior is best understood in a social context.* To understand the dynamics of family behavior, one has to not only observe the behavior of individuals in the family context but also be aware of all the systems affecting the family's social interactions. The larger social systems of the community affect the family economically, socially, and politically and give impetus to survival processes and family beliefs about these larger systems. Unless the family is viewed in light of *all* the interacting systems, counselors cannot hope to understand behavior in a minority family and its ultimate effect on the individual.

2. *Behavior is motivated by the need to belong.* Human beings have a basic inclination toward being a part of the larger whole. We have a need to belong and a desire to contribute to the betterment of the group. Adler called this *gemeinschaftsgefuel*—social interest (Ansbacher & Ansbacher, 1967). Many minority groups, such as Native Americans, Hispanic Americans, and African Americans, already operate under this framework of social interest. Minority families, too, are striving to belong, to be part of the greater whole. This need is revealed in the psychological cohesion and banding together of minority groups. It is also understood in the anger manifested when minorities are the victims of exclusionary practices by white society. The need to belong and participate is basic to all.

3. *Behavior is understood in terms of striving for significance.* The family is seen as the primary social group in which each individual strives to find a significant place. When this sense of worth is established, the individual moves toward the goals of significance and recognition in the larger society.

   This striving for significance is a movement toward establishing a unique identity and is considered the master force behind all individual and collective human activity. For minority families, this master force takes on even greater import, as the striving for identity is more pronounced. Rather than subscribe to the "melting pot" concept, minority families seek to achieve their own sense of significance by maintaining their unique culture.

4. *Each individual is considered equal and has value.* The notion of equality is inherent in Adlerian psychology: "There is an ironclad law of social living—all people are equal" (Dreikurs, Corsini, Lowe, & Sonste-

gard, 1959). People are of equal value; therefore, the family and the cultural group have inherent rights to mutual respect and equal treatment. In recognizing the value of equality, minority families are no longer tolerating cultural oppression from the dominant society. Counselors can no longer operate under the guise of ideological equality; they have to operationalize human value with all people.

5. *Behavior is a function of perception.* Behavior is perceived subjectively. This phenomenological view includes the cultural interpretations families make and share with their own group. Therefore, perceptions of the systems that affect a particular cultural group and its families are a *reality* and must be dealt with as such. The inner, subjective experience of any cultural group is its subjective truth. As counselors, we must value and accept this truth—even when we may not perceive it as such.

Counselors need to be involved in a continuing process of understanding a minority family's collective view and hearing the messages the family is hearing. Faulty perceptions then can be mutually examined, analyzed, and placed in a perspective that provides the family and the counselor with a more comprehensive and realistic view.

6. *Behavior is ideographically interpreted.* The ideographic view of behavior requires that the family counselor have a generic understanding of minority groups and an understanding of the interactions between minority groups and the dominant group. Even more important is an understanding of how minority group individuals interpret these processes. The counselor needs to understand the views of the cultural group as a whole along with views of the family.

The counselor needs to understand how a minority family acquired its beliefs and value system and how the family presently perceives the systems affecting not only the cultural group as a whole but their own family as well. In this way, the counselor can begin to understand how the minority family processes decisions, establishes goals, and sets the values by which its members live.

7. *Behavior is viewed in terms of use rather than possession.* People *use* their behavior for their own purposes: "One will do that which is most useful or which best accomplishes one's purpose and striving; that which interferes with one's goal is not done" (Dinkmeyer, Pew, & Dinkmeyer, 1979). The important issue is what individuals *do* with what they *perceive* to have, rather than with what they actually possess. When minority groups are stereotyped and labeled, they sometimes come to believe this fiction and use it in counterproductive ways. The counselor needs to see how the family and the culture determine the use of behavior. The focus is on family processes and how to use them in productive ways.

8. *Behavior is seen as a unified whole with discernible patterns.* Behavior is best understood as a unified whole. The individual and family are seen

in the context of their subjective view, including the milieu of their interacting systems. Behavior is interpreted in light of the patterns established by the family cultural lifestyle.

CROSSCULTURAL FACTORS

Much of the criticism of minority group counseling is directed at the interactions that occur between counselor and client. Counseling is seen as a process of interpersonal interaction and communication that requires accurate sending and receiving of verbal and nonverbal messages. When the counselor and the client come from different cultural backgrounds, barriers to communication are likely to develop, leading to misunderstandings that destroy rapport and render counseling ineffective.

The starting point for counselors who wish to facilitate positive interactions with minorities rests with the counselors themselves. Family counselors must be knowledgeable about the culture of the minority family and must acquire generic cultural information through reading and firsthand knowledge. The sensitivity of family counselors to cultural issues has an effect on how minority families perceive them. Equally important is the counselor's cautious interpretation of generic ethnic information to the specific family. Too often, the counselor projects institutional stereotypes without a conscious awareness that this is occurring.

When implementing Adlerian premises in a family counseling setting, several cultural factors should be noted. The following should be considered in gathering information, and integrated into the family counseling process (Arciniega & Newlon, 1983).

Language

In counseling minority families that still use their language of origin, understanding the language is not enough. Language must be understood for both content and contextual meaning. In addition, the counselor must be able to assess the language dominance of the various family members; all members may not have the same degree of fluency in the language of origin or in English. And if English is the spoken language, it may still reflect the culture. For example, in Spanish the reflexive is often used in sentence structure and it may be carried over into the English translation.

Responsibility regarding material things is reflected differently in the Native American and Hispanic cultures and, subsequently, in their language. For example, "se cayo el lapiz" (the pencil fell) is a direct translation from Spanish, as opposed to "I dropped the pencil." This does not connote irresponsibility, but a fact.

Code switching—mixing and combining words in new and creative expressions that operate from a distinct cultural base—occurs when two languages come in contact. Adjectives are placed differently in Spanish—e.g., "The dog spotted ran" as opposed to, "The spotted dog ran." Many families use black English and

Calo (Hispanic communication style), depending on their location and need to be understood.

Cultural Identity

Counselors should be aware of the self-referent labels that families choose when referring to their cultural group. Self-referent identifiers are a sensitive issue in many minority families and may be different even for various members within the family. For families of Mexican or Latin American descent, the identifiers may be Mexican American, Hispanic, Chicano, Americans of Mexican descent, or Latinos. For families of African descent, these may be Negro, Black, African, or West Indian. For Native Americans, identifiers may be Indian, Native American, Red, or even more important tribal names. For Asian Americans, the identifiers may be Oriental, Asian, or Asian American.

Generation

The families' generational factors (first, second, third generations in this country) should be assessed to try to determine the degree of acculturation that has occurred. First-generation families obviously will have more ties to the traditional culture, and these ties will be reflected in the family dynamics. The acculturation process is unique for each minority family. Contrary to some current beliefs, as the family becomes acculturated, it does not drop its former cultural ways but, rather, adds new ones and synthesizes both the new and the old in a creative manner.

Cultural Custom Styles

In addition to the obvious cultural customs of foods, dress, and traditions, several cultural styles of responsibility and communication have to be considered. For example, the Hispanic and Native American cultures emphasize the responsibility of the oldest child to younger siblings. Oldest children assume this responsibility as part of tradition. The counselor should not view this behavior as taking away responsibility from younger siblings. As another example, the Asian family's expectations of unquestioning obedience may cause problems when exposed to American values emphasizing independence and self-reliance.

The style of communication in traditional Native American and Hispanic American families stresses patience and respect. The children of these families may show respect by looking down and not into the eyes of the authority figures. When counseling with families from these groups, the verbal question/answer approach is often ineffective in obtaining behavior cues. Cultural contextualizing (or cultural interpretation) by a family member who is more bicultural may provide needed information.

With African American families, verbal interaction moves at a faster pace, and sensitive confrontation is accepted more readily than with traditional Hispanic, Native American, or Asian families. Counselors need to be aware of their own interactional cultural style to determine if any major difference exists in the interaction.

Geographical Location and Neighborhoods

Ethnic groups from different geographical locations exhibit distinct geocultural traditions and customs. Counselors cannot assume that the same customs apply to seemingly similar cultural groups. An African American family from the South manifests the culture in a different way that an African American family from the West Coast. This concept of geographical differences also applies to Asian American, Hispanic American, and Native American families. The counselor also should note rural and urban influences in the family's present situation and within the family history. The closer the family is to its country of origin, the more traditional are the values, beliefs, and language.

Neighborhoods where the families reside have a great deal to do with how they see themselves. A minority family living in a totally ethnic area views itself differently than a family living in an integrated neighborhood.

Family Constituency

In most minority families kinship networks help to satisfy important cultural needs for intimacy and interpersonal relations. Extended families where more than one generation lives in the same household and where formalized kinship relations exist are common among minority groups. The culturally sensitive family counselor must be able to comprehend this concept within each culture. In many Hispanic families significant adults may extend to uncles, grandparents, cousins, close friends, and godparents. These adults often play a significant part in child-rearing and perhaps should be considered for inclusion in the family counseling process.

Children occupy a special place in the families of most minorities. Love and protection of children are pronounced, creating an environment where children can develop strong feelings of self-worth despite the lingering effects of discrimination and racism. In some instances, minority group families function as buffers against society's attempt to impose a negative self-image.

Psychohistorical and Religious Traditions

This history of the ethnic group's origin, along with the history of the ethnic group in the United States, is part of the information counselors need. Minority families reflect the psychohistory of the family through child-rearing practices.

Many facets of child-rearing are rooted in the history of minority groups and are distinct from the dominant culture in which the family presently lives.

Spiritual and religious practices traditionally have been strong within most minority families. These, too, affect the family dynamics. Religion provides the medium through which minority group members deal with forces and powers that are mysterious and beyond rational control. It also provides a basis for social cohesion and support. Historically, the minority church has been a resource for personal counseling, a place where minorities are accorded personal respect and given opportunities to hold positions of responsibility, and a refuge from a hostile environment. Counselors must take this factor into account in working with the individuals and families.

Individuality

Minority groups view the concept of individual responsibility differently. Native Americans, for instance, judge their worth primarily in terms of whether their behavior serves to better the tribe. Tribal culture places a high value on the harmonious relationship between an individual and all other members of the tribe. The concept of cooperation within certain ethnic groups has been documented (Kagan & Madsen, 1971). Family counselors must be wary of assigning individual responsibilities at the expense of cooperativeness already manifest in these children. Responsibility to the family is a major value found in many minority families and should be considered and encouraged. Chinese and Japanese children feel a much greater sense of obligation toward the family and parents than do white children. Individual responsibilities are of secondary value, after the family.

COUNSELOR AWARENESS

Why is it important for counselors to understand minority groups and their cultures? The number and variety of persons they have the potential to impact— especially in today's world, where they are expected to provide effective helping services to all people— is staggering. Thus, counselors have a special responsibility to understand more than one frame of reference.

Most counselors are white and middle class. Many minority group members are of lower socioeconomic status. In addition to cultural differences, counselors and clients have class differences in attitudes, behaviors, beliefs, and values. The impact of social class differences on counseling in general acquires added significance when considering that existing counseling techniques are middle-and upper-class based (Singleton, 1982).

Counselors frequently impose their own cultural values upon minority clients in ignorance. For example, one of the most highly valued aspects of counseling entails self-disclosure. Self-disclosure may be contrary to the basic cultural values of some minorities. Chinese American clients who are taught at an early age to refrain from emotional expression feel threatened by a counselor's direct and subtle demands for self-disclosure. Hispanic American and Native American clients have reported similar conflicts.

Stereotyping

Stereotyping is a major problem in all forms of counseling. It may be defined as rigid preconceptions that are applied to all members of a group or to an individual over time, regardless of individual variation. Stereotypes often are institutionalized, and counselors have to be conscious of this process, because most counselor training institutions do not train family counselors from a culturally pluralistic concept.

The preconceived notions that counselors have about families who differ from them ethnically, racially, or socioeconomically affect their reactions to minority families, and they may unwittingly act upon these beliefs, approaching families from a monolithic, dominant point of view. Or in an attempt to avoid stereotyping and treat the client as just another client, counselors may demonstrate "color or culture blindness." In this case, the counselor may avoid discussing differences. The content of the counseling also may be restricted by counselors' fear that the client will detect conscious or unconscious stereotyping on their part.

Self-Concept

Counseling inherently deals closely with clients' self-concept. Counselors should be aware that the development of minority members' self-concepts has distinct characteristics that are not found in the self-concept development of members in the dominant culture. The unique cultural values of minority families are part of their identity and part of their self-concept. These are cognitively learned through the interaction of the family culture and the dominant group environment. Thus, a bicognitive self-concept (concept of self within family and concept of self in relation to the dominant group) becomes evident and may be manifested in cultural conflict. Counselors have to be aware of this conflict in order to provide a place of acceptance, confirmation, and encouragement to resolve this conflict and enhance the healthy development of minority families.

Diagnosing Behavior

Counselors must exercise caution when diagnosing behavior in minority families. A diagnosis that is appropriate when viewed in the majority culture may be inaccurate when considering cultural variables. The goals of misbehavior, as identified and discussed by Dreikurs (1950), for example, have to be interpreted in light of the family's culture. The goal of power may be misdiagnosed in the minority child. A minority child's hesitancy or "non-doing" may be misinterpreted, resulting in an inaccurate hypothesis. The same misperception may occur when diagnosing the goal of revenge or assumed disability.

The diagnosis of *assumed disability* is particularly subject to scrutiny. Minority children may not have learned the language sufficiently well or acculturated enough to know how to respond to the counselor. Again, the counselor must analyze the cultural context of the behavior before making a diagnosis. Many minority children have been misdiagnosed as needing special education when, in reality, the problem has been a lack of cultural understanding on the part of the institution.

Attributes of Effective Counselors

Some studies have shown that the ethnicity of counselors is not always the significant variable in determining the efficacy of counseling. Certain family counselors who are of different ethnic groups than their clients seem to have enough skill and understanding to be effective. These counselors manifest an attitudinal mind-set and belief system that project certain assumptions. This belief system and process of understanding appear to be the intervening variables that constitute viable counseling approaches with minority families. Counselors who facilitate positive interaction with minority families:

— personally acknowledge that cultural diversity exists within the United States and that diversity implies difference, not inferiority.
— confront and resolve personal cultural variation through study and interpersonal contact.
— examine the historical and present interaction between minorities and the dominant culture.
— expand interactions with minority and dominant cultural group persons.

CONCLUSION

Cultural considerations integrated into Adlerian psychology have been presented as a base for working with minority families. Adlerian theory most approximates the belief structure necessary when working in a crosscultural family counseling setting. Specific counseling techniques and approaches serve no purpose unless the proper belief structure undergirds their implementation. Adlerian theory's basic premise of equality is the cornerstone of successful crosscultural family counseling.

When counseling with minority families, counselors must keep in mind the following points:

1. The extent of acculturation is not the same for all members of the same family. Each member conceivably could be at a different point on the continuum.
2. Counseling must begin as an educational process more for the counselor than the minority family.
3. Counseling must incorporate a systemic approach. The institutional systems in which the family operates often have to be interpreted.
4. The theoretical approach is not nearly as important as the counselor's underlying beliefs and assumptions, which must include a belief in the value of all people and the inherent equality of all groups.
5. Counselors have to be aware of and challenge their own personal and institutional experiences involving stereotypes, racism, and oppression.

Although application of these principles does not guarantee effective counseling with minority families, the principles do give the counselor a foundation for understanding minority clients. Implementation of the pluralistic counseling model will affect not only the minority families being counseled but also will enhance the development of the counselor as a person.

REFERENCES

Ansbacher, H., & Ansbacher, R. (Eds.). (1967). *The individual psychology of Alfred Adler.* New York: Harper & Row.

Arciniega, M., Casaus, L., & Castillo, M. (1982). *Parenting models and Mexican Americans: A process analysis.* Albuquerque, NM: Pajarito Publications.

Arciniega, M., & Newlon, B. (1981). A theoretical rationale for cross-cultural family counseling. *School Counselor, 29*(2), 89–96.

Arciniega, M., & Newlon, B. (1983). Cross-cultural family counseling. In O. Christensen & T. Schramski (Eds.), *Adlerian family counseling: A manual for counselor, educator and psychotherapist.* Minneapolis: Educational Media Corp.

Atkinson, D., Morten, G., & Sue, D. (1983). *Counseling American minorities: A cross-cultural perspective.* Dubuque, IA: Wm. C. Brown Publishers.

Christensen, O., & Schramski, T. (Eds.). (1983). *Adlerian family counseling: A manual for counselor, educator, and psychotherapist.* Minneapolis: Educational Media Corp.

Daniels, R. (1971). *Concentration camps, USA.* New York: Harper & Row.

Dinkmeyer, D. C., Pew, W., & Dinkmeyer, D. (1979). *Adlerian counseling and psychotherapy.* Monterey, CA: Brooks/Cole.

Dreikurs, R. (1950). *Fundamentals of Adlerian psychology.* New York: Greenburg Publishers.

Dreikurs, R., Corsini, R., Lowe, R., & Sonstegard, M. (1959). *Adlerian family counseling: A manual for counseling centers.* Eugene, OR: University Press, University of Oregon.

Gordon, M. (1958). *Social class in American society*. Durham, NC: Duke University Press.

Kagan, S. & Madsen, M. (1971). Cooperation and competition of Mexican, Mexican American, and Anglo American children of two ages under four instructional sets. *Developmental Psychology, t, 32*.

LeVine, E., & Padilla, A. (1980). *Crossing cultures in therapy: Pluralistic counseling for the Hispanic*. Monterey, CA: Brooks/Cole Publishing Co.

Manaster, G., & Corsini, R. (1982). *Individual psychology: Theory and practice*. Itasca, IL: F.E. Peacock Publishers.

Okun, B., & Rappaport, L. (1980). *Working with families: An introduction to family therapy*. North Scituate, MA: Duxbury Press.

Richardson, E. (1981). Cultural and historical perspectives in counseling American Indians. In D. W. Sue, *Counseling the culturally different: Theory and practice*. New York: John Wiley & Sons.

Ruiz, R., & Padilla, A. (1977). Counseling Latinos. *Personnel & Guidance Journal, 7*, 401–408.

Singleton, D. (1982). *Counseling approaches for enhancing self-esteem of minorities*. Ann Arbor, MI: School of Education.

Sue, D. (1973). Ethnic identity: The impact of two cultures on the psychological development of Asians in America. In D. Sue & N. Wagner (Eds.), *Asian-Americans: Psychological perspectives*. Palo Alto, CA: Science & Behavior Books.

United States Department of Commerce. (1980). *Supplementary report PC80-S1-1, Provisional estimates of social, economic, and housing characteristics, 1980 census of population and housing*. Washington, DC: Bureau of the Census.

Vacc, N. & Wittmer, J. (1980). *Let me be me: Special populations and the helping professional*. Muncie, IN: Accelerated Development, Inc.

RELATED READINGS

Boyd-Franklin, N. (1989). *Black families in therapy: A multisystems approach*. New York: Guilford Press.

Cheathan, H. E., & Stewart, J. B. (Eds.). (1990). *Black families: Interdisciplinary perspectives*. New Brunswick, NJ: Transaction Publishers.

Delworth-Anderson, P., & McAdoo, H. P. (1988). The study of ethnic minority families: Implications for practitioners and policymakers. *Family Relations, 37*, 265–267.

London, H., & Devore, W. (1988). Layers of understanding: Counseling ethnic minority families. *Family Relations, 37*, 310–314.

McGoldrick, M., Pearce, J. K., & Giordano, J. (Eds.). (1982). *Ethnicity and family therapy*. New York: Guilford Press.

Pinderhughes, E. (1990). Legacy of slavery: The experience of black families in America. In M. P. Mirkin (Ed.), *The social and political contexts of family therapy* (pp. 289–306). Boston: Allyn & Bacon.

12

Counseling the Elderly

Douglas R. Gross

Old age is not for sissies.
-variously ascribed

The increasing number of elderly persons within our population and the lengthening lifespan currently are having, and will continue to have, a profound impact on all areas of counseling. Today, 28 million people are age 65 or older. Based upon the projections of Siegel and Davidson (1984), this figure will climb to 35 million by the year 2000. This impact has been addressed by many authors including Sterns, Weis, and Perkins (1984), Kart, Metress, and Metress (1988), Gross (1987), Myers and Shelton (1987), Myers (1988), and Gilkison and Drummond (1988). The growing body of literature dealing with counseling and intervention strategies for elderly people speaks directly to the emerging recognition that this population will continue to present itself in growing numbers to the counseling professional.

Based upon education and training, are today's counseling professionals prepared to deal with this growing population? Ganikos (1979) implied that most practicing counselors have had little or no experience or training in working with older people. More recently, authors such as Waters (1984), Wellman and Mccormack (1984), Cavallaro and Ramsey (1988), and Cunningham and Brookbank (1988) speak not only to the growing needs of this population but also address issues that indicate counselors' increasing competence to effectively work with this population. Much is being accomplished, but much still has to be done to prepare counselors to adequately address the concerns and problems that the elderly confront.

THE NATURE OF THE PROBLEM

From a psychological viewpoint the emotional and psychological problems of elderly people differ slightly from the emotional and psychological problems of their younger counterparts. For example, feelings of anxiety, frustration, guilt, loneliness, despair, worthlessness, and fear are prevalent across all age levels. The young, as well as the old, must learn to cope daily with a multitude of life situations that test their emotional stability. The process of aging, however, brings with it a set of circumstances not only unique but also telescoped into a brief period of years. These circumstances—physiological, situational, and psychological in nature—force elderly people into changing patterns of behavior and lifestyles developed and ingrained over long periods.

A sample of the changing life circumstances that the elderly person is forced to confront includes:

- Loss of work role identity.
- Loss of significant person(s) in his or her life.
- Geographical relocation.
- Increased physiological disorders.
- Decreased financial support.
- Loneliness and separation.
- Excessive amounts of leisure time.
- Peer group restructuring.
- Family group restructuring.
- Increased dependence.

When these major life changes are viewed in terms of the rapidity of their onset, the lack of preparation for them, and society's negative attitudes regarding the elderly in general, the prevalence of emotional and psychological problems in the elderly is brought into clear focus. Any one of these changing life situations can generate emotional and psychological difficulties for the individual. In combination, they place the individual in a situation in which the development of coping strategies is mandatory.

John, 72, and his wife Laura, 70, live in a small home in a retirement community in Arizona. John had spent 40 years as a production worker for General Motors, and Laura was a secretary for the same corporation. Their decision to leave Michigan 3 years ago was based on their desire to be closer to two of their three children. Since their move, the following situations have become problematic:

- Leaving friends of many years and knowing no one other than their children has made developing new friendships difficult.
- The difference in cost of living between Michigan and Arizona has placed a strain on their fixed retirement income.
- Although they see their children more often, they have growing feelings of resentment and rejection. Their children often are too busy to include John and Laura in their activities.
- Both John and Laura have had trouble filling the large amount of leisure time with significant activities. Most of their life has been structured around work, so they seem to have no model for structuring it around leisure activities. Both have tried to find part-time work, but the employment conditions and their age have worked against them.
- The loneliness they feel and the separation from familiar locations and friends are creating stress, which impacts both their health and their relationship. They often discuss returning to Michigan but are concerned about the financial outlay such a move would require.

In attempting to deal with the myriad of physiological, situational, and psychological changes that accompany the aging process, elderly persons turn for assistance to family, friends, the church, physicians, counselors, and state and federal agencies. In doing so, they encounter both personal and societal barriers, including:

- Lack of recognition of the need for help.
- Personal values and fears regarding seeking assistance.
- Ageism on the part of helping professionals.
- Society's negative attitudes regarding the elderly population.
- Practical considerations such as transportation and financial limitations.
- Lack of awareness of existing support services.
- Family pressure to keep problems within the family.

These factors place the elderly at risk—not only based upon personal attitudes and values that keep them from seeking needed assistance but also from lack of attention by the many professionals who could serve this population. Counselors are part of this professional service group and, based upon demographic projections, will more and more see elderly persons as clients. Therefore, counselors must become aware of what techniques and interventions are most appropriate and how to expand upon their existing skills to better serve this population.

Counselors who work with elderly clients need specialized training in the area of gerontological counseling, which places special emphasis on areas such as personal and social values related to the aging process and foundational information regarding the physiological, psychological, and sociological aspects of aging. In the area of personal and social values, counselors should be exposed to a series of values clarification activities to aid them in understanding the values they place on their own aging and what values are prevalent within the larger social context. Educational seminars and workshops such as those conducted through the American Association of Counseling and Development, the Association for Adult Development and Aging, and the American Association of Gerontology would be most helpful to counselors who wish to work with this population. Many universities are adding programs in gerontology to address these same issues.

Understanding the aging process from a physiological, psychological, and sociological perspective is mandatory for anyone interested in working in this field. Information of this type is available in gerontological programs in higher education, through workshops, and through the professional literature. A comprehensive overview of this area can be found in Ganikos (1979) and Cunningham and Brookbank (1988).

COUNSELING STRATEGIES

A basic premise of this chapter is that a common core of counseling strategies is applicable across the lifespan. Skills in rapport building, active listening, and the ability to demonstrate caring, support, respect, and acceptance are as applicable to the client of 8 as the client of 80. According to Waters (1984):

Regardless of the age of your client, you as a counselor need to communicate clearly, respond both to thoughts and feelings, ask effective questions, and confront when appropriate. It also is important to help people clarify their values and their goals in order to make decisions and develop action plans to implement these decisions. (p. 63)

Counseling is not age-related. The goal of all counseling is to assist individuals in problem resolution and behavior change, regardless of age. When working with elderly clients, counselors need not put aside their basic skills and techniques and adopt a new set. What they have to do is to develop an awareness of the aging process and the factors within it that may necessitate adapting existing skills and techniques to more effectively meet the needs of elderly clients.

This kind of adaptation is best understood in terms of a set of general counseling strategies that perhaps are more applicable to older than younger clients. These strategies are directed at compensating for some of the changing life situations and barriers listed earlier. The strategies have general applicability to both individual and group counseling.

1. Counselors should expend more effort in enhancing the dignity and worth of elderly clients. Based upon ageist attitudes within society and often within the helping professions, elderly clients often are led to believe that their value is less than that of their younger counterparts. Counselors will have to devote time and energy in restoring self-esteem

and encouraging clients to review their successes, accomplishments, and positive aspects of their changing lifestyles.

For example, counselors could spend time in life review activities emphasizing the positive events in the individual's life. These might include the successful rearing of children, career recognition, charitable activities, educational achievements, or perhaps the individual's ability to survive various crises successfully across the lifespan. Too often these are forgotten in the midst of the day-to-day struggles of aging.

2. Counselors must expend more effort in "selling" the client on the positive benefits to be derived from counseling. Based upon long-established values and attitudes, elderly clients may view counseling and seeking the assistance of counselors as a sign of weakness and thus place little value on the positive results of the counseling process. The counselor will have to reinforce the client's seeking assistance and demonstrate, through actions, the positive results that are possible through counseling.

   Counselors wishing to respond to this aspect may want to identify a presenting concern of the clients that can be dealt with in a timely manner. A client who needs medical attention could receive an immediate referral to a physician; a client who would benefit from a legal opinion may be referred to a lawyer; a person who has a need for assistance with food or housing might be guided in interfacing with the appropriate social agency in an expedient manner. Demonstrating that results can be obtained expeditiously should reinforce the elderly client's view of the positive results of the counseling process. Further support for this strategy can be found in Sargent (1980).

3. The counselor has to attend more to the physical environment of counseling than might be necessary with younger clients. Based upon decreasing physical competencies, attention must be directed at factors such as noise distractions and counselor voice levels if clients have a hearing loss, adequate lighting for those with visual impairments, furniture that will enhance clients' physical comfort, thermostatic control to protect against extremes in either heat or cold, office accessibility, and the removal of items that impair movement. Shorter sessions also may be appropriate because of the difficulty elderly people may have in sitting in one position for a long time. Further support for this strategy can be found in Waters (1984).

4. For the issue of counselor-client involvement and the role of counselor as advocate, the counselor may have to take a much more active/doing role to better serve elderly clients. This active/doing may involve making telephone contact with agencies to secure answers to clients' concerns; bringing family members into the counseling process to inform them of ways they can assist the client; securing legal opinions from attorneys to

provide clients with answers to pressing questions; or contacting social support personnel who offer services such as meals on wheels, involvement in senior centers, or selection of full-care residence facilities. It could entail transporting the client or taking counseling services to the client, as would be the case with shut-ins or those who are incapacitated. This active/doing role allows the counselor not only to demonstrate the positive aspects of counseling but also to be an advocate. In the advocate role the counselor represents the client in dealing with the myriad of bureaucratic systems that often confuse or frighten the elderly.

5. The counselor should establish short-term goals that are clear-cut and emphasize the client's present life situation. Many of the problems that the elderly client presents deal with day-to-day living situations. These problems often center on physical condition, use of medication, costs of medication, decreasing financial assets, housing, transportation, and daily interaction with a variety of social agencies designed to assist the elderly. In aiding the client to find solutions to these problems, not only will it reinforce positive aspects of the counseling process but also will encourage the client to continue seeking assistance.

6. Based upon changing life circumstances, elderly people often are forced into a more dependent lifestyle. The reasons vary from client to client but most likely relate to health, finances, and family. The counselor has to realize that a certain degree of dependence may benefit elderly clients and that they need to be encouraged until they are ready to assume an independent role once again. For example, elderly clients with health problems may have to depend on family, friends, and other professionals until they regain their health. The counselor could reinforce this dependence and, at an appropriate time, help the client move back to a more independent role. Most elderly people have functioned somewhat independently a large portion of their adult lives. They often need assistance in seeing that it is still possible.

7. The counselor must be sensitive to the possible age differential and the differing cultural, environmental, and value orientations that this difference in age may denote. With the exception of peer counseling, counselors are usually much younger than their clients. This age difference could precipitate client resistance, anger, or resentment. The counselor has to be aware of this and learn to deal with it appropriately. The counselor, based upon his or her attitudes regarding aging, may have some of the same reactions. Dealing with this at the beginning should enhance the probability of success.

The counselor also should have some perspective on client's "place in history" and the significance this place holds in determining values and attitudes. Individuals whose significant developmental period took place during the depression years of the 1930s or the war years of the 1940s may well be espousing values characteristic of that time. Elderly clients not uncommonly held the following values and attitudes:

- Lack of trust in banks and other financial institutions because of losses suffered during the depression.
- Belief in the rightness of war, stemming from the patriotic national attitude that surrounded the United States involvement in World War II. This attitude justified war as a means of saving the world from Nazi domination.
- Ultimate trust in the family doctor and a willingness to accept his or her diagnosis, medication, and treatment regimen without question. This may result from a history of being treated by a family doctor who saw all members of the family for all disorders.
- A belief in one's ability to solve his or her own problems and the idea that seeking assistance is a sign of weakness.
- A belief in the strength of the family and the expectation that it will provide for them when they are in need.

The counselor should accept these values and attitudes and not expect the person to easily incorporate values and attitudes descriptive of the 1990s.

In using diagnostic tools with this population, the counselor must exercise caution. Unlike their younger counterparts, older persons have limited recent experience with test instruments, and their use may create undue anxiety. Many of the diagnostic instruments applied in mental health have not been normed for this population and, therefore, the results obtained are questionable. Also, many of these instruments contain content that is inappropriate for this population. Elderly clients often do not understand the rationale for standardized tests or many of the test-taking procedures.

A second point that should be taken into consideration in using standardized instruments with an elderly population is the individual's physical ability to attend to completion of the instruments. Failing eyesight may make reading for extended periods fatiguing. The length of time a person might have to remain stationary to complete standardized instruments could prove physically uncomfortable for the elderly. Too, test completion demands concentration, and the elderly often complain about their inability to remember or to concentrate for any length of time. Prior to using diagnostic tools, the counselor should evaluate if this is the best means of gaining the types of data needed. For more information regarding the problems associated with this strategy, a review of Gallagher, Thompson, and Levy (1980) is recommended.

COUNSELING PROCEDURES

Based on the premise that counseling is not age-related, all theoretical systems, techniques, and intervention styles would appear to have applicability to the older population and currently are being utilized. In a review of the outcome research in counseling older persons, Wellman and Mccormack (1984) reported the results of more than 90 studies. In this report a myriad of approaches—including psychoanalytic (Brink, 1979), developmental (Kastenbaum, 1968), brief task-centered therapy (Saferstein, 1972), behavior management (Nigl & Jackson, 1981), and cognitive behavioral (Meichenbaum, 1974)—were cited. The results are varied, but all approaches seem to support the use of psychological intervention with this population.

According to Wellman and Mccormack (1984), much of the research reviewed suffered from methodological weaknesses centering on controls, sampling, and sound theoretical rationales. They indicate, however, that the following procedures seem to hold promise in working with the elderly:

1. Regular continued contact.
2. Brief psychotherapy approaches.
3. Task-oriented and structured activities.
4. High levels of client involvement.
5. Multidisciplinary team and peer counseling.
6. Group work.

Based upon the Wellman and Mccormack review, the following goals for counseling with the elderly appear often:

1. to decrease anxiety and depression
2. to reduce confusion and loss of contact with reality
3. to increase socialization and improve interpersonal relationships
4. to improve behavior within institutions
5. to cope with crisis and transitional stress
6. to become more accepting of self and the aging process. (p. 82)

These six counseling goals are indicative of the types of concerns that elderly persons often bring to the counseling setting. Many of these are not unique to the elderly. Anxiety, depression, socialization, interpersonal relationships, and coping with crisis and transitional stress are as applicable to the young as they are to the older person. The reason that these appear often for the elderly client rests more in the challenges that the aging process presents. Changing roles, geographical transitions, physical decline, and changing peer and family relationships compound those problems for the elderly, and do so in a somewhat telescoped time period. The more unique aspects of this listing for the elderly are the ones dealing with reality orientation, institutional behavior, and acceptance of the aging process. Elderly clients, more than their younger counterparts, will have to confront many realities in effectively facing the aging process. Institutional confinement, confusion, loss of degrees of reality, and lowering degrees of self-acceptance are often the outcomes of the aging process. In combination, these six areas speak to the need for increased counseling support for this population.

Both individual and group approaches to working with the elderly are supported in the literature (Myers & Shelton, 1987; Barry, 1984; Glass & Grant, 1983; Pelsma & Flanagan, 1986; Allred & Dobson, 1987; Kelly & Remley, 1987). Which is the most appropriate depends upon the client, the nature of the presenting problem, the resources available to both the client and the counselor, and the setting in which the counseling takes place.

Along with the concerns identified earlier, the counselor should keep in mind that elderly clients bring to treatment the same variety of problems that younger clients present. Issues dealing with alcohol and drug use, abuse, loss, family, marriage, divorce, suicide, and career and avocational areas often are found to be continuing concerns in elderly people. Although data are not available addressing this commonality of presenting problems, counselors working with the elderly should keep in mind that although the aging process brings with it certain unique problems, ineffective behavior patterns developed over the lifespan do not magically disappear as one reaches age 65. Counselors who select an individual approach have a variety of techniques, intervention strategies, and theoretical systems available to them; the only limitations seem to be those related to the counselor's skill and expertise.

Counselors selecting a group approach with elderly clients can gain a great deal of information and direction from reviewing articles such as Waters (1984), Capuzzi and Gross (1980), Burnside (1978), and Capuzzi, Gossman, Whiston, and Surdam (1979). Those authors suggest special considerations for working with elderly people in groups, such as:

- Shorter meeting times to accommodate for the physical discomfort that elderly persons might face when they are required to sit for long periods.
- Time parameters to meet the needs for routine and consistency, which are important to many elderly people.
- Member selection and group size addressing issues such as age cohorts, similarity of concerns, and smaller groups than otherwise might be formed, to reduce confusion and to enable better communication for those who are hearing impaired.

Those authors also give suggestions for the types of groups that have been utilized successfully with this population. Some of the advantages of the group approach, as mentioned, include discovering common bonds, teaching social skills, alleviating loneliness, offering mutual assistance, presenting an opportunity to share feelings, and providing shared purposes.

Whether selecting an individual or a group modality for working with elderly clients, specific approaches to both individual and group work have been designed to deal with the elderly population from a rehabilitative perspective. The needs of an individual in a life-care facility may be quite different from those of an elderly person who maintains an independent lifestyle.

For Clients in Life-Care Facilities

In working with the individual in a life-care facility, the following selected approaches have proven to be helpful:

REALITY ORIENTATION THERAPY

This form of therapy, which combines both individual and group work, is directed at the individual who has experienced memory loss, confusion, and time-place-person disorientation. The thrust of reality orientation therapy is the repetition and learning of basic personal information such as the individual's name, the place, the time of day, day of the week and date, the next meal, time of bath, and so on. If utilized within the care facility, it should be adopted by all persons who have contact with the elderly person.

Instructional programs in reality orientation therapy usually are provided to the entire staff within a care facility, done on-site either by a professional staff member or by someone the institution employs. Providing this training on-site allows the staff to practice the skills under direct supervision and allows for more immediate incorporation into the existing program. On a formal basis, reality orientation therapy is done in a class setting. Informally, it is done on a 24-hour basis by those who have contact with the individual.

MILIEU THERAPY

This approach, which may use both individual and group work, is based on the concept that the social milieu of the care facility itself can be the instrument for treatment. the environment is organized to provide a more homelike atmosphere, with the individual taking more responsibility, trying new skills, and being involved in decision making in a somewhat safe environment.

A care facility utilizing milieu therapy gives the individual an opportunity to take more responsibility for his or her environment. In doing this, the facility encourages the individual in making decisions regarding routine, environmental decor, rules and regulations governing behavior, and in determining what role the individual will play in overall operation of the facility. In this environment, individuals are encouraged to utilize their skills, talents, and knowledge to benefit not only themselves but other people and the facility as well. Increased levels of activity, improvement in self-care, and increasing degrees of self-worth have been reported.

REMINISCING GROUPS

These groups, designed to encourage the sharing of memories within groups of six to eight members, are conducted in both institutional and noninstitutional settings. This approach is similar to the "life review" process and, in a group setting, enhances a cohort effect, helping members to identify and share accomplishments, tribulations, and viewpoints, while at the same time increasing opportunities for socialization.

For example, elderly persons who are suffering from low self-esteem and diminished concepts of self might benefit from a group experience in which the "life review" process is directed at bringing out discussion of the successes and accomplishments in each of their lives. Because of the negative impact that the aging process often engenders, individuals have lost perspective as to positive impacts they have had and can continue to have on significant others. Often music, visual aids, and memorabilia aid in stimulating group discussion.

REMOTIVATION THERAPY

This approach, which can be done in either a group or an individual setting, encourages the moderately confused elderly patient to take a renewed interest in his or her surroundings by focusing attention on the simple, objective features of everyday life. Common topics, such as pets, gardening, and cooking, are selected, and the clients are encouraged to relate to these topics by drawing upon their own life experiences.

For Independent Clients

In working with the greater percentage of older people who continue to live independent lives, self-help groups, assertiveness training groups, growth groups, support groups, and the variety of special topic groups find equal applicability in work with the elderly as they do with a younger client population. Is counseling with the elderly different from work with younger clients? The answer seems to be one of selective emphasis. In both individual and group work, all counseling interventions are applicable to the elderly, but the counselor has to adapt his or her approach to accommodate the unique factors that parallel the aging process.

RECOMMENDATIONS

As the number of elderly persons increases, more and more of them will be seen in counseling. Counselors who have been trained, through education, personal values clarification, and skills adaptation, to work primarily with a younger population should be prepared to work with the elderly. The following recommendations address these issues:

1. Counselors should secure information regarding the aging process and the physiological, sociological, and psychological factors that impact this population. This knowledge, gained through formal education or through workshops and reading, will equip counselors to serve this population better. Understanding the normal/expected aspects of the aging process is important so this information can be applied to educate and facilitate the effective transition of the client from one life stage to another.

2. Counselors must clarify their values regarding aging, from both a personal and another perspective. Ageism exists not only in our society in general but also more specifically within the helping professions. Values clarification, as this relates to the elderly, is mandatory for anyone who wishes to work with this population. Counselor problems in this area stem from lack of acceptance of our own aging, our difficulties in dealing with aging relatives, confrontation with our own destiny, and ageist attitudes that tell us younger clients hold more promise for change. Attitudes such as these, if not confronted prior to service delivery, will impede, not enhance, success with the elderly.

3. In adapting current skills, counselors will have to pay more attention to the physical setting in which counseling takes place. What is needed is a facilitative environment that will encourage, not discourage, elderly clients' participation. Attention should be given to areas such as: (a) ease of access based on physical condition; (b) adequate temperature control to provide for the changing body temperatures associated with aging; (c) differing time parameters that take into account decreased attention spans; and (d) reduction of noise levels to accommodate older people who have hearing deficits.

4. Counselors should view their role with elderly clients from an advocacy perspective. They will have to be more actively involved with the client's day-to-day life. The image of the client who appears for his or her appointment at a specified time once a week does not always fit for the elderly. Counselors may have to leave their offices to go to the client; they may have to transport the client to other social agencies in an attempt to surmount many of the bureaucratic barriers that exist for the elderly; and they may have to seek the assistance of family and peers. As with any at-risk population, efforts to reduce the risk call for more active participation.

5. Counselors who have been trained and are used to working with younger populations sometimes have fears and apprehensions about involvement with the elderly. At times, apprehensions associated with their relationships with their own aging relatives are transferred to their

elderly clients. As counselors gain more experience with the elderly, they should begin to see the extent of similarity across the life span, and this will do much to reduce the initial fears and apprehensions.

6. Counselors should use their elderly clients' longevity factor to advantage. These individuals have proven qualities of survival. They have developed coping strategies that counselors can call upon to work on improving self-esteem, interpersonal relations, family problems, loneliness, and a myriad of other concerns representative of this population. The counselor should reinforce these survival/coping qualities to aid elderly clients in dealing with their current life situations.

The common theme of these recommendations is that counselors must pay more attention to, and show more concern for, elderly people. Counselors must recognize their unique needs and, more important, treat them as fully deserving of the care counselors provide for younger people. Unfortunately, our society and mental health professionals have not always followed those principles. Perhaps counselors need to remind themselves that how they treat elderly people is how they deserve to be treated if they are fortunate enough to arrive at this stage of life.

REFERENCES

Allred, G., & Dobson, J. (1987). Remotivation group interaction: Increasing children's contact with the elderly. *Elementary School Guidance & Counseling, 21*(3), 216–220.

Barry, J. (1984). Responsibility-inducing interventions with older clients. *Journal of Counseling & Development, 63*(1), 51–52.

Brink, T. L. (1979). *Geriatric psychotherapy.* New York: Human Sciences Press.

Burnside, I. M. (1978). *Working with the elderly: Group process and technique.* North Scituate, MA: Duxbury Press.

Capuzzi, D., Gossman, L., Whiston, S., & Surdam, J. (1979). Group counseling for aged women. *Personnel & Guidance Journal, 57*(6), 306–309.

Capuzzi, D., & Gross, D. (1980). Group work with the elderly: An overview for counselors. *Personnel & Guidance Journal, 59*(4), 206–211.

Cavallaro, M., & Ramsey, M. (1988). Ethical issues in gerocounseling. *Counseling & Values, 32*(3), 221–227.

Cunningham, W., & Brookbank, J. (1988). *Gerontology.* New York: Harper & Row.

Gallagher, D., Thompson, L. W., & Levy, S. M. (1980). Clinical psychological assessment of older adults. In L. W. Poon (Ed.), *Aging in the 1980's* (pp. 120–138). Washington, DC: American Psychological Association.

Ganikos, M. L. (Ed.). (1979). *Counseling the aged.* Falls Church, VA: American Personnel & Guidance Association.

Gilkison, B., & Drummond, R. (1988), Academic self-concept of older adults in career transition. *Journal of Employment Counseling, 25*(1), 24–29.

Glass, J., & Grant, K. (1983). Counseling in the later years. *Personnel & Guidance Journal, 62*(4), 210–218.

Gross, D. (1987). Aging and addiction: Perspective and recommendations. *Arizona Counseling Journal. 12*(1), 29–35.

Kart, C., Metress, E., & Metress, S. (1988). *Aging health and society.* Boston/Portola Valley: Jones & Bartlett Publishers.

Kastenbaum, R. (1968). Perspectives on the development and modification of behavior in the aged: A developmental field perspective. *Gerontologist, 8,* 280–283.

Kelly, S., & Remley, T. (1987). Understanding and counseling elderly alcohol abusers. *AMHCA Journal, 9*(2). 105–113.

Meichenbaum, D. (1974). Self-instructional strategy training: A cognitive prosthesis for the aged. *Human Development, 17,* 173–280.

Myers, J. (1988). The mid/late life generation gap: Adult children with aging parents. *Journal of Counseling & Development, 66*(7), 331–335.

Myers, J., & Shelton, B. (1987). Abuse and older persons: Issues and implications for counselors. *Journal of Counseling & Development, 65*(7), 376–380.

Nigl, A. J., & Jackson, B. (1981). A behavior management program to increase social responses in psychogeriatric patients. *Journal of the Geriatric society, 29,* 92–95.

Pelsma, D., & Flanagan, M. (1986). Human relations training for the elderly. *Journal of Counseling & Development, 65*(1), 52–53.

Saferstein, S. (1972). Psychotherapy for geriatric patients. *New York State Journal of Medicine, 72,* 2743–2748.

Sargent, S. S. (Ed.). (1980). *Nontraditional therapy and counseling with the aging.* New York: Springer.

Siegel, J., & Davidson, M. (1984). *Demographic and socioeconomic aspects of aging in the United States* (Current Population Reports, Special Studies Series P-23, No. 138). Washington, DC: U.S. Department of Commerce, Bureau of the Census.

Sterns, H., Weiss, D., & Perkins, S. (1984). A conceptual approach to counseling older adults and their families. *Counseling Psychologist, 12*(2), 55–61.

Waters, E. (1984). Building on what you know: Techniques for individual and group counseling with older people. *Counseling Psychologist, 12*(2), 63–74.

Wellman, F., & Mccormack, J. (1984). Counseling with older persons: A review of outcome research. *Counseling Psychologist, 12*(2), 91-96.

RELATED READINGS

Bohm, L. C., & Rodin, J. (1985). Aging and the family. In D. C. Turk & R. D. Kerns (Eds.), *Health, illness, and families: A life-span perspective* (pp. 279–310). New York: John Wiley & Sons.

Hansson, R. O., Nelson, R. E., Carver, M. D., Nee Smith, D. H., Dowling, E. M., Fletcher, W. L., & Suhr, P. (1990). Adult children with frail elderly parents: When to intervene? *Family Relations, 38,* 153–158.

Mercier, J. M., Paulson, L., & Morris, E. W. (1988). rural and urban elderly: Differences in the quality of the parent-child relationship. *Family Relations, 37,* 68972.

Qualls, S. H. (1988). Problems in families of older adults. In N. Epstein, S. E. Schlesinger, & W. Dryden (Eds.), *Cognitive-behavioral therapy with families* (pp. 215–253). New York: Brunner/Mazel.

Waters, E. B., & Goodman, J. (1990). *Empowering older adults: Practical strategies for counselors.* San Francisco: Jossey-Bass.

Weiler, P. G. (Issue Ed.). (1988). Aging and health promotion. Special issue of *Family & community Health, 11*(3), whole issue.

13

Counseling and Child Abuse: A Developmental Perspective

Judith Cooney

Anger in a house is like a worm in a plant.

Talmud

Child abuse is a term that has been defined by every state, the federal government, and a myriad of professionals. The general public defines child abuse as something other people do to their children. Abusive parents also believe that abuse is something *other* people do. Thus, parents who rely on spanking for discipline would not include spanking in their definitions of abuse. Those who spank with objects (spoons, switches, belts, hangers, electrical cords, fan belts) do not consider this abusive behavior. Sexually abusive parents describe what they do to their children as teaching, training, initiating, or preparing a child for adulthood.

Despite the unwillingness of any parent to admit to being abusive, the number of reported cases of abuse and neglect increases each year. It is not possible to determine if these numbers reflect an actual increase in the incidence of abuse or represent a heightened community awareness of reporting responsibilities.

All states have mandated reporting laws that define, in general terms, the reportable conditions for abuse and neglect. The trend in revising these laws is to enlarge the group of people required to report (Education Commission of the States, 1977). Included in reporting laws is the general definition of child abuse as the emotional, physical and/or sexual maltreatment of a minor by a parent or an

225

adult caregiver. In some states (Illinois, for example), "minor" may include mentally handicapped adults who have the mental age of a child. Definitions of neglect also are included in mandated reporting laws. Child abuse is an act of commission; neglect is an act of omission. Family dynamics and treatment procedures for neglected children differ from those related to abused children.

Whether in private practice or employed in schools or agencies, counselors are mandated reporters. They deal with both victims and perpetrators of abuse. To be effective, counselors must understand the nature of child abuse and its developmental effects. Although the term "child abuse" emerged in the 1960s, the problem is much older.

HISTORICAL PERSPECTIVE: EMOTIONAL ABUSE

The history of emotional abuse is difficult to document. Novels recounting the experiences of children in work houses and orphanages give some clues about emotional maltreatment of children in the 18th and 19th centuries. The industrialized society used children as cheap labor. Those children faced long hours and dangerous conditions with no laws to protect them. The emotional abuse that occurred in conjunction with physical and sexual abuse in the past can only be imagined. What were the thoughts of a child about to be sacrificed to ensure a bountiful harvest or a successful business? What were the feelings of a child sold into slavery or prostitution?

To this day, emotional abuse is difficult to identify and document. For this reason, the courts investigated it or dealt with it, for the most part, as a secondary effect of physical abuse or neglect (Garbarino, Guttmann, & Seeley, 1986).

HISTORICAL PERSPECTIVE: PHYSICAL ABUSE

As tempting as it may be for some to blame physical abuse on drugs, alcohol, televised violence, or junk food, the reality is that child abuse has existed as long as there have been children and adults. Radbill (1974) has pointed out that, throughout the ages, physical maltreatment of children has been justified on religious or educational grounds. Children were beaten to drive out the devil. Whippings on Innocents Day in England were meant to remind children of the death of infants under King Herod's decree.

The Bible includes many references to the harsh treatment and sacrifice of children. *Proverbs* 13:24 states: "He that spareth the rod hateth his son, but he that loveth him correcteth him betimes." This has been abbreviated over centuries to "spare the rod; spoil the child" and has been used as a justification for everything from corporal punishment in the schools to ritualized beatings by religious cults. The Old Testament is replete with stories of cannibalism and the sacrificing of young children to appease an angry God. Infanticide is a recurring Biblical theme, as evidenced by Herod's slaying of the innocents and the story of the infant Moses escaping the Pharaoh's death sentence.

Piers (1978) has pointed out that infanticide always has been associated with famines, war, and hopelessness. Infants have been considered less than human. In the Middle Ages and well into the 19th century, wet nurses were commonplace in Europe; mothers who could gain some income by nursing children of the wealthy routinely disposed of their own newborn infants. No questions were asked about the whereabouts of these children. Unwed mothers in Europe faced a terrible dilemma. If they were found out, they would be excommunicated from the church and forced to live as outcasts; if they killed their infants and were discovered, they would be put in a sack and thrown into a river or decapitated (Chase, 1975). Female babies were considered a curse rather than a blessing in many societies. In India, China, and Papua, the killing of females continued into the 20th century. The role of the geisha in Japan provided an option for parents of females there. Salisbury (1969) described the disappearance of children who ventured outside during the World War II siege of Leningrad; they were victims of a starving population, not a foreign invader.

Killing deformed children was an acceptable practice in ancient Rome, Greece, and Egypt. Radbill (1974) reported that in 16th-century Europe, Martin Luther advocated drowning mentally defective infants whom he considered to be instruments of the devil. During this same period, children were buried alive in the foundations of new buildings to ensure the longevity of the buildings.

Children have been mutilated to fulfill specific societal roles. Castration guaranteed "safe" guards for a master's harem, as well as high voices for church choirs. Parents have mutilated their children for begging purposes. It is suspected that such practices continue today in impoverished nations.

Acceptability of violence toward children has been a theme of many nursery rhymes, children's songs, and fairy tales (Chase, 1975; Walters, 1975). The original versions of *Hansel and Gretel, Snow White* and *Little Red Riding Hood* all dealt with children who were destined to be devoured. The words to "Rock-a-Bye, Baby" have been put to a lovely melody, but the image of the baby and cradle falling from the treetop does not facilitate sweet dreams. Children's jump rope songs often refer to beatings or whippings. Even the "old woman who lived in a shoe" whipped all of her children before sending them to bed.

HISTORICAL PERSPECTIVE: SEXUAL ABUSE

Sexual contact between children and adults in ancient Rome and Greece was a common practice (Mrazek, 1981). Boys in particular were victimized by teachers, masters, and other adult men. Boy brothels flourished in the cities, with community approval. Epstein (1967) has pointed out the inconsistency of ancient Jewish law regarding adult-child sexual relations. Although sex with young children was not considered a serious offense, the penalty for sexual contact with a child over age 9 was death by stoning. The attitude that a young child is less than a person continues today in the United States, Europe, Sri Lanka, and many Moslem countries, where child prostitution and pornography are officially condemned but unofficially tolerated (Kempe & Kempe, 1984).

The incest taboo has not been as universal as one might believe. Marriages between parents and their children, as well as siblings and first cousins, were encouraged in royal families. This was especially true in Egypt, India, Persia, Peru, and Hawaii. Those marriages ensured that family riches would not be shared with outsiders. Throughout the Middle Ages, kings and popes were openly involved in incestuous relationships. Through the end of the 19th century, incest was accepted practice among some groups in the United States (Cooney, 1987; Justice & Justice, 1979; Mrazek, 1981).

FORMS OF ABUSE AND THEIR EFFECTS

As the literature reveals, all forms of child abuse have existed throughout time. Historically, children have been treated as the property of their parents. They could be bought, sold, beaten, or killed depending upon the whims of their adult caregivers. Children have had neither rights nor legal protection. The fact that hundreds of thousands of children are the subject of all forms of abuse every year in the United States is an indication that, for many, the status of children has undergone little change from antiquity.

While considering each form of abuse separately, it is important to be aware that often they are not separate. The child who is physically or sexually abused usually is emotionally abused as well. Preceding a physical assault on a child, the caregiver is likely to have been screaming at the child, shouting names, or swearing. Perhaps these adults have threatened the child with physical harm before the actual attack. It is difficult to conceive of physical abuse preceded by silence. Thus, the physically abusive parent is probably an emotional abuser as well. I have found that helping abusive parents to stop physically abusing a child is relatively easy; helping parents to stop emotionally abusing their children is much more difficult. This requires learning an entire new method of communications.

Sexual abuse also is accompanied by emotional abuse. The abusive adult may threaten the child with a variety of punishments that keep the child from telling anyone about the abuse. Threats of destroying the family, sending the victim to an orphanage or jail, killing the nonabusive spouse, or physically harming the child are typical. Even more pervasive are the confusion, guilt, and subtle pressure imposed by a supposedly loving parent.

The combination of sexual abuse and other physical abuse directed by an adult toward the same victim is rare (Allen, 1980; Bass & Thornton, 1983; Brady,

1979), although the threat of physical abuse may be implied, stemming from the physical abuse of other children in the family. The message to the sexually abused child is: "Cooperate with me or suffer my wrath like the others!"

Emotional Abuse

Most parents would admit that they have said something unkind or unfair to their children at a time of stress; later they felt guilty about this and apologized or retracted the statement. Although these incidents may be upsetting at the time, the child experiences no long-term harm. In contrast, emotional abuse implies a pattern of continual attacks on a child's self-esteem, self-confidence, sense of belonging, or safety. The child who is emotionally abused may be the recipient of constant criticism, threats, or embarrassment. He or she may be a scapegoat, treated as an unwelcome intruder in the family. *Cinderella* and, more recently, *Mommy Dearest* recount the pain of being a less-than-equal family member.

There are innumerable ways of emotionally abusing a child. Eleanor Roosevelt grew up hearing constant criticism of her parents by her custodial grandmother. The message was obvious: "They were no good, and neither are you." Her grandmother forced her to dress in unfashionable clothing and kept her from playing with other children. Eleanor was tutored at home and did not attend grade school.

Some emotionally abused children are compared constantly to higher achieving siblings or other relatives. They are taught that nothing they accomplish will ever be acceptable. Other children live under threat of abandonment, exile, or punishment. The parents tell them that they will leave them or send them to boarding school, an orphanage, or even a correctional facility.

DEVELOPMENTAL EFFECTS OF EMOTIONAL ABUSE

Early Childhood (0-6)

Young children are especially vulnerable to emotional abuse. Their world and their contacts with adults, other than parents, are extremely limited. At this stage in a child's development, parents are considered all-knowing. If they say the child is clumsy, stupid, bad, or ugly, it must be true. All threats, no matter how outlandish, are real to a young child. Because young children take statements literally, a threat to "give you away to the garbageman" or to "leave you in the shopping mall" is a source of constant worry.

Garbarino et al. (1986) indicate that the effects of psychological maltreatment at any stage will vary depending upon the severity of the abuse. Those authors use a mild, moderate, and severe continuum of abuse. Mild emotional abuse creates "the risk of limited psychic damage confined to one aspect of functioning" (p. 23). An example of this is a father who tells his daughter that she is her grandfather's least favorite grandchild because she is so clumsy. As a result, the child is tense and subdued whenever she is in the presence of her grandfather, but this behavior is not generalized to all contacts with adults.

Moderate emotional abuse "prevents a child from achieving minimal success in important settings" (p. 23). The most important setting for children is likely to be school. Children who live with criticism develop low self-esteem. They believe they are what their parents say they are. They come to school expecting not to do well. The labels applied by abusive parents become self-fulfilling prophecies.

Severe emotional maltreatment is so extreme that the recipient is "crippled in one or more of life's primary settings—work, love, and play" (p. 23). The child has no opportunity to develop self-confidence or a feeling of self-worth. He or she may not be able to relate to other children or to adults. The inability to function in a normal classroom may result in being placed in a special class for socially maladjusted or behavior disordered children. By rights, Eleanor Roosevelt would fit into the latter category. Her noteworthy accomplishments become more so in light of her miserable childhood.

Young children who experience mild emotional abuse may be fearful of specific people or places. When faced with these people or places, they may become agitated or withdrawn. They may seem "clingy" under specific circumstances. Those who are subjected to moderate emotional abuse may demonstrate low self-esteem. In school they will be reluctant to volunteer information. They are children whose presence or absence has no effect on the class. Prompting by the teacher is required to get them to participate in any activities. They are likely to be loners in school.

Children who experience severe emotional abuse may never reach the regular classroom, because preschool screening may result in their being placed in classes for the developmentally delayed. If they manage to be placed in a regular classroom, others will likely consider them weird or strange. They may exhibit extreme shyness and poor socialization skills. In all likelihood they will be referred to a special class, where their adjustment will be minimal. They will still be on the "outside"—fearful, shy, and alone.

Childhood (6-12)

Emotionally abused children continue to have no self-confidence. In elementary school they may begin to act out to conceal a sense of inadequacy. They may call others the names they are called at home or make threats that have been made to them. If a child has been scapegoated at home, he or she may attempt to scapegoat a younger child on the school bus or playground. These children have been taught to alienate others and are very good at it. If they receive praise or commendation, they find it difficult to believe. Still on the outside of the peer group, with little hope of being accepted, they are suspicious of anyone who attempts to befriend them.

Adolescence (12-18)

By the time emotionally abused children become teenagers, they have developed a role in school. They may be considered troublemakers or as invisible persons who get by—barely. As troublemakers and low-achievers, they finally may have some peer contacts. These peers also will have low self-esteem, low motivation, and hostility toward adults in authority who seem to them to be copies of their abusive parents. Or, if the teen has taken the role of invisible person, it requires that he or she not act out or call attention to himself or herself in any way. Invisible adolescents drift through school, do what is required, but have no personal attachment to anyone in the school. If they move, their classmates and teachers do not even notice that they are gone.

Adulthood (18+)

Emotionally abused adults continue to have a low self-image, persisting in the belief that they are undeserving and inadequate. Though their parents may no longer have contact with them, they tell themselves the same negative things they were told as children. If they think they are worthless, they attract a mate who will confirm their worthlessness. Women with low self-esteem are inclined to marry men who affirm their unworthiness by emotionally or physically abusing them (Langley & Levy, 1977). Threats from childhood may influence the victim's behavior as an adult. Fear of the dark or of being alone may still be present.

Just as in school, the adult may seek attention through negative behavior, or may choose to be invisible. Typically, adults who were physically abused as children continue to be emotionally abused by their parents. Established family rituals limit the adult's ability to escape the abuse.

TREATMENT OF EMOTIONAL ABUSE

The primary treatment in emotional abuse cases requires parental retraining. Individual or group parent education provides the abusive parent with alternative ways of communicating with children. Because the concept of learning an entirely new manner of speaking to a child may be overwhelming to parents, the retraining should focus on one or two changes at a time. The process of retraining is a gradual one, and backsliding is to be expected. Groups such as Parents Anonymous have been effective in helping abusive parents. Other structured groups such as Parent Effectiveness Training (PET), Active Parenting, and the Systematic Training for Effective Parenting (STEP) program also can be helpful. It is important to reinforce small accomplishments in this uphill battle.

The focus of treatment for children includes two basic procedures. The first is manipulating their environment. This involves retraining the parents and exposing the children to positive adults. The school counselor enlists the cooperation of the classroom teacher, gym teacher, principal, music teacher, and so on, to build a positive environment for the discouraged child. As an elementary school counselor, I found a great resource in the highly regarded school custodian. Assisting Faliero was a sought-after privilege. The other approach is more direct; individual or group counseling, or both, to enhance self-esteem and confidence.

At times parents are unwilling or unable to break their negative communication patterns. If this is the case, the next best thing is to surround the child with positive adults and minimize parental effect. Children may thrive in an 8-week summer camp. They also may benefit from an after-school program in which their strengths will be emphasized. Involvement in extracurricular activities should be encouraged. The reduced contact with parents may result in their being less hostile and abusive toward the child.

Adults who have low-esteem as the result of emotional abuse can benefit from group counseling, as well as parent education. The victims must learn more positive ways to communicate with their own children.

Physical Abuse

The generic definition of physical abuse included in most reporting laws is that physical abuse is the nonaccidental injury of a child by a parent or caregiver. "Child" is defined in most states as a person under the age of 18. The unwritten definition that many child protection investigators use is that, to be considered abuse, there must be marks on the child.

Every year in this country thousands of children die as a result of being abused by parents and caregivers. It has been estimated (O'Brien, 1980) that between 7 and 15 children die each day from physical abuse. Many more suffer permanent injury to the brain or central nervous system. The highest risk category of children likely to be killed or seriously injured are those under age 3 (Kempe & Kempe, 1978; O'Brien, 1980). Young children are less able to anticipate parental anger and have less mobility to escape injury than their older siblings do.

Many parents who abuse their children were themselves abused as children (Alford, Martin, & Martin, 1985; Kempe & Kempe, 1978; Walters, 1975). They have learned inappropriate ways to discipline children, and they repeat the pattern with their own children. But what has been learned can be unlearned. Abusive parents can be taught nonabusive methods of discipline. Parents Anonymous groups are especially effective for retraining abusive parents. These groups are free to any parent who chooses to attend. A professional sponsor is present as a resource for group members. Parents learn new ways of relating to their children, as well as ways to deal with their anger and to relate to other adults.

DEVELOPMENTAL EFFECTS OF PHYSICAL ABUSE

Early Childhood (0-6)

As indicated previously, young children are at great risk for serious injury or death resulting from physical abuse. Many of these children are not in school or preschool and therefore are not visible to people outside of the family. Kempe and

Kempe (1978) identified several sources of stress for families with young children. Problems related to feeding, crying, and toilet training seem to lead to much of the physical abuse directed toward young children. Children who refuse food or reject a bottle may have injuries to the mouth and face in particular; children who have experienced a tear in the lip area or uvula possibly have had a bottle or food container forced into their mouths.

Some parents interpret their child's crying as defiance or a hostile attack against them. Or parents may consider a crying baby to be an indicator of their being an inadequate parent. When a caregiver assigns to a child a negative motive for crying, the child is at risk for physical abuse. Beating, smothering, or throwing a child to make him or her stop crying are some of the ways abusive parents have attempted to deal with their reactions to the crying.

Toilet training becomes a race for some parents. They want their child to be trained at an earlier age than their nieces or nephews. When the child cannot meet unrealistic goals, the parent may attribute the failure to willfulness on the child's part. Children who wet the bed often are subjected to humiliation as well as abuse. Young children who receive burns, especially on the legs or buttocks, may have been punished for some failure in the toilet training process.

Physical abuse results in physical and emotional damage to children. As a result of abuse, young children may become physically or mentally handicapped. They may never reach their potential for learning or living because of what abusive parents have done to them. Less extreme abuse is less likely to be noticed. Bruises, human bite marks, abrasions, cigarette or other burns, broken bones, and internal injuries are some of the physical effects of abuse on young children.

The emotional effects of physical abuse are varied. Some young children may seem shy and withdrawn. They may physically cling to their parents. They also may appear tense and fearful, always looking to an adult for approval and reassurance. At times young children may appear overly compliant. They will do anything to please the adults around them. But they may lack the spontaneity of a child in trying to measure up to adult demands.

Some young children who have been abused become hostile and aggressive. They are cruel to other children and go out of their way to destroy others' belongings. Kempe and Kempe (1978) identified a connection between abuse and extreme hyperactivity in young children, citing disorganizing anxiety as the basis for hyperactivity.

Childhood (6-12)

As physically abused children get older, they become more adept at recognizing danger signals that a parent may display prior to abuse. The child may develop a repertoire of coping or avoidance behaviors to minimize the abuse incidents. With age comes more freedom to be away from home and out of reach of the abusive parent.

School plays an important role in protecting children from abuse. Physical separation of the child from the parent during the school day can alleviate some of the stress in the relationship. The fact that someone at school might see marks may deter some parental abuse. Conversely, some abuse is school-related; parents may abuse children as a reaction to bad grades or a negative report from a teacher. For these parents, their children are reflections of themselves and reminders of their own failures.

Again, no one pattern of behavior fits all abused children. Some become bullies during this period. They have learned that violence is the way to get what they want. Not every child who harasses others is an abused child, but the possibility that this is learned behavior should always be considered. Abused children may exhibit learning problems that warrant special services. Anxiety may affect their speech or motor functions. Some become withdrawn in the presence of an adult who resembles their abuser. For instance, a girl who expresses concern about having a male teacher in an upcoming grade may be physically or sexually abused by her father or other adult male.

Many abused children manifest no overt behaviors that would suggest their home lives are exceptional in any way. They do not talk about how they are punished, nor do they think of themselves as abused. They are more likely to think of themselves as bad children who cannot please their parents. This low self-image may affect their social relationships and their academic achievement.

Adolescence (12-18)

Physical abuse sometimes subsides during the teen years. Emotional abuse continues, but the adolescent spends less time at home and is more likely to have developed ways of avoiding parental wrath. Some adolescents escape by running away from the abusive environment. Others move in with friends or become emancipated. By adolescence the negative self-image is deeply ingrained. Physically abused children are still trying to please the parent who finds them unsatisfactory. In between incidents of physical or emotional abuse, the relationship with the abusive parent may seem similar to those in "normal" families. The normal times give the abused adolescent hope that things may be improving, but the next abusive attack temporarily shatters that hope.

Adulthood (18+)

The child who lives through physical abuse and survives to adulthood does so with physical and emotional scars. The cycle of abuse is continued in many instances by adults who have learned their parenting pattern from abusive parents. This cycle can be broken in several ways. One is that the adult who was abused marries someone from a very different family environment, and the spouse who was not abused teaches nonabusive child-rearing methods through example and discussion. Another means by which the cycle is broken is if the abused adult has had close contact with a nonabusive family. For instance, if a child from an abusive family spends summers with loving relatives or friends, alternatives to abuse can be learned.

Sometimes an adult who was abused seeks counseling because of fears related to dealing with children. The prognosis for anyone who seeks help prior to actually being abusive is very good. There is not a one-to-one correlation between a history of abuse and abusive parenting. Not all children who were abused become abusive parents. Not all parents who abuse were abused themselves. Walters (1975) described the *situational abuser*, who abuses because of a set of circumstances that comes together. For instance, a mother has three preschoolers. Her husband is promoted to a job that requires extensive travel. While he is away, a major snowstorm occurs, and the husband cannot return home. The wife cannot take the children outside, nor can visitors come out in the storm, which rages for days. At some point the washing machine breaks down, the children are restless, and the mother explodes. Regardless of the fact that she came from a loving environment, the stress of these circumstances results in a single incident, probably never to be repeated.

Adults who were abused as children may continue to have low self-esteem, which limits their choices and experiences. As adults they may still be trying to please the parents who abused them. They may continue to be subjected to emotional abuse from their parents. Often the parents are extremely critical of their grandchildren and the way they are being reared. The adult still feels like an unsuccessful child in the eyes of the parent.

TREATMENT OF PHYSICAL ABUSE

Children who have been physically abused may require medical treatment. After the physical problems have been tended to, the emotional damage must be confronted. They may be fearful of adults and ashamed that they have been bad and deserving of punishment. Counselors can assist classroom teachers in providing esteem-building experiences for abused children. Individual counseling to help the child deal with changes in the family, guilt, and anger may be indicated.

If their parents are receiving help, children will be confused by changes in the parent's behavior. Kids Anonymous groups are available in some areas for children of parents receiving help through Parents Anonymous. As they get older, children who have been abused need parenting education to learn alternatives to abusive parenting.

Abusive parents usually have many problems that create stress in their lives. These problems have to be identified so that necessary referrals can be made. As sources of stress are identified and eliminated, the possibility that a parent will continue to abuse becomes more remote.

Sexual Abuse

Sexual abuse has been defined as "sexual contact with a child by an adult or other person in a position of authority or control over the child" (Bulkley, 1982, p.

3). Not limited to sexual intercourse, sexual abuse encompasses a range of sexual activity including genital exposure, fondling, forced touching, inappropriate kissing, oral sex, and intercourse. Typically, sexual abuse occurs over a period of years with gradual escalation of sexual demands. If intercourse occurs, it is likely to begin in puberty or prepuberty.

Because the effects of sexual abuse are much more subtle than those of physical abuse, sexual abuse is underreported. The presence of a sexually transmitted disease in a child is a conclusive indicator of sexual abuse. Other physical evidence may take the form of genital lesions or infections. Pregnancy of a minor can result from sexual abuse. For the most part, however, the effects of sexual abuse are emotional rather than physical. Mandated reporters most often become aware of sexual abuse because the victim tells them about it rather than that the reporter observes specific indicators.

Statistics indicate that one of four girls and one of four or five boys will be sexually abused before reaching age 18 (Waterman & Lusk, 1986). Previous estimates (Giaretto, 1982) indicated one of seven boys, but there is growing awareness that boys are victimized more frequently than anyone had imagined previously. Boys are less likely than girls to report sexual abuse, for several reasons. They have been taught that they are supposed to take care of themselves, and asking for help implies an inability to do this. If the abuser is also a male, the male victim is concerned about being labeled a homosexual. If the abuser is female, the victim may be concerned about being taken seriously or believed. Because media attention has focused on father-daughter sexual abuse, male victims sometimes do not realize that the term applies to them as well.

The effects of sexual abuse vary depending on the duration of the abuse, the age of onset, and the closeness of the relationship of the victim to the abuser. A child who is abused by her father beginning at age 3 and continuing through high school is more likely to experience intense emotional reactions than is a child who was molested by a cousin on two occasions at age 8. Children who are sexually abused experience many of the following: the loss of childhood, guilt, low self-esteem, fear, confusion, depression, anger, inability to trust others, a sense of helplessness, and distorted attitudes toward sexuality (Cooney, 1987).

DEVELOPMENTAL EFFECTS OF SEXUAL ABUSE

Early Childhood (0-6)

Young children who are sexually abused exhibit a variety of behavioral indicators. Some appear very withdrawn and may seem retarded to the untrained observer. Others act out and display sexual behavior or knowledge beyond their years. Regression to earlier developmental stages may occur. Psychosomatic effects include stomachaches, headaches, encopresis, enuresis, and sleep disturbances (Lusk & Waterman, 1986). Depression and anxiety are common in these children. A preschool teacher might observe sexual overtures toward other children or adults or excessive masturbation.

Childhood (6-12)

Children who have been sexually abused may appear to be distracted or daydreaming in the classroom. They often have learning problems that require special attention. Because of their premature introduction to sexual activity, they feel older and different from their peers. As a result, they tend to be loners who have no friends or who seek older companions. The fact that they also have been warned of dire consequences if their secret becomes known discourages them from making close friendships with anyone.

In a two-parent family, the relationship between the victim and the nonabusing parent is usually poor. These children may express hostility or disinterest in the parent who has failed to protect them from abuse. Anxiety, depression, and low self-esteem contribute to social and educational failure. The prepubescent child may dress or behave seductively. Children are not naturally seductive. The child who acts out in this manner has been trained to be sexual. Such behavior should be explored rather than condemned.

Adolescence (12-18)

Sexual abuse often begins when the victim is 3 or 4 year old. It may continue into adulthood. Victims who reveal sexual abuse frequently do so while in junior high or high school. They may indirectly reveal abuse by acting out promiscuously, running away, abusing drugs or alcohol, or attempting suicide. They may directly disclose abuse to a caring teacher or counselor.

Several precipitating factors might motivate a sexual abuse victim to risk disclosure:

1. The abuser is beginning to demand full sexual intercourse. When the victim reaches puberty, the abuser rationalizes that she or he is now an adult.
2. The abuser becomes more possessive and restricts the victim more. The teen may not want to live with the rules and innuendos about dating. Other members of the family may attempt to intervene when the parent is obviously unreasonable, and the resulting family arguments make it more difficult for everyone to ignore the inappropriate relationship.
3. The teen becomes more informed about sexuality. The relationship that the abusing parent described as normal is no longer considered normal by the adolescent.
4. The teen becomes aware that the abuser is a threat to other siblings. Even though disclosure is painful, it may be the only recourse for the adolescent who wants to protect younger family members.

Adulthood (18+)

There is no magical age at which sexual abuse ceases. Some victims report that long after they left home, their abusers attempted to molest them when they returned for family visits (Allen, 1980; Bass & Thornton, 1983). Adults who have been abused may never feel safe or comfortable at family gatherings. If the secret has never been discussed, the victim may continue to experience tension, fear, and depression. If the victim has confronted the abuser and revealed the abuse to other family members, he or she may not have been believed, may have been labeled "crazy," and may have been ostracized by the family.

Childhood fears of the dark, nightmares, insomnia, eating disorders, and other somatic symptoms may continue throughout adulthood. Without intervention, the adult victim is likely to experience a deep sense of guilt and responsibility about the abuse. Sexual dysfunction is a common problem for these victims. Kempe and Kempe (1984) wrote that the number of adult prostitutes who report childhood sexual abuse is extremely high. The adult lifestyle is profoundly influenced by the trauma of abuse.

The intergenerational occurrence of sexual abuse is becoming clearer. Many mothers of sexually abused children were sexually victimized as children themselves (Damon & Waterman, 1986) and feel just as helpless to protect their children as they were to protect themselves. Men who were molested as children tend to identify with the abuser. The abusive father repeats what was done to him (Cooney, 1987).

TREATMENT OF SEXUAL ABUSE

The Child Sexual Abuse Treatment Program (CSATP) in Santa Clara County, California, provides a model for treatment of sexual abuse that has proven to be highly successful. The program, in existence since 1971, has provided services to over 10,000 families (Giaretto, 1981, 1982). There are satellites of CSATP throughout the United States.

A combination of individual, group, dyad, triad, and family counseling services are provided to the family members. There are also groups for adults who were molested as children. Play therapy, puppetry, and art therapy are used with young children. Great emphasis is placed on working with the nonabusing spouse and victim together. Giaretto has found that this relationship is the key to healing in the family. The longer it takes to reconstruct the parent-child bond, the less likely it is that the victim can return to the home.

The judicial system plays a significant role in the treatment program. The perpetrator is removed from the home, ordered to participate in the treatment program, and given conditional work release in many instances. Failure to participate in treatment can result in forfeiture of work release, as can attempts to contact the victim.

Parents attend Parents United groups; victims attend Daughters and Sons United groups. Eventually all members of the triad, and possibly other family members, are brought together. In this process the abuser must take full responsibility for what has been done to the child, and the nonabusive spouse must take responsibility for failing to protect the victim.

COUNSELOR RESPONSIBILITIES

Child abuse presents specific responsibilities for counselors in school or agency settings.

1. *Awareness*

Many myths are associated with the topic of child abuse. The professional counselor must be aware of the facts about abuse, including indicators, high-risk children, characteristics of abusive parents, reporting mandates, and community resources. Accurate information can be obtained through reading and participating in state and national professional conventions.

Each state has an office of child protection services, which publishes timely brochures and statistical reports. Counselors who are informed about abuse will be better prepared to recognize victims and perpetrators with whom they work. Counselors who know that abuse occurs across all socioeconomic levels will be alert to the possibility of abuse with all clients. They will be better prepared to approach the subject. Too often, adults who may have been in counseling for years have never broached the topic of their prior abuse with the counselor. Why? Because the counselor never asked! The aware counselor knows how and when to ask and is prepared to deal with the client who has been victimized.

2. *Reporting*

The requirement to report suspected abuse is both a legal and an ethical one (Knapp, 1983). Mandated reporters must report suspected abuse. They are not expected to investigate cases; this is the responsibility of the state protective service agency. At times counselors misunderstand the issue of confidentiality in reporting abuse; the counselor's legal responsibility takes precedence over the desire to provide confidentiality (Callis, Pope, & DePauw, 1982). The judicious counselor will make the exceptions to confidentiality clear from the outset of the counseling relationship. Reporting will be most effective if:

—the agency or school has a written policy specifying reporting procedures. Fraser (1977) provides an excellent model for school districts, which could easily be adapted for agencies.
—a positive relationship has been developed between protective service workers and the counselor. This may require that the counselor take the

initiative in meeting and talking with the worker(s) assigned to the local area.

—confidentiality is maintained with colleagues and co-workers. The report should never be general knowledge in the staff lounge.

—the counselor's attitude toward reporting is positive. Reporting is not "ratting" or tattling but, instead, the first step toward securing help for a troubled family.

3. *Follow-Up*

The knowledge that an investigation of suspected abuse is taking place will be upsetting to family members. The victim will be under great pressure to "explain away" physical abuse or retract charges of sexual abuse. If the counselor has access to the victim, daily support should be provided. Other family members should be encouraged to continue participation in counseling. The counselor should be a resource to the child regarding future scenarios based on protective service procedures.

4. *Cooperation in the Investigation*

The child protective services worker and the counselor are on the same side. The counselor must be aware of state laws and regulations regarding access to records and to the victim, as well as the rights of parents in abuse investigations. Jargon-free communication with the caseworker will expedite the investigation.

5. *Staff Development*

The counselor in a school or agency can be a leader in educating co-workers about abuse. Local resource personnel can be extremely helpful in inservice programs.

6. *Prevention*

Child abuse is preventable. Counselors in any setting can provide prevention activities including parent education groups for teen and adult parents, parenting classes for children and adolescents, self-esteem workshops and groups for parents and children, assertiveness training, and training in problem solving. At the community level, counselors can encourage support services for children including elementary school counselors, after-school programs; 24-hour emergency child-care centers, and personal safety programs.

CONCLUSION

Child abuse is a topic that elicits more questions than answers, more emotions than solutions. In 1959 the United Nations issued a Declaration on the rights of the child. The gap between these rights and reality for the abused child is painfully evident. According to the declaration, all children have the right to:

—affection, love, and understanding.
—adequate nutrition and medical care.
—free education.
—full opportunity for play and recreation.
—a name and nationality.
—special care, if handicapped.
—be among the first to receive relief in times of disaster.
—learn to be useful members of society and to develop individual abilities.
—be brought up in a spirit of peace and universal brotherhood.
—enjoy these rights regardless of race, color, sex, religion, national or social origin.

The counselor who is willing to be a child advocate can help to make this list more than a dream for all children.

REFERENCES

Alford. P., Martin, D., & Martin, M. (1985). A profile of the physical abusers of children. *School Counselor, 33*(2), 143–150.

Allen, C. V. (1980), *Daddy's girl.* New York: Berkley Books.

Bass, E., & Thornton, L. (Eds.), (1983). *I never told anyone: Writings by women survivors of child sexual abuse.* New York: Harper & Row.

Brady, L. (1979). *Fathers' days: A true story of incest.* New York: Dell.

Bulkley, J. (1982). The law and child sexual abuse. In J. Bulkley, J. Ensminger, V. Fontana, & R. Summit (Eds.), *Dealing with sexual child abuse* (pp. 3–9). Chicago: National Committee for Prevention of Child Abuse.

Callis, R., Pope, S., & De Pauw, M. (1982). *Ethical standards casebook* (3d ed.). Falls Church, VA: American Personnel & Guidance Association.

Chase, N. (1975). *A child is being beaten: Violence against children, an American tragedy.* New York: Holt, Rinehart & Winston.

Cooney, J. (1987). *Coping with sexual abuse.* New York: Rosen Press.

Damon, L., & Waterman, J. (1986). Parallel group treatment of children and their mothers. In K. MacFarlane, J. Waterman, S. Conerly, L. Damon, M. Durfee, & S. Long (Eds.). *Sexual abuse of young children* (pp. 244–298). New York: Guilford Press.

Education Commission of the States. (1977). *Trends in child abuse and neglect reporting statutes.* Denver: Author.

Epstein, L. (1967). *Sex laws and customs in Judaism.* New York: KTAV Publishing.

Fraser, B. (1977). *The educator and child abuse.* Chicago: National Committee for Prevention of Child Abuse.

Garbarino, J., Guttmann, E., & Seeley, J. (1986). *The psychologically battered child: Strategies for identification, assessment, and intervention.* San Francisco: Jossey-Bass.

Giaretto, H. (1981). A comprehensive child sexual abuse treatment program. In P. Mrazek & C. H. Kempe (Eds.), *Sexually abused children and their families* (pp. 179–197). New York: Pergamon Press.

Giaretto, H. (1982). *Integrated treatment of child sexual abuse: A treatment and training manual.* Palo Alto, CA: Science & Behavior Books.

Justice, B., & Justice. R. (1979). *The broken taboo: Sex in the family.* New York: Human Sciences Press.

Kempe, R., & Kempe, C. H. (1978). *Child abuse.* Cambridge, MA: Harvard University Press.Kempe, R., & Kempe, C. H. (1984). *The common secret: Sexual abuse of children and adolescents.* New York: W. H. Freeman.

Kempe, R., & Kempe, C. H. (1984). *The common secret: Sexual abuse of children and adolescents.* New York: W. H. Freeman.

Knapp, S. (1983). Counselor liability for failing to report child abuse. *Elementary School Guidance & Counseling, 17*(3), 177–179.

Langley, R., & Levy, R. (1977). *Wife beating: The silent crisis.* New York: Pocket Books.

Lusk, R., & Waterman, J. (1986). Effects of sexual abuse on children. In K. MacFarlane, J. waterman, S. Conerly, L. Damon, M. Durfee, & S. Long (Eds.), *Sexual abuse of young children* (pp. 101–118). New York: Guilford Press.

Mrazek, P. (1981). Definition and recognition of sexual child abuse: Historical and cultural perspectives. In P. Mrazek & C. H. Kempe (Eds.), *Sexually abused children and their families* (pp. 5–15). New York: Pergamon Press.

O'Brien, S. (1980). *Child abuse: A crying shame.* Provo, UT: Brigham Young University Press.

Piers, M. (1978). *Infanticide.* New York: W. W. Norton.

Radbill, S. (1974). A history of child abuse and infanticide. In R. Helfer & c. H. Kempe (Eds.), *The battered child* (2d ed.) (pp. 3–21). Chicago: University of Chicago Press.

Salisbury, H. (1969). *The 900 days: The siege of Leningrad.* New York: Avon.

Walters, D. (1975). *Physical and sexual abuse of children: Causes and treatment.* Bloomington: Indiana University Press.

Waterman, J., & Lusk, R. (1986). Scope of the problem. In K. MacFarlane, J. Waterman, S. Conerly, L. Damon, M. Durfee, & S. Long (Eds.). *Sexual abuse of young children* (pp. 3–12). New York: Guilford Press.

RELATED READINGS

Ammerman, R. T., & Hersen, M. (1991). *Case studies in family violence.* New York: Plenum.

Baxter, A. (1987). *Techniques for dealing with family violence.* Springfield, IL: Charles Thomas.

Dale, P. (1986). *Dangerous families: Assessment and treatment of child abuse.* London: Tavistock Publications.

Daro, D. (1988). *Confronting child abuse: Research for effective Program design.* New York: Free Press.

Davis, L. (1990). *The courage to health workbook: For women and men survivors of child sexual abuse.* New York: Harper & Row.

Shengold, L. (1989). *Soul murder: The effects of childhood abuse and deprivation.* New Haven: Yale University Press.

Tower, C. C. (1989). *Understanding child abuse and neglect.* Boston: Allyn & Bacon.

14

Counseling
Children of Alcoholics

Judith A. Lewis

It will never happen to me!

Claudia Black

As Hastings and Typpo (1984) have pointed out, "Living in a family where drinking is a problem is a lot like living with an elephant in the living room." In a workbook designed for use by preadolescent children of alcoholics, they suggest that children imagine the "elephant's" role as follows:

> People have to go through the living room many times a day and you watch as they walk through it very . . . carefully . . . around . . . the . . . ELEPHANT. No one ever says anything about the ELEPHANT. They avoid the swinging trunk and just walk around it. Since no one ever talks about the ELEPHANT, you know that you're not supposed to talk about it either. And you don't.
>
> But sometimes you wonder why nobody is saying anything or why no one is doing anything to move the ELEPHANT . . . You wonder if maybe there is something wrong with you. But you just keep wondering, keep walking around it, keep worrying and wishing that there was somebody to talk to about the ELEPHANT.

Growing up in a home dominated by the huge, gray elephant of parental alcoholism places an obvious strain on children. Not only must they spend their preadolescent and adolescent years attempting to cope with a unique set of difficulties, but they also are frequently forced to address these problems within a framework of family secrecy. The alcohol problem of one member is likely to affect the functioning of the entire family unit, and the issues the alcoholic family system presents have important implications for the psychological, social, and even physical development of each child.

THE FAMILY AS A SYSTEM

Any discussion of alcohol's impact on family dynamics and child development must begin with the recognition that the family is an ongoing system characterized by consistent modes of interaction. The notion of the family as a system depends on general systems theory (von Bertalanffy, 1968), an epistemology that can be contrasted with the reductionistic thinking underlying Newtonian science. Traditional Newtonian thinking was reductionistic in its attempt to break down complex phenomena into the smallest possible parts, and linear in its attempt to understand these parts as a series of less complex cause-and effect relationships.

Systems theory represents an entirely different mode of thought, viewing all living things as open systems best understood by examining their interrelationships and organizing principles. Attention is paid not to linear, causal relationships but, rather, to consistent, if circular, patterns of interaction.

> If a system is defined as a set of units or elements standing in some consistent relationship or interactional stance with each other, then the first concept is the notion that any system is composed of elements that are organized by the consistent nature of the relationship between these elements. Consistency is the key; consistent elements are related to each other in a consistently describable or predictable fashion. (Steinglass, 1978, p. 305)

Living organisms are *open systems* in that they interact with their environments, taking in and discharging information or energy through boundaries that are sufficiently permeable to allow these interactions to take place. The system itself also encompasses *subsystems*, which interact in a predictable manner within the context of the larger system. Clearly, the family unit as we know it conforms to these principles.

> The human family is a social system that operates through transactional patterns. These are repeated interactions which establish patterns of how, when, and to whom to relate . . . Repeated operations build patterns, and these patterns underpin the family system. The system maintains itself within a preferred range, and deviations which pass the system's threshold of tolerance usually elicit counterdeviation mechanisms which reestablish the accustomed range. (Minuchin, 1979, p. 7)

Thus, each family has it own *homeostasis*, or preferred steady state, which may or may not be "healthy" but is monitored through feedback and control mechanisms and protected by the system as a whole. Each family has a set of rules that governs its interactions and makes them predictable. Each includes subsystems (e.g., spousal, parental, sibling) that have specialized functions and attempt to preserve the integrity of the overall system. Each is an organized whole, making intervention in one part impossible to consider without taking the other parts into account.

As family therapists have learned, one cannot legitimately separate the individual from the family, the "sick" from the "well," the cause of a dysfunction from the effect. "Rather than seeing the source of problems or the appearance of symptoms as emanating from a single 'sick' individual, the . . . approach views that person simply as a symptom bearer—the identified patient—expressing a family's disequilibrium" (Goldenberg & Goldenberg, 1985, p. 7).

THE ALCOHOLIC FAMILY SYSTEM

In a family characterized by the alcohol dependence of one or more members, the disequilibrium makes individual adjustment difficult.

> Trapped (or at least thinking they are trapped) in this highly disordered system, how do family members adjust? The only healthy response would be not to adjust to it but to open it up by voicing honestly their practical problems, their mental confusion, and their emotional pain and frustration. This course would protect their own psychological well-being and offer the best hope of bringing the [alcohol] Dependent [person] to treatment as well. But few family members choose it, for they risk losing the whole matrix of their lives. Instead, they opt for preserving the family system at whatever cost. Left with only unhealthy alternatives, they choose . . . the same defense as the Dependent: they hide their true feelings behind an artificial behavior pattern, a supporting role in the alcoholic drama, which seems to promise some kind of reward in a system that offers few. (Wegscheider, 1981, p. 84)

Thus, each family member plays his or her role in an ongoing system patterned around the alcohol or drug use of one member. Like any other presenting problem, substance abuse can be seen as a "systems-maintaining and a systems-maintained device" (Kaufman, 1985, p. 37). Abusive substance use is often central to a family's functioning—becoming a primary organizing factor in the system's structure. A family with an alcoholic member learns to maintain its homeostasis around the continued drinking of the alcohol-dependent individual.

Alcohol may even be a stabilizing factor, producing "patterned, predictable and rigid sets of interactions which reduce uncertainties" (Steinglass, 1979, p. 163). A number of families Steinglass (1978) and his associates studied seemed to use the alcoholic's intoxicated state as a way of dealing with conflict and restabilizing their interactions.

> The transition from sober to intoxicated behavior appeared to serve a specific functional role for . . . marital couples, a role that was felt to be primarily problem-solving in nature. Although it was felt that three different types of problem-solving activities were associated with alcoholism (problem-solving associated with individual psychopathology, intrafamilial conflict, or conflict between the family and the external environment), in each case the emergence of the intoxicated interactional state appeared to temporarily restabilize the marital system. (pp. 357–358)

These findings do not mean that unstable family dynamics "cause" alcohol problems or that the homeostasis found by alcohol-affected families should be considered a healthy or positive state. What they do imply is that families develop consistent, predictable methods for adapting to alcoholism, just as they create rules and interactional styles for dealing with other kinds of problems. At the same time, alcohol or drug abuse also may be one method—if a spectacularly ineffective one—for coping with the stresses of a family system.

> Drinking behavior interrupts normal family tasks, causes conflict, shifts roles, and demands adjustive and adaptive responses from family members who do not know how to appropriately respond. A converse dynamic also occurs: marital and family styles, rules, and conflict may evoke, support, and maintain alcoholism as a symptom of family system dysfunction or as a coping mechanism to deal with family anxiety. (Kaufman, 1985, pp. 30-31)

EFFECTS ON CHILDREN

The problems inherent in the alcoholic family system have important implications for the development of children who must learn to adjust. Although families affected by substance abuse obviously vary, they do tend toward some common patterns, at least as far as child-rearing is concerned.

In a family affected by parental alcoholism, at least one parent is likely to be somewhat impaired in the ability to provide consistency in child-rearing practices. Interactions with the alcoholic parent may have extreme variations, with the parent being effective or ineffective, warm or cold, distant or affectionate, depending on alcohol consumption at the time. The nonalcoholic parent also may show variations in parenting as a result of his or her focus on the partner's drinking. Thus, in some alcoholic families neither parent is truly available to the child on a consistent basis.

The structure and boundaries of the alcoholic family system also may be problematic. Within the family unit, boundaries between subsystems may be weak, with the unity of the parental subsystem broken and children taking on what should be adult responsibilities. At the same time, boundaries between the family and its environment may be overly rigid as the family tries to maintain secrecy about the alcohol problem. Children who are unable to count on solid support from their parents also may be prevented from reaching out beyond the family for fear of breaking the family's rule of silence. The delicate homeostasis of the alcoholic family system is maintained—but at high cost to the development and self-esteem of individual family members.

Children reared in these circumstances may need to work to provide consistency and order that otherwise are lacking in their home lives.

> Children need consistency and structure. As an alcoholic progresses into alcoholism, and the co-alcoholic becomes more and more preoccupied with the alcoholic, children experience decreasing consistency and structure in the family unit, and their lives become less and less predictable. Some days, when dad is drinking, no disruption or tension occurs, but on other days when he is drinking, he becomes loud, opinionated and demanding in his expectations of the children. Mom, at times, reacts to this disrupting behavior by being passive and ignoring it; and other times, she makes arrangements for the children to go to

the neighbors until dad goes to bed, or tells them to go outside and play until she calls for them. The children don't know what to expect from dad when he drinks, nor do they know what to expect from mom when dad drinks. When structure and consistency are not provided by the parents, children will find ways to provide it for themselves. (Black, 1981, pp. 17–18)

Individual children differ in the mechanisms they use to adjust to their family situations. Some writers and counselors believe that children of alcoholics play a limited number of identifiable roles that give their family systems a semblance of order. Wegscheider (1981) identified four basic roles that children may adopt in alcoholic families: (a) the family hero, (b) the scapegoat, (c) the lost child, and (d) the family mascot.

The "family hero" takes over many functions that normally would be carried out by adults, assuming responsibility for solving family problems and providing stability for himself or herself and for other children in the family. This leadership is carried over into other childhood situations, including school, and into adulthood, making the family hero a success at most tasks attempted. The "scapegoat" is identified as the troublemaker in the family and tends to receive attention for his or her misbehavior. The "lost child," in contrast, remains in the background and seems to need little in the way of attention from the family. The "mascot" becomes the focus of attention as a way of lessening anxiety; he or she uses clowning as a way of distracting other family members from tension-provoking problems. These roles are used as coping mechanisms and by the family system as a set of transactions to maintain homeostasis.

A typology of family coping roles taken on by children reared in alcoholic families also has been suggested by Black (1981), who labeled these as the *responsible one*, the *adjuster*, and the *placater*. Like Wegscheider's family hero, the responsible one provides consistency and structure in the home environment, taking over parental roles on a routine basis.

> The responsible child makes life easier for the parents by providing more time for the alcoholic to be preoccupied with drinking, and for the co-alcoholic to be preoccupied with the alcoholic. Whether . . . responsible children are blatantly directed into this role or more subtly fall into it, it is typically a role which brings them comfort. Playing the responsible role provides stability in the life of this oldest, or only, child and in the lives of other family members. These responsible children feel and are very organized . . . (They) have learned to rely completely on themselves. (pp. 19–20)

The adjuster copes with a disorganized family system by detaching, by going along with events as they occur and thinking about them as little as possible. Black's placater, like Satir's (1967), focuses on the needs of others. In the alcoholic system this process tends to involve an attempt to salve the family's wounds.

> The placater finds the best way to cope, in this inconsistent and tension-filled home, by acting in a way which will lessen his own tension and pain, as well as that of the other family members. This child will spend his early and adolescent years trying to "fix" the sadness, fears, angers and problems of brothers, sisters, and certainly of mom and dad. (Black, 1981, p. 24)

To identify and label a limited number of roles that children of alcoholics play and to assume that these roles differ substantially from those that children of nonsubstance-abusing parents play may be an oversimplification. But understanding that the alcoholic family is at risk of being dysfunctional and recognizing that children of alcoholics might be required to develop extraordinary mechanisms for coping are important in working with these families.

Black (1986) pointed out that children of alcoholics have to cope with a great deal of stress and at the same time may have fewer physical, social, emotional, and mental resources available to them than do children living in more functional family systems. Their physical resources may be sapped because they are tired as a result of lack of sleep at night, because they have internalized stress, or because they have been abused. (They also may be the victims of fetal alcohol syndrome, which can cause developmental problems in the infants of women who consume large amounts of alcohol during pregnancy.) In some cases, social resources also may be limited; hesitancy to bring other children into the home or to share information about the family may interfere with the formation of intimate relationships. Emotional resources are affected by the pain, fear, and embarrassment that come with unstable living arrangements, financial difficulties, broken promises, accidents, and public intoxication. Even mental resources may be affected by a lack of parental help and by difficulties in maintaining regular school attendance.

Children in this situation are not necessarily poorly adjusted. In many cases they are exceptionally competent. Even children who appear to be coping effectively, however, may share some of the feelings Morehouse (1986, pp. 128–129) described as characteristic of children of alcoholics.

1. Children feel responsible directly or indirectly, for their parent's drinking . . . . (They may feel, for instance, that their misbehavior upsets the parent and therefore makes drinking an inevitable response.)
2. Children equate their parent's drinking with not being loved.
3. Children feel angry with the nonalcoholic parent for not making things better and for not providing protection.
4. Children fear that the alcoholic will get hurt, sick, or die as a result of being intoxicated.
5. In situations in which the alcoholic parent is more permissive or affectionate while intoxicated, the adolescent may want the parent to drink but then feels guilty.
6 Children feel confused by the difference between "dry" behavior and "drunk" behavior.
7. Parents' inconsistent behavior makes adolescents reluctant to bring friends home because they never know what to expect.
8. Once children are old enough to realize that alcoholic drinking is frowned upon by others or is "different," they feel shame and embarrassment.

Children who are forced to deal with this kind of pain can benefit from the attention of counselors and other helping adults. They deserve the opportunity to share their previously unexpressed feelings, to hear that they are not to blame for their families' difficulties, to learn less personally taxing mechanisms for coping with distress, and to gain the kind of support that we know people of all ages need.

COUNSELING YOUNG CHILDREN OF ALCOHOLICS

Counseling for children who still live in the alcoholic home environment should concentrate on providing empathy and support and on helping clients to develop coping skills that can serve them effectively both in the current situation and in the future. Ideally, this process should help children deal with their present uncertainties and, concurrently, prevent the development of chronic emotional problems from developing.

One way to look at the appropriate direction for counseling to take is to consider Ackerman's (1983) conceptualization of the family's potential for progressing from a "reactive" to an "active" phase of development.

> The reactive phase is consistently dominated by the behavior of nonalcoholic family members reacting to the alcoholic's behavior. During this time most family members become extremely cautious in their behavior in order to avoid or to further complicate the existing problems of alcoholism. However, by being reactive they are constantly adapting their behavior in order to minimize or survive an unhealthy situation. (p. 11)

Thus, the reactive phase is characterized by family members' attempts to deny the existence of the alcohol problem—even to themselves. Parents try to protect children from the situation by covering up problems and by avoiding discussion of unpleasant realities. The reactive phase is characterized by social disengagement, with the family becoming isolated from others. Emotional disengagement also occurs, with children learning to deny their negative emotions.

The kinds of coping roles described by Wegscheider and by Black may become rigidified. Ackerman's notion, however, is that a family can move from a reactive to an active phase.

> The main difference between the active and reactive phases is the response of the nonalcoholic family member even though the alcoholic is still drinking. Rather than being passive to the effects on themselves from alcoholism, they begin to take an active interest in themselves . . . . In this manner, the family begins to "de-center" itself from alcoholism . . . . They are willing to abandon their anonymity in exchange for help and a viable alternative to how they have been existing. (Ackerman, 1983, p. 28)

The most useful approach to take with children of alcoholics may be to help them move from a reactive to an active state. If children are isolated in their home environments, counseling should help them reach out to others. If children are afraid of their feelings, counseling should help them recognize and express their previously forbidden emotions. If children feel they are alone in their situations, counseling should convince them that others share their problems. Children of alcoholics also need to know that their attempts to meet their own needs are in no way detrimental to other family members. These counseling goals probably can be accomplished most successfully in group, rather than individual, settings.

As Brown and Sunshine (1982) pointed out:

> One of the primary tasks in the treatment of the latency-age child from an alcoholic home is to help the child bear the burden of the shameful and frightening family secret by bringing it out in the open. This process is immediately relieving to the child and causes her or him to feel less isolated. For this reason and because children from alcoholic homes often have deficits in the areas of social development and peer interaction, group is the treatment of choice. (p. 70)

Morehouse (1986) stated that a group situation is also most appropriate for treatment of adolescent children of alcoholics, suggesting that participation in a group reduces isolation, presents a chance to learn about new ways of coping, encourages peer support, provides a laboratory for practice in sharing feelings, allows for confrontation when needed, and enhances readiness for participation in Alateen (a self-help group movement for young people in alcoholic homes).

Group counseling for children of alcoholics should follow a structured process that helps group members understand more about substance dependence but that goes beyond the cognitive dimension to deal with affect and with skill acquisition. A good example of a structured approach is provided by Hastings and Typpo (1984) in a children's book designed to be utilized by a counselor with a child or a group of children. Their design includes materials dealing with the kinds of topics that are likely to meet the needs of the target population, including:

1. Drinking and drug problems (a knowledge-building module discussing the effects of alcohol and other drugs).
2. Feelings (exercises designed to elicit awareness of negative and positive emotions and to explore the use of defenses).
3. Families (discussions of family rules, feelings, and relationships).
4. Coping with problems (exercises eliciting fresh ideas about coping methods, along with suggestions for dealing with some of the more prevalent alcohol-related family problems).
5. Changes (material encouraging children to make changes in the areas over which they do have some control, including taking care of themselves and handling their uncomfortable feelings).
6. Choices (decision-making exercises with an emphasis on the nature of choices).

This structured approach, like many others becoming available for counselors' use, is designed to help children develop the kinds of skills and resources they need for coping with family stress. Underlying most of these approaches is an emphasis on bringing hidden family dynamics to the surface—on recognizing and talking about "the elephant in the living room."

COUNSELING ADULT SONS AND DAUGHTERS OF ALCOHOLICS

People who grow up with that elephant in the living room may develop coping mechanisms that serve them poorly in adulthood. Only a minority of children of alcoholics respond by acting out; these individuals tend to receive some kind of attention or help during their adolescence. Most children in these situations respond instead by exerting control, burying feelings, and doing the best they can to adapt and survive.

Until recently these children received little notice. If anything, their behavior has been seen as mature and well adjusted. But they pay a price for this adjustment—one that many clinicians and writers believe leads to a common set of concerns in adulthood. Seixas and Youcha (1985), for instance, ask adult children of alcoholics whether they identify with the following list of feelings and attitudes;

Lack trust?
Feel isolated and lonely?
Deny or suppress deep feelings?
Feel guilty?
Feel unnecessarily embarrassed and ashamed?
Wish for closeness, yet fear it?
Have a low opinion of yourself?
Feel sad?
Need to control yourself?
Need to control others?
Split the world into all good or all bad?
Have an exaggerated sense of responsibility?
Want desperately to please?
Have trouble standing up for your own needs?
Overreact to personal criticism? (pp. 47–48)

Adult sons and daughters of alcoholics certainly are not the only people who exhibit these attitudes and behaviors. These problems are ubiquitous in our society. Many writers point out, however, that a significant number of adults from alcoholic homes (and, of course, from other dysfunctional family situations) are troubled by difficulty in trusting others, relinquishing control, identifying and expressing feelings, or abandoning behavioral rigidity (Ackerman, 1983; Black, 1981; Seixas & Youcha, 1985; Wegscheider, 1981). Clearly, adult children of alcoholics (ACOAs) who have the opportunity to participate in group situations addressing their specific concerns do seem to sense a commonality in their characteristics.

> We're often high achievers, even overachievers, but we also have a knack for sabotaging success, and certainly have difficulty enjoying it. We fear losing control to the point where we're often rigid. We may have terrific social skills, but we feel we're different from other people. We can be perfectionistic and are relentlessly unkind to ourselves, we're relentlessly critical of others. We have a pervasive sense of guilt and of sadness. We feel our heart is a stone, but we cry at dog movies. We lie when it would be just as easy to tell the truth, and we're often brutally honest when we shouldn't be. We have a high tolerance for the bizarre. We're extremely loyal even when loyalty is undeserved. We deal in extremes. We have low self-esteem. Some of us also wisecrack a lot. That was my specialty and I learned it at my mother's knee. (Malone, 1987, p. 54)

Coping mechanisms made necessary by a difficult childhood situation may be less appropriate in mature lifestyles. The counselor attempting to work with adult children of alcoholics should address these issues in a two-stage process. Black (1986) has suggested that clients must be encouraged to face their fears of loss of control and to express their guilt, sadness, and anger, but that this cathar- sis then must be replaced with an attempt to learn new behavioral skills. If coun- selors accept this idea, they then can approach these clients as they would any oth- ers—completing a careful assessment of each individual's strengths and deficits and developing a plan for behavioral change based on the client's unique needs.

If clients' needs are addressed through a group process, emphasis should be placed on the development of skills such as assertion, relaxation, stress manage- ment, and interpersonal communication, depending on the areas that group mem- bers need to have addressed. Although the group also can serve as a mechanism for providing information about substance abuse and its effects on family dynam- ics, it probably is less useful to focus on children of alcoholics as an alcoholism risk group than to stress the individual's potential for successful adaptation and self-control. Attempts to eliminate the individual's sense of isolation and guilt may work best in concert with a referral to one of the many self-help groups for adult children of alcoholics now available in a number of locations.

RESOURCES FOR SELF HELP

Thousands of adult sons and daughters of alcoholics are finding in the "ACOA movement" a chance to explore issues that they might have kept hidden for years. Of course, as with any broadly based movement, there are vast over- simplifications. Stark (1987), for instance, quoted an alcoholism program direc- tor's reaction to the publicity being given to children of alcoholics:

> I think the label is wonderful news. Finally a lot of these people can say, "Ah! That's what's the matter with me." (p. 62)

Human behavior is too complex to allow an individual to attribute all of his or her personal problems to a single causal agent, just as systems are too complex for people to believe that families with alcoholic members are unique in their dysfunctional characteristics. With this caveat in mind, however, specialists in counseling and human development should recognize the benefits that the self-help phenomenon can offer.

As one woman wrote about her feelings on attending her first ACOA workshop:

> ACOAs are people who have spent the bulk of our lives not feeling. Beneath the shock of recognition that these 40 strangers carried my secret, there was also the recognition that if I kept on with this process, the pain would get much worse before it got better. And beneath that, barely breathing, lay a tiny newborn of hope . . . .When the workshop leader started asking questions and people started answering them, I never doubted that this direction was where health lay. I was hearing my experience validated over and over again. (Malone, 1987, p. 54)

This validation of personal experience provides the underpinning of activities that are becoming available to children of alcoholics for the first time. The resources that people seem to find useful take two general forms: (a) written and audiovisual materials designed to guide personal exploration, and (b) organizations encouraging interpersonal networking among affected individuals.

Written and Audiovisual Material

A body of self-help literature has appeared in recent years. A number of books written for the general public describe the experience of growing up with an alcoholic parent. Of particular interest are several publications that take the form of manuals, providing guidelines and exercises designed to take an individual or group through a healing process. Among the manuals available in popular bookstores are:

Black, C. (1985). *Repeat after me*. Denver: M.A.C. Printing and Publications.
This popular work contains a number of sentence completion exercises that help the individual reader to recognize the effects of past losses and to move ahead unencumbered by blame and judgment. The step-by=step process begins with a series of warm-up exercises and goes on to consider feelings, self-esteem, and family issues.

Tessmer, K. (1986). *Breaking silence: A workbook of adult children of alcoholics*. Santa Rosa, CA: ACAT Press.
This book uses CAT family stories, adapted from the author's earlier work for children, to help ACOAs deal with issues such as anger, fear, guilt, grief, sex roles, relationships, and parents. Guidelines for letter writing to parents, as well as a personal "bill of rights," are included.

McConnell, P. (1986). *Adult children of alcoholics: A workbook for healing*. San Francisco: Harper & Row.
McConnell's book is divided into two general sections. The first section, "The Hurt," focuses on recognizing the beliefs, behaviors, and roles governing the individual's life and making the decision to change. Section Two, "The Healing," helps the individual to confront issues of anger and control and to concentrate on healing, forgiveness, and self-empowerment.

Seixas, J. S., & Youcha, G. (1985). *Children of alcoholics: A survivor's manual*. New York: Harper & Row.

The "survivor's manual" begins with a look back to childhood ("Living in Chaos"), goes on to examine "hangovers from childhood," and, like the other manuals, extends its focus to "climbing out of the trap."

Several films—also appropriate for the lay public—focus on issues relating to alcoholic family systems and on the problems faced by children of alcoholics and other substance abusers. Among these films are:

Alcoholism and the Family (FMS Productions, 1888 N. Vine St., Los Angeles, CA 90028)
This film discusses the impacts of both active alcoholism and sobriety on the family system. (42 minutes)

Alcoholism: A Family Problem (Health Sciences Consortium, 200 Eastowne Dr., Suite 213, Chapel Hill, NC 27514)
Based on a stage theory of alcoholism, this film shows the effects on the family during each of three stages in problem development. (13 minutes)

All Bottled Up (AIMS Media, 626 Hustin Ave., Glendale, CA 91201)
This film depicts a child's viewpoint regarding alcoholic parents. (29 minutes)

Children of Alcoholics (Addiction Research Foundation, 33 Russell St., Toronto, Ontario, Canada M5S 2S1)
This film examines treatment programs for children of alcoholics. (15 minutes)

Children of Denial (A.C.T., P.O. Box 8536, Newport Beach, CA 92660)
This film focuses on children of alcoholics and the issues they face in childhood, adolescence, and adulthood. (28 minutes)

The Family Trap (Onsite Training and Consulting, Inc., P.O. box 3790, Minneapolis, MN 55403)
A general overview of the impact of alcoholism as a "family illness" is followed by the benefits of intervention and counseling. (30 minutes)

She Drinks a Little (Learning Corporation of America, 1350 Avenue of the Americas, New York, NY 10019)
This is the story of an adolescent girl with an alcoholic mother. (31 minutes)

Soft is the Heart of a Child (Maryland Center for Public Broadcasting, 11767 Bonita Ave., Owings Mills, MD 21117)
This dramatization shows the effects of alcoholism on children and other family members. (30 minutes)

The Summer We Moved to Elm Street (McGraw-Hill films, 330 West 42nd St., New York, NY 10036)
A father's alcoholism and its impact on a 9-year-old girl and her family are dramatized in this touching film. (30 minutes)

Organizations

A number of organizations provide assistance and opportunities for networking to children of alcoholics. Among the organizations that can provide information concerning COA and ACOA issues are:

Al-Anon Family Group Headquarters, Inc., P.O. Box 182, Madison Square Station, New York, NY 10010

Children of Alcoholics Foundation, Inc., 200 Park Ave., New York, NY 10166

National Association for Children of Alcoholics, 31706 Coast Highway, Suite 201, South Laguna, CA 92677

National Clearinghouse on Alcohol Information, Box 2345, Rockville, MD 20852

National Council on Alcoholism, 12 West 21st St., New York, NY 10010

CONCLUSION

What is an adult child of an alcoholic (ACOA)? A person who, when she's drowning, sees someone else's life pass before her eyes. That life is the drinking parent's. (Malone, 1987, p. 50)

The effects of being raised in a family with an alcoholic parent often linger, affecting the individual's attitudes and behaviors long after the acute problems seem to have passed. From childhood through adolescence and adulthood, sons and daughters of alcoholics use survival skills that have helped them cope with the stress of an alcoholic family system but that may serve them poorly as long-term styles of living. Specialists in human development can help affected individuals to surmount these difficulties, first by recognizing the pain and isolation of children of alcoholics and then by providing the kind of support, assistance, and information that can enhance the individual's attempts to move ahead.

REFERENCES

Ackerman, R. J. (1983). *Children of alcoholics: A guidebook for educators, therapists and parents* (2d ed.). Holmes Beach, FL: Learning Publications.

Black, C. (1981). *It will never happen to me.* Denver: M.A.C.

Black, C. (1986, March 14). *Children of alcoholics.* Paper presented in Chicago.

Brown, K. A., & Sunshine, J. (1982). Group treatment of children from alcoholic families. *Social Work with Groups, 5*(1), 65–72.

Goldenberg, I., & Goldenberg, H. (1985). *Family therapy: An overview.* Monterey: Brooks/Cole

Hastings, J. M., & Typpo, M. H. (1984). *An elephant in the living room.* Minneapolis: CompCare Publications.

Kaufman, E. (1985). *Substance abuse and family therapy.* Orlando: Grune & Stratton.

Malone, M. (1987). Dependent on disorder—Children of alcoholics are finding each other and paths to a better life. *Ms., 15*(9), 50–62.

Minuchin, S. (1979). Constructing a therapeutic reality. In E. Kaufman & P. Kaufmann (Eds.), *Family therapy of drug and alcohol abuse* (pp. 5–18). New York: Gardner Press.

Morehouse, E. R. (1986). Counseling adolescent children of alcoholics in groups. In R. J. Ackerman (Ed.), *Growing in the shadow.* Holmes Beach, FL: Learning Publications.

Satir, V. M. (1967). *Conjoint family therapy (2d ed.).* Palo Alto, CA: Science & Behavior Books.

Seixas, J. S., & Youcha, G. (1985). *Children of alcoholism: A survivor's manual.* New York: Harper & Row.

Stark, E. (1987). Forgotten victims: Children of alcoholics. *Psychology Today, 21*(1), 58–62.

Steinglass, P. (1978). The conceptualization of marriage from a systems theory perspective. In T. J. Paolino & B. S. McCrady (Eds.), *Marriage and marital therapy: Psychoanalytic, behavioral, and systems theory perspectives* (pp. 298–365). New York: Brunner/Mazel.

Steinglass, P. (1979). Family therapy with alcoholics: A review. In E. Kaufman & P. Kaufmann (Eds.), *Family therapy of drug and alcohol abuse* (pp. 147–186). New York: Gardner Press.

von Bertalanffy, L. (1968). *General systems theory,* New York: George Braziller.

Wegscheider, S. (1981). *Another chance: Hope and health for the alcoholic family.* Palo Alto, CA: Science a& Behavior Books.

RELATED READINGS

Bepko, C., & Krestan, J. A. (1985). *The responsibility trap: A blueprint for treating the alcoholic family.* New York: Free Press.

Kaufman, E. (1985). *Substance abuse and family therapy.* Orlando, FL: Grune & Stratton.

Lewis, J. A., Dana, R. Q., & Blevins, G. A. (1988). *Substance abuse counseling: An individualized approach.* Pacific Grove, CA: Brooks/Cole.

Schlesinger, S. E., & Horberg, L. K. (1988). *Taking charge: How families can climb out of the chaos of addiction.* New York: Simon & Schuster.

Steinglass, P., Bennett, L. A., Wolin, S. J., & Reiss, D. (1987). *The alcoholic family.* New York: Basic Books.

15

Counseling Families
Affected by AIDS

Loretta J. Bradley and Mary A. Ostrovsky

*In the face of whatever frustration, resentment, anxiety, or stress
we may encounter, can we open our hearts and offer those suffering from the effects of AIDS our intelligence, our integrity, our
selflessness and our compassion?*
Craig D. Kain

As recently as 1981, few Americans had heard the term *acquired immunodeficiency syndrome* (AIDS), and the few Americans who had heard the term had
little information about the disease's cause or prevalence. Yet today, only a few
years after the discovery of AIDS, there are definite signs that Americans not only
are aware of, but also are very fearful of, AIDS.

In a recent study by the National Center of Health Statistics (1988), the Center reported that the U.S. public's awareness of AIDS includes virtually everyone.
The study reported that 99% of adults 18 years and older have heard of AIDS.
The majority of participants (90%) stated that they are certain that AIDS leads to
death, 86% said they realize that AIDS has no cure, 78% said that they think anyone with the AIDS virus can transmit it through sexual intercourse, and 73% said
they believe a pregnant woman can transmit AIDS to her baby.

With the increased awareness of AIDS, many Americans express fear and
dread when the term AIDS is mentioned. The fear is real, especially when one
recognizes that AIDS is spreading in epidemic proportions.

Prior to the discovery of AIDS, infectious disease was no longer considered
a real threat for Americans. Although at one time infectious diseases such as ty-

phoid, measles, diphtheria, and polio were definite health threats, the American health community conquered these problems, mainly with the advent of vaccines. During the past decade Americans have feared noninfectious diseases, such as heart attack, cancer, stroke, and diabetes, more than infectious diseases.

Consequently, for several years American health advances have been unprecedented in controlling infectious disease, and increased success had been achieved in controlling noninfectious disease. At least this was the scenario until the advent of AIDS. After many years of control over infectious disease, AIDS appeared. Suddenly Americans were thrust into the health arena with a new infectious disease that is spreading in epidemic proportions.

AIDS was formally recognized by the Center for Disease Control (CDC) in 1981. In less than 2 years from the initial report of five AIDS cases. CDC reported 5,550 AIDS cases in 1983. By 1985 more than 10,000 cases of AIDS had been reported. In mid-May, 1988, CDC reported 62,200 cases of AIDS—a cumulative total of more than 2½ times that of September, 1986 (Cooper, 1988). These data indicate that AIDS is spreading rapidly.

Kubler-Ross (1987) described the magnitude of AIDS cases as staggering, and she concluded that this is only the beginning. It has been predicted that by the end of 1991, an estimated 170,000 persons will have died within the decade since the disease was first recognized (Koop, 1986). In the year 1991 an estimated 145,000 patients with AIDS will need health and support services, at a total cost of between $8 billion and $16 billion (Kubler-Ross, 1987).

To say that AIDS is just another medical problem is an understatement. With new AIDS cases doubling every 10 to 12 months (Mason, 1985) and with public opinion surveys reporting that AIDS ranks third (behind cancer and heart disease) as the disease most Americans fear they will acquire (Mills, 1986), certainly AIDS ranks among significant issues facing Americans.

Although researchers have made advances in establishing the cause of AIDS,[1] the origin of the AIDS virus,[2] the high risk factors associated with AIDS,[3] testing for the AIDS virus,[4] and counseling with AIDS patients,[5] little research has been devoted to the family of the AIDS patient. In a literature search we found only nine articles that even mentioned the family of the AIDS patient,[6] and only two focused on the AIDS family.[7]

Given the incidence of increase of AIDS, by necessity many people are influenced by the presence of AIDS. Although most of the AIDS publications have focused on the medical aspects of AIDS or its impact on the AIDS patient, few studies have considered the effect of AIDS upon significant others. This chapter focuses on the family of the AIDS patient.

AIDS OVERVIEW

History

The Center for Disease Control (CDC) receives surveillance data from reports from state and local health departments. A report in June, 1981, alerted CDC to the presence of AIDS. The report described how in the past 8 months an extremely rare type of pneumonia caused by the protozoan *Pneumocyotis carinii* had been diagnosed in Los Angeles. The disease was so rare that the drug given to treat it was experimental and was dispensed solely by CDC. Between 1967 and 1979 only two cases of *P. carinii* pneumonia—a disease that usually attacks older persons whose immune system has been profoundly impaired—had been reported. Yet in the five new cases in 1981, the pneumonia had struck five young homosexual men whose immune system had no apparent reason for malfunctioning (Heyward & Curran, 1988).

Later in 1981 CDC received reports of an increase in the incidence of a type of cancer called Kaposi's sarcoma. Prior to 1981 this type of cancer seldom had been seen in the United States, and when it was, it occurred mainly in elderly men and older patients receiving immuno-suppressive therapy. In a 30-month span, however, 26 cases of Kaposi's sarcoma had been diagnosed in homosexual men living in New York and California. Several of these men had also contracted *P. carinii* pneumonia. Also in 1981, clinicians and epidemiologists noted an increased occurrence in homosexual men of lymphadenopathy (disease with enlarged lymph nodes) and a rare malignancy called diffuse, undifferentiated non-Hodgkin's lymphoma. The common denominator in all cases was a severely impaired immune system. This collection of clinical syndromes was recognized as an entirely new syndrome that became known in 1982 as acquired immunodeficiency syndrome, or AIDS (Heyward & Curran, 1988).

Through control studies in late 1981, researchers had evidence to illustrate that the factor differentiating homosexual patients with AIDS from homosexual controls was the number and frequency of sexual contacts. By 1982 researchers had evidence to strongly suggest that AIDS was transmitted by sexual relations in active homosexual males. Later in that year researchers had evidence indicating that other modes of transmission of AIDS existed. These included injection with blood or blood transfusions and were confirmed among hemophilia patients and intravenous (IV) drug abusers who shared hypodermic needles.

In December, 1982, a baby was born with AIDS. Thus, by the end of 1982, evidence strongly suggested that AIDS could be transmitted by sexual intercourse and blood. In January, 1983, researchers had evidence to illustrate the presence of AIDS cases in heterosexual partners of male IV drug abusers. Later in 1983 cases of AIDS were reported in central Africa and Haiti in individuals without any homosexual or IV drug abuse history.

Because AIDS was known to be transmitted by sexual contact and by blood, researchers were convinced that AIDS was caused by a class of infectious agents called retroviruses (Gallo & Montagnier, 1988). In two years, from mid-1982 to mid-1984, a new virus, the *human immunodeficiency virus* (HIV), was isolated by Montagnier and his colleagues at the Pasteur Institute in Paris and by Gallo and his colleagues at the National Cancer Institute. The HIV was isolated and shown to cause AIDS. Soon after the discovery of HIV, laboratory tests were developed to detect the presence of HIV in the blood (Heyward & Curran, 1988).

AIDS Risk

Ever since the AIDS pandemic was recognized, it has aroused mysterious dread in the United States. At first Americans believed they were safe if they were not homosexual or bisexual. As more information about AIDS has become known, however, it is apparent that several groups are at a higher risk for AIDS.

Table 15.1 shows the distribution of AIDS among higher risk groups. Although the table presents data via type of group, the reader should be aware that individuals engaging in unprotected vaginal sex, oral sex, and IV drug use are at a higher risk for contracting AIDS regardless of whether the individual is in one of the higher risk groups.

TABLE 15.1
Diagnosed Cases of AIDS by Risk Group (Adults)

Risk Group	% of Diagnosed AIDS Cases[*]
Homosexual or bisexual men	63%
Heterosexual IV drug abusers	19%
Homosexual or bisexual IV drug abusers	7%
Heterosexual men and women	4%
Recipients of blood or blood products	3%
Persons with hemophilia or other coagulation disorders	1%
Other or undetermined	3%

[*]Adapted from Center for Disease Control data as of 7/4/88.

As Table 15.1 indicates, 63% of the AIDS cases have occurred in homosexual or bisexual men, and 19% have occurred in heterosexual intravenous (IV) drug abusers. An additional 7% of the cases have occurred in homosexual or bisexual IV drug abusers. When the percents for those three groups are added, it becomes apparent that most of the AIDS cases have occurred in homosexual or bisexual men and IV drug abusers (89%). The 5% of the total AIDS cases attributed to heterosexual man and women occurred in persons who either had sexual contact with a person infected by HIV or were born in a country where heterosexual transmission of AIDS is the primary mode of transmission.

Further, Table 15.1 indicates that 3% of the AIDS cases occurred from blood contamination, and another 1% occurred in hemophiliacs. Because blood has been screened for the HIV since 1985, most of the AIDS transmission from blood transfusions occurred before 1985.

Contrary to popular belief, the fastest growing group of AIDS cases has occurred in children. Heyward and Curran (1988) reported 502 new cases of AIDS in children under 13 years of age; this represented a 114% increase over the previous year. Table 15.2 gives percentages of diagnosed AIDS cases in children by risk group. More than three-fourths (77%) of the children diagnosed with AIDS acquired it from their mothers during the prenatal period, with the original mode of transmission being IV drug abuse on the part of the mother or her sexual partner. As this table further shows, 13% of the AIDS cases in children occurred among children who had received blood or blood transfusions, and 6% of the cases were found in children with hemophilia.

TABLE 15.2
Diagnosed Cases of AIDS by Risk Group (Children)

Risk Group	% of Diagnosed AIDS cases[*]
Children who contracted AIDS prenatally from their mothers	77%
Recipients of blood or blood products	13%
Persons with hemophilia or other coagulation disorders	6%
Other or undetermined	4%

[*]Adapted from Center for Disease Control data as of 7/4/88.

With regard to AIDS across race, the data show a disproportionate amount of AIDS infections in Blacks and Hispanics. Heyward and Curran (1988) reported:

> In the U.S. 59 percent of the reported AIDS cases among adults and 23 percent of the cases among children have been white; Blacks have accounted for 26 percent of adult cases and 53 percent of pediatric cases, and Hispanics for 14 percent of adult and 23 percent of pediatric cases. Such figures are in striking contrast to the respective percentage of Blacks (11.6 percent) and Hispanics (6.5 percent) in the general U.S. population. (p. 78)

Although gaps remain in understanding the transmission of AIDS, cumulative data indicate that some groups are at higher risk for AIDS transmission. Even so, no one should assume that because he or she is not in one of the higher risk groups, AIDS presents no threats.

THE AIDS FAMILY

Ozzie and Harriet Syndrome

For years Ozzie and Harriet represented the ideal American family. The Nelsons personified the American dream family. It included a husband, a wife, two bright, healthy children, a nice home, and a car. Dad (Ozzie) was the breadwinner of the family. Each day he left for work in a suit and tie with briefcase in hand, and accompanied by a happy smile. Mom (Harriet) was the loyal, loving wife who stayed home and cared for the family. Although her life centered on the family, she played bridge with neighbors and participated in volunteer work. She was always home when the children arrived from school, and she was available with her station wagon to transport her children and their friends to their after-school activities. When Dad arrived home from work, she had a nice meal ready for him and the children to enjoy. The family frequently interacted with neighbors. The family was happy and enjoyed being together. Such was the American dream.

In reality, the American dream falls apart with only a cursory look at the data. Today many Americans are divorced, and single parenting is becoming more frequent (Craig, 1989). Many married couples are electing to remain childless. Women are no longer staying home but instead are entering the workforce in increasing numbers. The American family is fast becoming a two-paycheck family. Although the idea of the American dream with its Ozzie and Harriet family may still be a *dream* for the American family, for most Americans it is merely a dream and not reality.

One group that does not fit the traditional syndrome depicted by the Nelson family is the family in which a member has AIDS, a disease the American family does not want to encounter. The dread of AIDS in American families is precipitated by a number of factors. Fear of a disease for which there is no known cure and dread of the social stigma associated with AIDS contribute to a large portion of the fear. Certainly AIDS in a family does not fit the American expectation. Consequently, many families have ignored the AIDS epidemic and have assumed that AIDS will not penetrate their family system. Erroneously, parents have concluded that if their son is not gay or is not on drugs, AIDS should not be a concern for them. But try as the family might to ignore AIDS, it doesn't work. With more than 62,000 cases of AIDS diagnosed in 1988 and more than 260,000 cases projected by 1991 (Cooper, 1988), AIDS is a reality with which the American family must reckon.

Traditionally the American family consisted of father, mother, and children. But the AIDS family has caused Americans to reexamine and expand its traditional definition of the family to include not only the biological family but also lovers and friends. Family members of persons with AIDS (PWA) are usually from one of the following three groups: (a) biological family and spouses, lovers, and friends of homosexual and bisexual men, (b) biological family, spouses and lovers of IV drug users, and (c) spouses, lovers, and other family members of hemophiliacs (Donlou et al., 1985; Greif & Porembski, 1987; Mason, Olson, & Parish, 1988).

Common Family Responses

Upon learning that a family member has AIDS, the family typically experiences the following four reactions:

1. *Negative reaction.* Learning that a family member has AIDS almost always evokes a negative response from family members. A common statement is, "I never expected this . . . .this is awful."
2. *Surprise.* Although family members may realize that an individual may have been exposed to the AIDS virus via sexual contact or IV drug use, they don't expect that person to contract AIDS. Upon being told that a family member has AIDS, the other members are surprised and, in many cases, don't believe it. They typically say, "I just can't believe that Jim has AIDS . . . .surely this can't be true."
3. *Helplessness.* Upon learning that one if its members has AIDS, the family often experiences a feeling of helplessness. This is often manifested in their feeling of being out of control. A comment that typifies this feeling is, "Our Jim has AIDS, a disease without a known cure. Is there anything we can do? I feel so helpless."
4. *Loss.* Knowledge of an AIDS diagnosis often evokes a feeling of loss and a feeling that the loss doesn't seem right. Most parents expect to die before their child does, but with an AIDS diagnosis the child is likely to die before the parents do. Most spouses and lovers expect many years in a satisfying relationship, but with an AIDS diagnosis the relationship is likely to be shortened. With an AIDS diagnosis comes the inevitable feeling of impending loss. The feeling of loss often is verbalized as, "I just can't believe that Jim is terminally ill and we're going to lose him."

Family of Origin of Homosexual and Bisexual Men

Because the greatest number of AIDS cases presently are in homosexual and bisexual men ages 20–40 years, most of their parents are 40–65 years old. According to developmental research conducted by Erikson and Erikson (1981), individuals between 40 and 65 years of age are dealing with the developmental task of establishing themselves as generative persons. Generativity is defined as *the effort to perpetuate oneself through something lasting and meaningful to the world.*

Some individuals express generativity through productivity in their work. Others may achieve generativity through creation and nurturance of a family (Craig, 1989). Thus, at this stage of life, parents usually are involved in rearing children and preparing for retirement. But AIDS may cause parents and other family members to return to earlier life roles, especially the role of caregiver. Kubler-Ross (1987) captures the essence of this predicament in summarizing the roles of mothers of AIDS victims: "They had to train themselves to be moms again for little helpless children in a grown-up body (p. 32)." Additionally, the prolonged illness of the PWA may drain family members emotionally and physically and deplete family resources (Flaskerud, 1987; Wolcott, Fawzy, & Pasnau, 1985).

Family members, especially parents, may find themselves geographically isolated from their child. Although they may want to offer their support, they may experience great situational stress in trying to find accommodations during visits or wanting to provide support and being unable to do so because of distance and finances. In other cases involving previous conflicts between the PWA and the family about issues concerning sexual preference and lifestyle, the family members may reject the PWA and desire greater geographic and psychological distance.

Because AIDS has attacked a minority group that lacks full acceptance by society, the family of the AIDS victim may feel as much stigma as the child does. This often is expressed in the form of anger, fear, guilt, and grief. Parents of PWAs frequently feel guilty because they erroneously believe that if they had reared their child differently, the child would have been neither gay nor ill (Wolcott, Fawzy, & Pasnau, 1985). The parents often admonish themselves by stating, "If only I had spent more time with him, this wouldn't have happened" or Did I do something wrong to cause my son to be gay and contract AIDS?"

Although both fathers and mothers usually experience guilt, they do so for different reasons. Mothers feel guilt because they traditionally have been responsible for their children's actions (Flaskerud, 1987). Fathers experience guilt because they see their son's orientation as a reflection of their own masculinity. As might be anticipated, researchers have reported that gay men perceive their mothers as more supportive of their sexual orientation than their fathers (Skeen & Robinson, 1985).

Upon learning of the AIDS diagnosis, parents and other biological family members often grieve. The grief is acute initially, and then, in the case of prolonged illness, chronic. The sequence is similar to the five stages of grief that Kubler-Ross (1969) described as denial, anger, bargaining, depression, and acceptance. The case of John depicts the grief process, as well as some of the family dynamics involved.

Case Illustration: John

John, a 23-year-old male, has just been diagnosed with AIDS. One of his greatest fears is telling his family that he has AIDS. He still remembers the trauma of 8 years ago when he told his family he was gay. On hearing that his son is gay, John's father at first was shocked and then outraged. His mother, although sad that her son is gay, tried to be understanding, but even she was often influenced by her husband.

With time the father became a little more tolerant of the situation and talked with John about almost any topic except John's sexual orientation. Although his mother was usually kind and caring, at times even she would remind John that, "This is upsetting to your father, who only wants you to be like other men." The parents nevertheless worked hard and sent John to college. John graduated from college with an engineering degree and reported that he had never been happier.

Sequentially, then, upon learning that John has AIDS, his father and mother couldn't believe they were hearing correctly. First they had to live with John being a homosexual, and now AIDS. Initially John's parents were very upset with him, and in the beginning they said some hurtful things to him. In fact, John returned to Chicago thinking he never wanted to see them again. After several phone calls from his mother, John decided to visit his parents. Although the visit was strained, his parents made an attempt to be friendly. At one point his mother said, "We love you no matter what." John thought about the statement and realized its intent was to convey that no matter how difficult his being gay, and now AIDS, has been, they love and accept him as their son.

Stages of Loss Related to Counseling Interventions

Counselors should understand how family members react to the news that a member has AIDS, for the reaction will determine the counseling interventions. Table 15.3 presents a means to conceptualize what is likely to occur within the family system. The first column names the stage, the second contains an explanation of it, and the third provides an example of the family's reaction at a specific stage. The stages of grief may or may not be experienced sequentially. Some families do not reach the fifth stage (acceptance). Almost all experience stages 1 and 2 (denial, anger), and most experience stage 3 or 4 (bargaining, depression). An article by Barret (1989) substantiates evidence for the passage of stages. It mainly discusses stages 1 and 2 and then adds a stage between stages 2 and 3, which might be labeled stage 2A, guilt. The counselor should realize that although reaching stage 5 is desirable, this doesn't always happen.

In the case of John's family, initially both parents experienced denial, and then John's father expressed a great deal of resentment. When families are experiencing stage 1 and 2 reactions, they often will not accept family counseling. Sometimes one of the family members (often the mother) will seek individual counseling. Usually at stage 1, however, the family wants concrete information and seems to benefit from a concrete educational approach in which questions are answered.

At stage 2 individual counseling should be encouraged as an avenue for family member(s) to express feelings (often anger) in a safe environment rather than venting it on the PWA. Because many hurtful expressions can emerge at stage 2, the PWA often needs to seek the help of counselors and significant friends. In the example of John, the counselor should help him express his feelings toward his family's anger. By stage 5, a family intervention approach is likely to be beneficial.

Not all (actually many) families respond the way that John's family responded. Some respond by almost total rejection. Often the family does not know that the PWA is homosexual or bisexual, and the revelation may be a "double whammy." In other instances one family member may know about the AIDS diagnosis but hadn't told other family members—a situation that may cause friction and distrust within the family (Deuchar, 1984; Donlou, Wolcott, Gottlieb, & Landsverk, 1985; Faltz & Mandover, 1987; Flaskerud, 1987). In still other instances a family member (usually parent) may have known about the PWA's sexual orientation, and the diagnosis of AIDS just confirmed his or her worst fears. Robinson, Skeen, and Walters (1987) reported that 71% of the parents of gay men worried that their child might contract AIDS.

AIDS and Family Stress

To say that AIDS is a stressor in the lives of the parents and the AIDS victim is an understatement. Indeed, AIDS is a major stressor. In some families AIDS is the only stressor, but in most families additional stressors exist. Because stressors can accumulate and in turn influence family members' reactions toward the PWA, the counselor might check to see if other stressors are present.

One means for assessing life stressors is the Social Readjustment Rating Scale (Holmes & Rahe, 1967). This scale lists 43 major stressors, such as divorce, death, and fired at work, and places a mean value on the stressor. As examples, death is given a value of 100, divorce a value of 73, fired at job a 47, and sleeping habit change a 16. The values of each stressor are added. A total stressor value of over 300 indicates a high amount of stress. In contrast, a score under 100 indicates a lack of major stress in the individual's life.

The scale and its interpretive guide contain specific means for interpreting the score. The basic point is that counselors should realize that too much stress in a family member's life can indeed influence his or her acceptance or rejection of the AIDS diagnosis. In addition, these circumstances can take their toll on one's patience and health.

Spouses and Lovers of Homosexual and Bisexual Men

Spouses and lovers of persons with AIDS have some of the same reactions as parents of PWAs but often experience many different reactions as well. For example, they may fear for their own health and become hyper-vigilant about illness, especially AIDS. They also may feel guilty because they are not ill and their spouse (lover) is terminally ill with AIDS. Further, they may have escalating anticipatory grief as the PWA's death becomes more imminent. They may devote themselves to being the total caregiver of the PWA and often experience all of the stresses that are characteristic of those who provide care for terminally ill patients.

Sometimes the stresses become so great that the spouse (lover) may become immobilized to the point of avoiding the issue. If this occurs, the counselor might

TABLE 15.3
Family Reaction to AIDS and Loss

Stage	Explanation	Example
1. Denial	Most families respond with shock and disbelief when they are told that a member has AIDS. A typical response is, "Surely this isn't true."	Mr. and Mrs. Jones had just celebrated their 35th wedding anniversary. About a week after the celebration, they were told their oldest child has AIDS. Their response was, "I can't believe it . . . not my child."
2. Anger	After realizing that the AIDS diagnosis is true, many families become hostile and angry toward the member who has AIDS. The anger is directed not only toward the afflicted person, but it is often displaced toward others as well. They often look in envy at other families experiencing harmony.	Mr. and Mrs. Fine, a 45-year-old couple, had been model parents to their only son, John—at least they thought they were. Their response to John's diagnosis of AIDS was an outburst of anger with unpleasant name-calling. In discussing their plight, a constant theme emerged: "How dare he bring this on us. We've devoted our lives to him, and now look . . . .Why us?"
3. Bargaining	The family members realize the person with AIDS is getting worse by the day. The AIDS diagnosis is indeed true. They pray, "If you'll just give John another chance, we'll be better people."	Mr. and Mrs. Smith realize their child is going to die unless a cure is found for AIDS very soon. They ask the doctor, "Can't you do something to let him live just a litle longer?" They also pray, "Just let my child live long enough to graduate from college; then we'll let him go."
4. Depression	The family realizes the fight to save the AIDS member is lost. At this stage there is often a desire to spend a lot of time alone thinking. The days become so long and depressing that they dread getting out of bed each day. They're embarrassed and afraid that friends and neighbors will learn of the AIDS. They need emotional release. The mother cries alone, while the father refuses to give in to emotions. As they reach the depths of despair, emotional release comes. After the release, the deep depression begins to lift.	Mr. Ruiz, 50, and his wife Martha, 48, realize their child's life is almost over—a child who just turned 21 last week. Mr. and Mrs. Ruiz realize there is nothing they can do to save him. They would give their last dollar to cure him. As they think back over their lives, they remember their child's birth, first step, first days at school. The pain becomes depressing, and they find themselves alone, thinking about their child and AIDS. Finally they acknowledge their grief and cry their hearts out. The deep depression begins to lift.
5. Acceptance	The family at this stage doesn't like what has happened but nevertheless begins to accept the inevitable.	Mr. and Mrs. Smith, age 39, know they must accept the inevitable. Although it is not what they want, they realize that AIDS is winning. So with courage and dignity they conclude, "Time is almost up. We'll continue to help our child and do the best we can."

help the client remember critical decisions from the past. The accompanying exercise, entitled "A Critical Decision," contains 10 questions that help clients remember a past decision and how that decision was handled. The ninth question asks the client, "Do you see any similarities between the way you handled the past decision and the way you are handling your current decision (decision produced by the diagnosis of AIDS)?" The tenth question asks, "What is your greatest fear about your current decision?" This exercise can be helpful for the counselor to assist the client in looking at the past as a lever for understanding and improving the present.

In the case of the PWA, problems may arise regarding decision-making during the illness. These include important decisions such as which physician to select and who will make the decision(s). It is best if the PWA makes those decisions, but some PWAs either neglect to make the decisions or do not want to make them. In the absence of either verbal or written decisions by the PWA, parents and lovers may experience conflict in the decision-making process, especially if the parents did not know or did not accept the lover prior to the illness (Faltz & Mandover, 1987; Flaskerud, 1987; Wolcott et al., 1985).

In deciding who has the legal right to make decisions for the PWA when he or she becomes incapable of doing so, the legal right usually is awarded to the parents unless the PWA has given, via legal document, power of attorney to the lover. If legal power of attorney has not been provided, parents can make decisions for the PWA prior to death. After death, unless a legal will has been made, the parents can inherit all property, bank accounts, and the like that belonged to the PWA. This can be devastating to the lover, psychologically as well as financially. The counselor must be cognizant of the need to discuss these issues with the PWA, recognizing that some clients have attended to the legal issues via formal documents and others have not.

A Critical Decision

Directions to Client: Take a few minutes to think about a past situation that involved a major change in your life—a change that was unwanted. (After the client has identified the situation, proceed with the following 10 questions.)

1. What was the decision?
2. What major change did the decision involve?
3. What were your feelings at the time you were aware of your need to make the decision?
4. Did your feelings remain the same, or did they change during the decision process?
5. How did you proceed in making the decision? (Be specific as possible about the stages.)
6. What was the outcome of the decision?
7. How did you feel about yourself after you made the decision?
8. If you were to have opportunity to remake the decision, would you make any changes? (Be as specific as possible.)
9. Do you see any similarities between the way you handled the past decision and the way you are handling your current decision about your spouse (lover) and the AIDS diagnosis?
10. What is your greatest fear about your current decision? (Be as specific as possible.)

In the case of the bisexual PWA, the spouse may be shocked to learn of this sexual orientation. It is not uncommon for a wife to have assumed that her marriage has been monogamous for the past 10 years and then to learn, following the diagnosis of AIDS, that her husband is bisexual. The spouse, therefore, may experience denial, fear, and a high level of anger.

Further, the care and reactions of children may be a compounding issue in the family of the PWA. The counselor should try to explore three broad issues with the spouse (and with the children, if they are old enough to be cognizant of the issues): (a) survival issues, (b) personal issues, and (c) work/family issues.

In terms of survival issues, the counselor may need to help the spouse explore some of the following issues: Can she and the children survive financially? What is the medical prognosis for her husband? With regard to personal issues, the counselor might help the spouse explore her feelings upon learning that her husband is bisexual. How will the bisexual relationship impact their marriage? In terms of family issues, the counselor should explore what effect the bisexual relationship is having on the family as a system and on individual family members. What impact has the relationship had or will the relationship have on the family's interaction with acquaintances (friends, neighbors, co-workers)?

Friends of Homosexual Men, Bisexual Men, and IV Drug Users

Friends of homosexual men, bisexual men, and IV drug users may fear contagion because they identify with the PWA's lifestyle and activities. This in turn can force them to evaluate their own lifestyles. Further, they may overidentify with the PWA, resulting in worry-related anxiety states (Wolcott et al., 1985). Some individuals may overidentify so much that they may exhibit AIDS symptoms without being HIV-positive. Glaser (1987) related the feelings of this group to those experienced by survivors of the bombing of Hiroshima: Survivors may have the feeling that the whole world is dying around them.

Biological Families and Spouses/Lovers of Intravenous Drug Users

The percentage of AIDS cases related to IV drug use has been increasing steadily in the past few years. This is now a primary source of heterosexual and prenatal transmission of the HIV virus, from the sharing of needles and from having sexual contact with infected partners. In the United States, IV drug use is a risk factor in 25% of AIDS cases, including 8% in whom male homosexual activity is also a risk factor (Des Jarlais & Friedman, 1988).

AIDS can have a devastating effect on the family of the IV drug user. Family dynamics may include conflicts over illegal activities, estrangement, codependency, and child care.

In some instances in which the IV drug user is estranged from the family because of the drug use, the AIDS diagnosis may cause the family to evaluate its present situation and possibly reconcile. In other cases the AIDS diagnosis may lead to further alienation among members. For some families the AIDS diagnosis may lead to revelation of drug use or drug use/homosexual activity—a situation that may shock family members (Greif & Porembski, 1987).

In all of these situations, the family may be asked to be the primary caregiver for the PWA. The personal financial resources of many families may be too limited to allow proper care for the PWA. Children also may present a problem for this group, especially if the PWA is their primary caregiver. For these children for whom other resources are unavailable, the counselor might refer them to social service agencies. Finally, bereavement issues should be addressed to help the children deal with the loss of a parent.

Case Illustration: Sylvia

Sylvia is a bright 35-year-old woman. Upon graduation she moved to San Antonio, where she accepted a job with an accounting firm. She met a man at work, and together they began to smoke pot. One thing led to another, and they were into IV drug use. Sylvia experienced some symptoms similar to those of a cold or the flu. Despite medication, the symptoms would not go away. Sylvia's doctor said she was just "run-down," and with the new medication she would be well soon. The symptoms continued off and on for 6 months and Sylvia often felt even worse, so she visited her doctor again. After much testing, the doctor informed Sylvia by phone that she has AIDS and asked that Sylvia not return to his office but to seek medical help elsewhere (some physicians do not want to see AIDS patients; in addition to the fear of AIDS is the fear of losing other patient business).

About a year after the AIDS diagnosis, Sylvia decided to tell her parents. She recalls, "This was the most difficult decision of my life. I went home for the weekend and tried to tell my parents that I have AIDS. I just couldn't. I returned to San Antonio. A month later I visited my parents again. I told them together. My mother cried and cried. My dad did as I knew he would—he yelled and yelled at me. I hate to think what he said. His final statement was 'Get out! You are no child of mine. I don't ever want to hear or see you again . . . ever!' That was a year ago, I haven't heard from them."

In reviewing Table 15.3, Sylvia's father clearly is at stage 2, anger. Stage 2 can be a long one for many parents. For other parents, it is never lost, although parents who remain in stage 2 have a lot of parental guilt. Usually the guilt is reflected in a parental response, "Where did we go wrong?" Some parents, however, mask the guilt with overt anger directed at the PWA. Until the parents are ready to deal with their issues, they often reject the help a counselor can offer. In fact, during the early part of stage 2, many families do not consider counseling as an option.

If family therapy isn't feasible, the counselor might help the PWA locate other support. Often it is possible to increase the support from others such as friends, co-workers, other PWAs, and siblings. It should be noted that siblings sometimes substitute for their parent's rejection, and other times siblings follow their parent's path of rejection.

Although Sylvia's parents experienced a lot of anger, denial was likely their initial reaction. Sometimes counselors miss the importance of denial because it is camouflaged by the intense anger. The counselor should try to determine if denial occurred over a long period of time, and also why it occurred.

In the case of Sylvia's family, the intense anger could be the result of a fear of stigma. In many instances parents of PWAs are afraid to tell friends, co-workers, and other family members about their child having AIDS because they are afraid of their friends' reactions, the stigma it will produce, and the change in their community interactions. The display of anger can indeed mean, "Look what you've caused for us among our family and neighbors."

Counseling can be beneficial for these parents in many instances, because the counselor might be the only person to whom they dare say, "My child has AIDS." Even though counseling often begins on an individual basis, family support groups have been helpful in encouraging parents to talk with others about issues evolving from their child's diagnosis of AIDS (Flaskerud, 1987; Graham & Cates, 1987).

Families of Hemophiliacs

In the United States 92% of individuals with severe hemophilia A, the most common form of hemophilia, have been exposed to the HIV virus; in 1988, one in every 26 of these persons has acquired AIDS (Mason et al., 1988). Because hemophilia is a hereditary blood coagulation disease, entire families may be affected by the HIV virus.

Case Illustrations: Parrish and Teer Families

Mr. Aguilar, a school counselor, has two children in her school with AIDS. Both acquired HIV infections through contaminated blood products. She has been helping teachers, parents, and other children to provide the best learning experience for these children with AIDS. John Parrish is a 10-year-old fourth-grader whose mother is a hemophiliac carrier. Mr. and Mrs. Parrish talked with Mrs.

Aguilar about arranging for a visiting teacher to visit John at the hospital to prevent him from getting behind in his school work.

John has been hospitalized with esophageal candidiasis. When Mrs. Parrish came to talk to Mrs. Aguilar, she berated herself about her son's illness, saying, "I'm to blame for my son's illness! I should have never had children." Mr. Parrish also blames himself for his son's illness and expresses this through statements such as, "I knew that there were risks involved because of my wife's family history, and now our child is suffering. It's all our fault."

The Teer family also visits Mrs. Aguilar. When they talk about their son George's illness, they express more anger toward outside sources than anger toward themselves. George has been ill now for many months, and they do not think he will live to be released from the hospital. Mrs. Aguilar has been a source of support for the family since the beginning of George's illness a year ago.

In these two cases, attributions play a large role in the family's adjustment and acceptance of their child's illness. Figure 15.1 shows how attributions influence the family's coping style. As the figure illustrates, counselors need to be cognizant of how a family views the cause of the AIDS infection. Often this is expressed by internalizing or externalizing blame. Counselors should encourage families to stop assigning blame for AIDS. Instead, families should be encouraged to seek the most workable solution to the problem. Often this means that the counselor will need to help family members express their feelings about their child's illness without self-guilt being imposed.

CONCLUSIONS

AIDS is spreading in epidemic proportions. It is apparent from its incidence that AIDS is not a respecter of persons. It can be acquired by men, women, or children of any age. Further, AIDS is indiscriminate of membership in any social group or of socioeconomic level. It is typically spread by risky sexual practices, IV drug abuse, and contaminated blood or blood products.

AIDS has impacted, and will continue to impact, the American family system. At times the family affected by AIDS is the family of origin, especially the biological parents. In other instances the family is the *chosen family,* often the lover and close friends. In still other instances, family includes both the *biological and chosen family.*

Unlike other diseases, AIDS elicits strong, negative reactions, which often are accompanied by guilt. Counselors must be aware of the needs of the family of the PWA. These families often experience severe emotional, social, and financial trauma. Despite this, the family's needs have been largely underrecognized and unmet by society. Counselors can help fill these unmet needs by understanding the stages of loss and grief and the issues unique to members of these families.

Internal Attributions

Parental Statements
"Maybe I should not have had a child since I knew that hemophilia ran in my family."
"Where did I go wrong?"
"Could I have done something different?"

lead to self-depreciation, guilt, self-grief, depression

External Attributions

Parental Statements
"They should have checked the blood supply more closely!"
"People who donate blood should be sure they aren't HIV-positive!"

lead to anger at society and outside persons

Neutral Attributions

Parental Statements
"I'm upset that our child is ill, but I must do something now to provide her with the best quality of life possible."
"My child has died, and now I want to do something to see that other children will not get ill. I'm going to volunteer time working on the city's AIDS hotline."

lead to acceptance and action

FIGURE 15.1
The Influence of Attributions on Family Coping Style

REFERENCES

Baer, J., Hall, J., Holm, K., & Lewitter-Koehler, S. (1987). Challenges in developing an inpatient psychiatric program for patients with AIDS and ARC. *Hospital & Community Psychiatry, 38,* 1299–1303.

Baltimore, D., & Wolff, S. (1986). *Confronting AIDS: Directions for public health, health-care and research.* Washington, DC: National Academy Press.

Barret, R. L. (1989). Counseling gay men with AIDS: Human dimensions. *Journal of Counseling & Development, 67,* 573–576.

Bohm, E. (1987). AIDS: Effects on psychotherapy in New York City. *Journal of Psychosocial Nursing & Mental Health Services, 25,* 26–31.

Bor, R., Miller, R., & Perry, L. (1988). Systematic counseling for patients with AIDS/HIV infections. *Family Systems Medicine, 6,* 31–39.

Bruttn, J. G. (1989). Counseling persons with a fear of AIDS. *Journal of Counseling & Development, 67,* 455–459.

Center for Disease Control (1984). Antibodies to a retro-virus etiologically associated with AIDS in populations with increased incidence of the syndrome. *Morbidity & Mortality Weekly Reports, 33,* 377–379.

Coats, T., Temoshak, L., & Mandel, J. (1984). Psychosocial research is essential to understanding and treating AIDS. *American Psychologist, 39,* 1309–1314.

Cooper, T. (1988). *Confronting AIDS: Update 1988.* Washington, DC: National Academy Press.

Craig, E. (1989). *Human development.* Englewood Cliffs, NJ: Prentice Hall.

Des Jarlais, D., & Friedman, S. (1988). The psychology of preventing AIDS among intravenous drug users. *American Psychologist, 43,* 865–870.

Destounis, N. (1987). AIDS: A medical disaster. *European Journal of Psychiatry. 1,* 44–49.

Deuchar, N. (1984). AIDS in New York City with particular reference to the psycho-social aspects. *British Journal of Psychiatry, 145,* 612–619.

Donlou, J., Wolcott, D., Gottlieb, M., & Landsverk, J. (1985). Psychosocial aspects of AIDS and AIDS-related complex: A pilot study. *Journal of Psychosocial Oncology, 3,* 39–55.

Erikson, E., & Erikson, J. (1981). On generativity and identity: From a conversation with Erik and Joan Erikson. *Harvard Educational Review, 51,* 249–269.

Essex, M., & Kanki, P. (1988). The origins of the aids virus. *Scientific American, 259,* 64–72.

Faltz, B., & Mandover, S. (1987). Treatment of substance abuse in patients with HIV infections. *Advances in Alcohol & Substance Abuse, 7,* 143–257.

Flaskerud, J. (1987). AIDS: Psychosocial aspects. *Journal of Psychosocial Nursing & Mental Health Services, 25,* 8-16.

Galea, R., Lewis, B., & Baker, L. (1988). Voluntary testing for HIV antibodies among clients in long-term substance abuse treatment. *Social Work, 33,* 265–268.

Gallo, R. C. (1987). The AIDS virus. *Scientific American, 256,* 45–56.

Gallo R. C., & Montagnier, L. (1988). AIDS in 1988. *Scientific American, 259,* 40–50.

Ginzberg, H. (1984). Intravenous drug users and AIDS. *Pharm-Chem Newsletter, 13,* 1–9.

Glaser, C. (1987, Sept.). AIDS and A-bomb disease. *Christianity & Crisis,* pp. 311–314.

Gold, M., Seymour, N., & Sahl, J. (1986). Counseling HIV seropositives. In L. McKusick (Ed.), *What to do about AIDS.* Berkeley: University of California Press.

Graham, L., & Cates, J. (1987). AIDS: Developing a primary health care task force. *Journal of Psychosocial Nursing & Mental Health Services, 25,* 21–25.

Grant, D., & Anns, M. (1988). Counseling AIDS antibody-positive clients: Reactions and treatment. *American Psychologist, 43,* 72–74.

Greif, G., & Porembski, E. (1987). Significant others of I.V. drug abusers with AIDS: New challenges for drug treatment programs. *Journal of Substance Abuse, 4,* 151–155.

Heyward, W., & Curran, J. (1988). The epidemiology of AIDS in the U.S. *Scientific American, 259,* 72–82.

Holmes, T. H., & Rahe, R. (1967). The social readjustment rating scale. *Journal of Psychosomatic Research, 11,* 213–218.

Jaffe, L., & Wortman, R. (1988). Guidelines to the counseling and HTLV-III antibody screening of adolescents. *Journal of Adolescent Health Care, 9,* 84–86.

Koop, C. (1986). From the Surgeon General, U.S. Public Health Services. *Journal of the American Medical Association, 256,* 2783.

Krieger, I. (1988). An approach to coping with anxiety about AIDS. *Social Work, 33,* 263–264.

Kubler-Ross, E. (1969). *On death and dying.* New York: Macmillan.

Kubler-Ross, E. (1987). *AIDS: The ultimate challenge.* New York: Macmillan.

Lomax, G., & Sandler, J. (1988). Psychotherapy and consultation with persons with AIDS. *Psychiatric Annals, 18,* 253–259.

Mason, J. (1985). Public health service plan for the prevention and control of acquired immuno-deficiency syndrome. *Public Health Reports, 100,* 453–455.

Mason, P., Olson, R., & Parish, K. (1988). AIDS, hemophilia, and prevention efforts within a comprehensive care plan. *American Psychologist, 43,* 971–976.

Mejta, C. L. (1987). Acquired immunodeficiency syndrome (AIDS): Implications for counseling and education. *Counseling & Human Development, 20.* 1–12.

Mills, S. (1986). Attitudes and trends: Public perception of AIDS. *Focus: A review of AIDS Research, 2,* 1–3.

Morin, S., Charles, R., & Malyon, A. (1984). The psychological impact of AIDS on gay men. *American Psychologist, 39,* 1288–1293.

National Center of Health Statistics. (1988). AIDS knowledge and attitudes for September 1987: Provisional data from the National Health Interview Survey. *Advance Data from Vital and Health Statistics, No. 148,* (Ditas Pub. No (PHS) 88–1250). Hyattsville. MD: Public Health Service.

Nichols, S. (1985). Psychosocial reactions of persons with the acquired immunodeficiency syndrome. *Internal Medicine, 103,* 765–767.

Posey, E. C. (1988). Confidentiality in an AIDS support group. *Journal of counseling & Development, 66,* 226–227.

Robinson, B., Skeen, P., & Walters, L. (1987). The AIDS epidemic hits home. *Psychology Today, 21,* 48–52.

Skeen, P., & Robinson, B. (1985). Gay fathers' and gay nonfathers' relationship with their parents. *Journal of Sex Research, 21,* 86–89.

Stevens, L., & Muskin, P. (1987). Techniques for reversing the failure of empathy towards AIDS patients. *Journal of the American Academy of Psychoanalysis, 15,* 539–551.

Stulberg, I., & Smith, M. (1988). Psychosocial impact of the AIDS epidemic on the lives of gay men. *Social Work, 33,* 277–281.

Widen, H. (1987). The risk of AIDS and the defense of disavowal: Dilemmas for the college psychotherapist. *Journal of American College Health, 35,* 268–273.

Witt, M. (Ed.). (1986). *AIDS and patient management: Legal, ethical and social issues.* Owings Mills, MD: Rynd Communications.

Wolcott, D., Fawzy, F., & Pasnau, R. (1985). Acquired immune deficiency syndrome (AIDS) and consultation-liaison psychiatry. *General Hospital Psychiatry, 7,* 280–292.

RELATED READINGS

Bor, R., Perry, L., & Miller, R. (1989). A systems approach to AIDS counseling. *Journal of Family Therapy, 11,* 77–86.

Greif, G., & Porembski, E. (1989). Implications for therapy with significant others of persons with AIDS. *Journal of Gay and Lesbian Psychotherapy, 1,* 79–86.

Hopkins, K. M., Grosz, J., Cohen, H., & Diamond, G. (1989). The developmental and family services unit: A model AIDS project serving developmentally disabled children and their families. *AIDS CARE, 1*, 281–285.

Kain, D. D. (Ed.) (1989). *No longer immune: A counselor's guide to AIDS.* Alexandria, VA: American Association for Counseling & Development.

Kelly, J., & Sykes, P. (1989). Helping the helpers: A support group for family members of persons with AIDS. *Social Work, 34*, 239–242.

Lovejoy, N. C. (1990). AIDS: Impact on the gay man's homosexual and heterosexual families. *Marriage and Family Review, 14*, 285–316.

Lynch, R. D. (1989). Psychological impact of AIDS on individual, family, community, nation, and world in a historical perspective. *Family and Community Health, 12*, 52–59.

Macklin, E. D. (1988). AIDS: Implications for families. *Family Relations, 37*, 141–149.

Mason, P. J., Olson, R. A., Myers, J. B., Huszti-Heather, C. (1989). AIDS and hemophilia: Implications for interventions with families. *Journal of Pediatric Psychology, 14*, 341–355.

Mays, V., Albee, G. W., & Schneider, S. F. (Eds.), *Primary prevention of AIDS: Psychological approaches.* Newbury Park, CA: Sage Publications.

Meintz, S. L., & Jackson, M. M. (issue editors). (1989). AIDS: Community perspectives. Special issue, *Family & Community Health, 12*(2), whole issue.

Olson, R. A., Huszti, H. C., Mason, P. J., & Seibert, J. M. (1989). Pediatric AIDS/HIV infection: An emerging challenge to pediatric psychology. *Journal of Pediatric Psychology, 14*, 1–21.

Ross, M. W. (1989). Married homosexual men: Prevalence and background. *Marriage and Family Review, 14*, 35–57.

Tiblier, K. B., Walker, G. & Rolland, J. S. (1989). Therapeutic issues when working with families of persons with AIDS. *Marriage and Family Review, 13*, 81–128.

Walen, S. R., & Perlmutter, R. (1988). Cognitive-behavioral treatment of adult sexual dysfunctions from a family perspective. In N. Epstein, S. E. Schlesinger, & W. Dryden (Eds.), *Cognitive-behavioral therapy with families* (pp. 325–360). New York: Brunner/Mazel.

NOTES

[1]Center for Disease Control, 1984; Gallo, 1987; Gallo & Montagnier, 1988.

[2]Essex & Kanki, 1988.

[3]Baltimore & Wolff, 1986; Bohn, 1987; Center for Disease Control, 1984; Ginzberg, 1984; Heyward & Curran, 1988; Mason, 1985; Witt, 1986.

[4]Galea, Lewis, & Baker, 1988.

[5]Bor, Miller, & Perry, 1988; Coats, Temoshak, & Mandel, 1984; Gold, Seymour, & Sahl, 1986; Grant & Anns, 1988; Jaffe & Wortman, 1988; Krieger, 1988; Lomax & Sandler, 1988; Mejta, 1987; Morin, Charles, & Malyon, 1984; Nichols, 1985; Posey, 1988; Stevens & Muskin, 1987; Stulberg & Smith, 1988; Widen, 1987.

[6]Baer, Hall, Holm, & Lewitter-Koehler, 1987; Barret, 1989; Bruttn, 1989; Destounis, 1987; Deuchar, 1984; Faltz & Mandover, 1987; Flaskerud, 1987; Graham & Cates, 1987; Greif & Porembski, 1987.

[7]Greif & Porembski, 1987; Robinson, Skeen, & Walters, 1987.

Author

Information

Jack S. Annon
Consultant
Honolulu, Hawaii

Miguel Arciniega
Arizona State University
Tempe, Arizona

Leroy G. Baruth
Appalachian State University
Boone, North Carolina

Loretta J. Bradley
Texas Tech University
Lubbock, Texas

Margaret Z. Burggraf
University of South Carolina
Columbia, South Carolina

Jon Carlson
Governors State University
University Park, Illinois

Judith Cooney
Governors State University
University Park, Illinois

Brenda Rifkin Faiber
Counselor
Orlando, Florida

Dan Fullmer
Consultant
Honolulu, Hawaii

Douglas R. Gross
Arizona State University
Tempe, Arizona

Bree A. Hayes
University of Georgia
Athens, Georgia

Richard L. Hayes
University of Georgia
Athens, Georgia

Charles H. Huber
New Mexico State University
Las Cruces, New Mexico

Judith A. Lewis
Governors State University
University Park, Illinois

J. Barry Mascari
Private Practice
New Jersey

Betty J. Newlon
University of Arizona
Tucson, Arizona

Mary A. Ostrovsky
Neuropsychology Clinic
Abilene, Texas

Ron J. Pion
Consultant and Clinical Professor,
 U.C.L.A. Medical School
Los Angeles, California

Bonnie E. Robson
The Hospital for Sick Children
University of Toronto
Toronto, Ontario, Canada

Aviva Sanders-Mascari
Private Counseling and Consulting
 Practice
New Jersey

Robert L. Smith
University of Colorado-Denver
Denver, Colorado

Index of

Contributors